IMAGES OF ENLIGHTENMENT
Tibetan Art in Practice

IMAGES OF ENLIGHTENMENT
Tibetan Art in Practice

Jonathan Landaw and Andy Weber

Snow Lion Publications
Ithaca, New York

Snow Lion Publications
P.O. Box 6483
Ithaca, New York 14851 USA

Printed in Canada

ISBN 1-55939-024-7

Library of Congress Cataloging-in-Publication Data
Landaw, Jonathan.
    Images of enlightenment : Tibetan art in practice / Jonathan
Landaw and Andy Weber. — 1st ed.
        p.   cm.
    Includes bibliographical references and index.
    ISBN 1-55939-024-7
    1. Tankas (Tibetan scrolls)   2. Painting, Buddhist—China—Tibet.
3. Buddhist art and symbolism—China—Tibet.   I. Weber, Andy, 1951-
. II. Title.
ND1432.C58L36   1993
    755′.943923—dc20   93-40283
                                                                          CIP

Contents

List of Illustrations

LIST OF COLOR PLATES

LIST OF FIGURES

LIST OF TABLES

Introduction

THE ORIGINS OF THIS WORK

The majority of the thirty-two full color Tibetan-style paintings, or *tangkas*,* that form the core of the present work were commissioned in 1983 from the artist Andy Weber by Hugh Clift, presently the head of Tharpa Publications in London. Since their creation, these paintings have hung in the meditation hall of Manjushri Institute in northern England where they have been viewed by the hundreds of visitors who pass through that buddhist center every year. These visitors, and many others who have seen the paintings in reproduction as cards and posters,[1] often ask who the figures in these tangkas are and what they represent. Although many books have been written in the past two decades about Tibetan art and culture, we found there was very little source material to which the serious inquirer could be referred for satisfactory answers to these questions. Much of what was available either demanded a great deal of prior knowledge to be understood properly, was too sketchy to be useful, or treated the images of Tibetan buddhist art as if they were lifeless artifacts of a lost civilization. It was very rare for us to find anything that conveyed the spark of inspiration we ourselves had found so attractive in this

---

*Terms appearing in italics may be found in the glossary at the end of this text.

1

art, or that showed how these figures form an integral part of a remarkable spiritual tradition that is still very much alive.²

It is our conviction that the only way of understanding the images of this art in anything more than a superficial manner is by becoming acquainted with the path of spiritual self-transformation they are meant both to illustrate and facilitate, namely, the *Vajrayana*. Although the author and artist have barely set foot on this demanding path of inner realization, we nevertheless have had the extreme good fortune of receiving instructions from leading masters of all four major Tibetan schools of Vajrayana Buddhism: the Nyingma, Sakya, Kagyu and Geluk. From the enlightening example of these inspiring teachers we have seen that this path, when followed with sufficient diligence and persistence, produces beings of undeniable wisdom, compassion and energy. This work is an attempt to repay a small fraction of the immeasurable kindness we have received from these masters by giving as accurate an account as we can of the spiritual path they have revealed to us, thereby making this path and its distinctive art more accessible to others.

It is far beyond the scope of this book, however, to provide a comprehensive overview of the teachings and art of all four Tibetan traditions of Vajrayana Buddhism. Although they hold many lineages in common and are equally rooted in the teachings of Shakyamuni Buddha, each tradition has its own particular manner of describing and presenting the spiritual path. Furthermore, each tradition has a particular set of images, or *meditational deities*, that it favors and not all, or even most, of these deities could possibly have been illustrated here. Therefore, in our attempt to provide a clear and coherent introduction to the vast world of Vajrayana buddhist thought and imagery, we have felt it wisest to concentrate on those deities and generally follow those explanations central to the tradition with which we ourselves are most familiar. This is the Geluk tradition of Je Tsong Khapa. Since this particular tradition was the last of the four to evolve in Tibet and, as a result, synthesized much of what is contained in the others, the material presented here should prove broadly applicable to Tibetan buddhist art as a whole. Anyone wishing to study in more depth the remaining Tibetan traditions should consult the notes and selected readings relating to Chapter Six, in which brief biographies of several of the most famous masters of these traditions are given.

It should be pointed out that although we have tried our best to remain faithful to the letter and spirit of the explanations we have received, we make no pretense that what follows is a definitive account of even one tradition of Vajrayana Buddhism. As will be obvious, the further one travels this path the more levels of meaning there are to uncover; thus the symbolism of any particular image, for example, can be interpreted in many more ways than we can possibly explain at present. Furthermore, the way the images and explanations have been arranged does not follow any traditional Tibetan model[3]; the grouping is strictly of our own creation and reflects our judgment as to which order best serves the purposes of this introduction to Vajrayana art and practice. Whatever inadequacies exist in this work are therefore no-one's responsibility but our own. We hope that the pure sources of our inspiration and the reader as well will be patient with these inadequacies, and that whatever errors in fact or interpretation we may have committed will be swiftly corrected.

INTRODUCTION TO THE VAJRAYANA

For centuries the spiritual and artistic treasure of Vajrayana Buddhism remained cloistered behind the nearly impenetrable Himalayan ranges, but with the Chinese occupation of Tibet in the 1950s and the subsequent attempts to obliterate this ancient culture and its sovereign identity, the situation has changed radically. A stream of refugees has made its way down from the Roof of the World, carrying the previously guarded treasure of the Vajrayana along with it. As these refugees settled first in neighboring Asian countries—most especially in India, the land where Vajrayana Buddhism was born and matured many centuries earlier—and then traveled around the globe in a modern-day Diaspora, thousands of people all over the world have been exposed to Tibet's unique, spiritually impregnated culture and the remarkable works of art it has produced. Interest in things Tibetan has been especially stimulated by the appearance on the world stage of His Holiness the Fourteenth Dalai Lama, the buddhist monk Tenzin Gyatso. As the temporal and religious leader of the Tibetan nation continues to live in exile from his native Land of Snow, he has been recognized as one of the most authentic and gifted spiritual leaders of our time, profoundly affecting people from all walks of life with his warmth, wisdom and simple humanity. Through the inspiration of the Dalai Lama and the disproportionately large number of spiritually advanced masters among the dispersed Tibetan refugee population, many people in both the West and the East have been moved to take sincere interest in Vajrayana Buddhism.

But what exactly is the Vajrayana? While the purpose of the commentary interspersed with the following color plates and line drawings is to provide a detailed answer to this question, a few brief remarks are in order now. *Vajrayana* is a Sanskrit term often translated as *Diamond Vehicle* and refers to the fullest flowering of the teachings that originated in India 2500 years ago with Shakyamuni, the historical Buddha (563-483 B.C.E.). *Vajra* means *indestructible, adamantine* or *diamond hard* and refers to the unshakeable, diamondlike awareness of reality that characterizes the fully awakened state of *enlightenment* (Skt. *bodhi*): the ultimate goal of the buddhist spiritual path. *Yana* means *vehicle* and refers to those means whereby this ultimate goal of spiritual awakening and fulfillment is reached.[4] Vajrayana Buddhism, therefore, includes the entire range of teachings and practices that can carry qualified and dedicated spiritual seekers to full enlightenment, or *buddhahood*, as swiftly and directly as possible. Because of the power and speed of this path, Vajrayana is also known as the *Lightning Vehicle*.

One of the outstanding features of the Vajrayana is its ability to channel all forms of physical, mental and emotional energy—even those generally deemed unmanageable and destructive by other religious systems—into the path of spiritual growth. Nothing that is part of the human experience is discarded or denied by the Vajrayana; instead, through its supremely skillful methods, every element of our being can undergo an alchemical transformation into spiritual gold. We can sense the vast scope of energies utilized by the Vajrayana by taking even a brief glimpse at the images reproduced in this book. Although they represent only a small fraction of Vajrayana art, they include such varied and apparently contradictory images as a smiling buddha absorbed in meditation (Plate 1) and a wrathful, demonic-looking figure encircled by flames (Plate 8); delicately beautiful goddesses (Plates 11 and 12) and an animal-headed creature possessing multiple arms and legs (Plate 20); a solitary figure of ascetic renunciation (Figure 4) and an embracing couple radiating fierce sexuality (Plate 22). Considering the wrathful and sensual nature of much of this imagery, it is understandable why some early European visitors to Tibet, unable or unwilling to discard their cultural preconceptions, were shocked by what they saw and therefore characterized the Vajrayana as a debased and degenerate form of Buddha's originally pure teachings.[5]

In fact, however, the Vajrayana originated with Shakyamuni Buddha himself and, far from being in contradiction to his teachings on moral self-discipline, compassion and insightful wisdom, is an integral part of the spiritual path he revealed. As will be explained in more detail later, the entire purpose for Buddha's having taught others is so that they might learn how to extricate themselves from their self-created miseries, overcome their self-imposed limitations, fulfill their highest potential and then help those who are still trapped to do the same. Because the aptitude, capability and temperament of those he taught varied so widely, Buddha reserved the most potent methods of self-transformation—those that employ the entire range of mental and physical energies in the task of spiritual evolvement—for those disciples with the capacity to practice them successfully. He also enjoined these disciples to keep these powerful (and potentially dangerous) methods hidden from those incapable of using them properly. That is one reason why the Vajrayana is also known as the *Secret Mantra Vehicle*: *mantra* here indicating the supreme protection offered the mind[6] by this profound path and *secret* referring to the injunction to keep these supremely powerful methods from those not yet ready to benefit from them.

Over time, various Vajrayana lineages matured and developed in India and were eventually disseminated at the great monastic universities that flourished in North India towards the end of the first millennium of the present era. At these universities and elsewhere the Vajrayana lineages were studied and put into practice by learned scholars (*panditas*) and accomplished meditation masters (*mahasiddhas*), and in this way they evolved and were transmitted for centuries. (It should be noted here that the texts recording those advanced teachings of Buddha upon which the esoteric Vajrayana is based are called the *tantras* and thus the practitioners of the Vajrayana are sometimes known as *tantrikas* and the vehicle they follow as *Tan-*

trayana. In this context, then, *tantra* is contrasted with those discourses of Shakyamuni, termed *sutra*, upon which the fundamental and more widely disseminated teachings of Buddhism are
founded.)

By the thirteenth century, when invading armies destroyed the
buddhist monastic system in India and Buddhism virtually disappeared from the land of its birth, these Vajrayana lineages had already been transplanted into Tibet where they continued to be practiced and transmitted right up through the first half of this century.[7]
Now, with the suppression of religious and political freedom in Tibet
and the subsequent attempts being made by the refugee community to perpetuate their severely threatened culture while in exile,
the precious Vajrayana has suddenly become available to the world
at large, and the artistic traditions so vital to the Vajrayana have likewise come into wider view.

VISUALIZATION OF VAJRAYANA IMAGES

The key for understanding the Vajrayana in general and its art in particular lies in the transmission of instruction and insight originating with Shakyamuni Buddha and passed down to the present day
through unbroken lineages of accomplished masters. Of particular
interest to us here is the way the images of Vajrayana art—specifically
those represented in Tibetan tangka paintings—play a vital part in
this process of enlightening transmission. To understand how these
images are used in the Vajrayana to transmit spiritual insights, we
must consider the centrally important meditational method known
as *visualization.*

Visualization is the process of becoming intimately acquainted with
positive and beneficial states of consciousness as they are envisioned
in our mind's eye in the form of enlightened beings and other images. Each visualized image functions as an archetype, evoking
responses at a very subtle level of our being and thereby aiding in
the delicate work of inner transformation. For example, by generating an image of Avalokiteshvara (Plate 5), the meditational deity
symbolizing enlightened compassion, and then focusing creatively
upon it with unwavering single-pointed concentration, we stimu-
late the growth of our own compassion. We automatically create a

peaceful inner environment into which the dissatisfied, self-centered thoughts of anger and resentment cannot easily intrude. The more we practice such visualizations—and the related disciplines, or *yogas*, that train our body, speech and mind in the appropriate manner— the more profound their effect. Eventually our mind can take on the aspect of its object to such an extent that we transcend our ordinary limited sense of self-identification and actually become Avalokitesh- vara: compassion itself, or whatever enlightened quality we have been concentrating upon.✔

For the process of visualization to have its most profound effect—to assist the process of enlightened self-transformation—it is clearly not enough to take an occasional glance at a particular image. Vajrayana paintings are not meant as decorative wall-hangings to be admired once in a while or looked at occasionally for fleeting inspiration. In- stead, their images are to be internalized to the point that we iden- tify with them intimately at the deepest level of our being. While we may begin by looking at the painting of a particular deity with our eyes, true visualization only takes place when we can hold this image clearly in our mind without forgetting it. Nor are we meant to be visualizing a flat, inert painting of limited dimensions but rather a living, radiant being of light who may appear infinitely large or small depending upon the specific meditation we are practicing. It is only by seeing the meditational deity as truly alive yet transpar- ent, radiant and empty of concrete *self-existence*,[8] that our mind— which itself is boundless, clear and luminous—can be transformed in the desired manner.

One reason the Vajrayana practitioner can see the various medita- tional deities as alive is that these figures represent forces possess- ing a vital reality of their own. They are not mere arbitrary creations of a limited mind or the fanciful product of an artist's imagination. Each particular image owes its existence to the fully enlightened mind from which it originally sprang and conveys the timeless qualities of such a boundless consciousness. Furthermore, the serious prac- titioner does more than merely chance upon a particular image some- where and casually decide to make it the central object of his or her meditation. Instead, the deity to be practiced is presented to the dis- ciple within the context of an *initiation*, or ceremony of *empowerment* (Skt. *abhisheka*; Tib. *wang*), presided over by a qualified tantric master in whom the disciple has already placed his or her confidence. This master has trained in the methods of the deity in question and can therefore transmit to the disciple all that is necessary for contacting its essence.

During the empowerment and the practices that follow, the disciple sees the deity and the master as indistinguishable from one another and from the lineage of enlightened masters stretching back to Shakyamuni Buddha himself. Far from being a static image, the meditational deity is revealed as the living embodiment of the enlightened energy and inspiration that pervades the entire external and internal universe. The sign of successful practice is the direct, intuitive experience that the mind of the spiritual master, the visualized meditational deity and the practitioner's own mind form an inseparable unity. When this experience is stable, the desired transformation has taken place, and the former disciple is now qualified to take his or her place in the ongoing lineage of accomplished masters and pass on the seeds of enlightening inspiration to others.

The underlying premise of all Vajrayana thought and practice is that the essential nature of each being's mind is pure and clear and that the main task along the spiritual path is to discover and identify with this essential purity, or *buddha-nature*. Visualization and other related practices involving the images of meditational deities assist this process of discovery and identification because these images directly communicate the experience of those who have already realized this essential purity to those who have not yet done so. The most important function of a realized spiritual master (Skt. *guru*; Tib. *lama*), is to reveal to us the true nature of our own mind. Thus the key to understanding Vajrayana art and following the Vajrayana path is found in the guru-disciple relationship; this is the true vehicle of enlightened inspiration.

We have attempted to convey the vital inspirational quality of the images presented in this work by focusing on the part played by each deity in exemplifying the Vajrayana path as a whole. Explanations of the symbolic meanings of each image are interspersed with some of the legends, myths and anecdotes Vajrayana masters tell about the meditational deity. For the sake of those readers who wish to explore in greater detail the topics touched upon here, notes have been provided throughout the text to indicate where this additional information can be found, and a list of further readings is given separately. A glossary and list of proper names in Sanskrit and Tibetan have also been provided. It should always be kept in mind, however, that those wishing to receive the full benefit of the Vajrayana tradition should not be satisfied with what can be found in books. Instead, they should try to make contact with accomplished Vajrayana masters and, through receiving their inspiration and following their advice, put the path of spiritual transformation and realization into practice for the sake of benefiting others.

OUTLINE OF THE TEXT

The images and their explanations have been organized into the following seven chapters:

One: The Founder and His Teachings. By way of introduction, this chapter begins with an abbreviated account of the life and basic teachings of Shakyamuni Buddha and includes a simple visualization practice. After this comes an explanation of the *twelve links of dependent arising*—the mechanism by which, according to Shakyamuni, ordinary beings are imprisoned by their ignorance and delusions and condemned to lives of dissatisfaction. Freedom from self-imprisonment within the *Wheel of Life*, as it is called, is indicated by an illustration of a liberated being, an *arhat*, and the chapter concludes with a representation of a *stupa*, a symbol of the fully enlightened mind.

Two: The Bodhisattva Path. In the first chapter the path to individual liberation from one's own suffering was outlined. In the second chapter we turn to those teachings that present the path of the *bodhisattva*, the supremely compassionate being intent on winning not mere self-liberation but the full enlightenment of buddhahood for the sake of benefiting others. This *Mahayana*, or *Great Vehicle*, path has its roots in those teachings of Shakyamuni known as the *Perfection of Wisdom Sutras*, and the first image in this chapter is that of the Great Mother, Prajnaparamita, the embodiment of these profound teachings. This is followed by illustrations of the three bodhisattvas—Avalokiteshvara, Manjushri and Vajrapani—who symbolize the three major attributes of a buddha's complete enlightenment:

unlimited compassion, unlimited wisdom and unlimited skillful means.

Three: The Five Buddha Families. The process of self-transformation culminating in full enlightenment is next illustrated by the *five buddha families* or lineages. These five represent the types of pristine awareness into which our accustomed delusions of ignorance and so forth are transmuted upon the attainment of complete spiritual awakening. In keeping with our stated interest in visual imagery, special mention is made here of the way in which color is used in Vajrayana art to effect and symbolize this transformation. Then the head of one of these five families, Amitabha Buddha, receives individual attention in an account of the *pure land* practices associated with this widely venerated figure.

Four: Enlightened Activity. Here the emphasis is on the ways in which an enlightenment-bound being puts compassion, wisdom and skillful means into service for others. The chapter begins with two forms of the female deity Tara, who embodies this enlightened activity, and then discusses Ushnisha Vijaya, Amitayus, Medicine Buddha and Vaishravana—deities whose practices confer long life, health and prosperity.

Five: The Path of Bliss and Emptiness. The Vajrayana methods of enlightened self-transformation are traditionally classified into four levels of increasing profundity and effectiveness, and most of what has been presented so far is from the viewpoint of the initial, most basic level of tantric practice. In this chapter the practices of the most profound level—*highest yoga tantra*—are introduced by focusing on some of the personal meditational deities, or *yidams*, associated with this level: Vajradhara, Vajrasattva, Guhyasamaja, Yamantaka and the protector Dharmaraja, Chakrasamvara, Vajrayogini, Vajradharma and the protector Mahakala.

Six: A Living Tradition. Throughout this work efforts have been made to show how all Vajrayana practices are dependent upon the vital link of the guru-disciple relationship. In this chapter we begin by giving a survey of the various traditions—the Nyingma, Kadam, Sakya and Kagyu—through which the essential qualities of this relationship have been transmitted since Vajrayana Buddhism was first introduced into Tibet. This survey is presented in terms of brief biographies of five of the most important masters of these traditions, namely Guru Rinpoche, Atisha, Sakya Pandita, Marpa and Milarepa. Lastly, a more detailed, though still abbreviated, account of the most recent of the major traditions—the Geluk—is given in terms of the life of its founder, Je Tsong Khapa.

Seven: The Future Buddha. To emphasize the continuity of the living tradition, this work concludes with an image of Maitreya, the buddha destined to reveal the spiritual path in a future age the way Shakyamuni Buddha has done in ours.

A PERSONAL NOTE

The seeds of the present work were sown in the mid-1970s in the Kathmandu Valley of Nepal. It was there, in the vicinity of the world-famous Boudhanath Stupa with its omniscient eyes of enlightenment, that the artist and the author of this book first met. Both of us had been drawn to this ancient and holy site by the presence in nearby Kopan Monastery of two extraordinary masters belonging to the Tibetan tradition of Vajrayana Buddhism: Lama Thubten Yeshe and his Sherpa disciple and heart-son, Lama Thubten Zopa Rinpoche. These lamas were to have a profound and long-lasting effect not only upon us, but upon an ever-growing number of students worldwide.

Prior to our first meeting, the artist—Andy Weber—had lived for several years in the small village that surrounds the Great Stupa, while the author had been studying first in Dalhousie, India and then in Dharamsala, home-in-exile of His Holiness the Dalai Lama. Since the early 1960s both Nepal and India had seen the influx of a large number of Tibetan refugees; it was through these uprooted yet nevertheless cheerful people that we were first introduced to the strange new world of Vajrayana Buddhism and its compelling spiritual and artistic traditions. Separately we met and studied with Geshe Ngawang Dhargyey, an esteemed meditation master and instructor now residing in New Zealand, and both of us formally entered the buddhist path under his guidance. Our connections with each other and the Vajrayana traditions were to deepen when, years later, we both coincidentally moved to England and began studying at Manjushri Institute. This is one of many buddhist centers founded by students who, like ourselves, had met the Vajrayana in the East and wished to pursue its teachings while back in their native lands.

During our stay at Manjushri Institute we both had many opportunities to receive instruction from the accomplished scholar and meditation master Geshe Kelsang Gyatso. We were also fortunate in being selected to illustrate and edit for publication several of the commentaries to buddhist thought and practice produced by this tireless lama. Eventually, at the kind instigation of Hugh Clift, who originally commissioned the paintings presented here, we undertook the task of producing this introduction to the sacred art of Tibet—a collaboration between writer and artist—attempting to convey the essence of what had so moved and inspired us during our own journeys to India and Nepal.

But we cannot speak of inspiration without making special mention of our most kind root guru, Lama Thubten Yeshe (1935-1984).[9] More than anyone else it was he who encouraged us to discover for ourselves, and then communicate through words and visual imagery to others, the living essence of the Vajrayana. Despite our many limitations, he urged us to convey to a larger audience whatever we understood of the *buddhadharma*. His profound faith in the power of Shakyamuni Buddha's pure teachings to benefit others—even when transmitted by imperfect vessels like ourselves—allowed us to proceed with sufficient borrowed confidence to bring a project such as this to conclusion. Therefore, if there is something of value in this present work, it is due to the kindness of our beloved Lama Yeshe, to whose memory *Images of Enlightenment* is hereby dedicated.

> Jonathan Landaw
> Capitola, California
> November 6, 1993
> Lha Bab Duchen
> Anniversary of Shakyamuni Buddha's descent from the celestial realms after teaching abhidharma to his mother

1 The Founder and His Teachings

To understand the significance of images presented in this work it is necessary to know something about the teachings of Buddhism and the founder of these teachings, Shakyamuni Buddha (Plate 1). According to one traditional interpretation, Shakyamuni achieved buddhahood eons in the past, long before his descent to this earthly plane 2500 years ago as the historical Buddha. The abbreviated account of his life story given below follows an alternative tradition according to which he gained his enlightenment during the current historical age.[1]

Shakyamuni was born in the sixth century B.C.E. as a prince and heir of the north Indian Shakya clan at Lumbini, in what is now southern Nepal, and was given the personal name Siddhartha. His father, King Shuddodana, was extremely desirous that his only son succeed him to the throne. Worried that Siddhartha's sensitive nature might lead him to choose a wandering religious life instead, he kept the prince a virtual prisoner in specially constructed pleasure palaces, cut off from the harsh realities of the outside world.

Eventually, after his marriage to Princess Yasodhara, the twenty-nine-year-old Siddhartha was allowed to tour the capital city of Kapilavastu—all unpleasant and potentially disturbing sights having previously been removed by order of the king. These precautions proved in vain, however, for during his first excursions outside

13

the protective walls of his palaces the prince encountered totally un-expected visions of old age, sickness and death. These so shocked and disillusioned Siddhartha that, when he subsequently met with the vision of a homeless seeker of truth, he was immediately inspired to renounce the royal life completely and search for a cure to the sufferings of which he had so suddenly and painfully become aware.

After escaping from his father's kingdom, Siddhartha studied tech-niques of deep meditative absorption under two leading spiritual teachers of the day, hoping that they would provide him with an ef-fective antidote to the world's misery. He soon mastered these tech-niques so thoroughly that his teachers were prepared to appoint him their spiritual heir. But Siddhartha felt that the skills he had mastered, though useful, were insufficient to uproot the deep causes of dis-satisfaction from his mind and decided that only through a course of strict asceticism could he gain the self-control needed to overcome suffering completely. And so he departed for the kingdom of Magadha in which was located a forest that ascetics had long used as the site for their austerities.

Siddhartha's practice of self-denial was so determined and inspir-ing that five other ascetic practitioners attached themselves to him in the hope of benefiting from his eventual success. But after six years of austerities so severe that his body was reduced to little more than a skeleton,[2] Siddhartha concluded that this path of self-denial was fruitless and, in fact, counter-productive, since his weakened phys-ical condition was seriously undermining the clear working of his mind. He realized that if he was ever to achieve his desired goal he would have to travel a middle path, avoiding the extremes of self-indulgence on the one hand and self-deprivation on the other. Then, in order to regain his health, he accepted an offering of milk rice from Sujata, wife of a local herder, much to the disgust of his five com-panions. Thinking that he had thereby abandoned the religious life, they departed for the Deer Park at Sarnath near the ancient city of Benares, determined to continue their practices without him.

In this way Siddhartha, nourished by the milk rice, was left to con-tinue alone. Making a cushion out of bundles of cut grass, he took his seat under what later came to be known as the Bodhi Tree, or Tree of Enlightenment, and resolved to remain there until he had discovered the path leading to the end of all suffering. It was the night of the full moon, and as he sat there in meditation beneath the tree he came under attack by the legions of Mara, the disturbing forces that interfere with those intent on purifying themselves of the causes of misery. In an all-out attempt to break Siddhartha's concentration, these demonic forces of delusion churned up fierce storms, filled the air with blood-curdling screams and tried to frighten him with nightmarish apparitions. But throughout this onslaught the meditator remained undisturbed, his radiant aura of love rendering the powers of hatred harmless and ineffectual.[3]

Having failed in this way to disturb Siddhartha's concentration, Mara then embarked on another tack: he would divert the meditator's attention by conjuring up images of extreme sensuality. Suddenly Siddhartha was surrounded by visions of the most sexually alluring women, but these also proved powerless to distract his mind or weaken his adamantine resolve.

The only hope Mara now had of preventing Siddhartha from gaining the victory that would mean defeat for the delusions was to sow the seeds of doubt in his mind. Dismissing his legions, he appeared directly before the meditator and began to mock him. How could someone who had squandered his life first in self-indulgence and then in fruitless self-denial ever hope to achieve the goal that had eluded so many far more qualified seekers? Who was the witness who could testify that Siddhartha was worthy to succeed where others had failed? Without breaking the train of his concentration, Siddhartha responded to these taunts by stretching out his right hand and touching the earth beneath his seat (see Plate 1). In this way he silently and confidently called upon the earth itself as his witness. Immediately the earth-goddess Vasundhara appeared and testified that over countless lifetimes in the past the meditator had practiced the *perfections* of generosity, discipline, patience, effort, concentration and wisdom, thereby preparing himself for the victory he would win that night. Mara was defeated and disappeared, leaving Siddhartha to continue his inward quest undisturbed.

During the course of that night the meditator entered deeper and deeper states of concentrated absorption.[4] He viewed the interrelated rise and fall of all phenomena, and directly perceived that nowhere in this entire universe was there even one atom that had the slightest independent self-existence. He also saw that every instance of suffering has its root in the ignorance that fails to understand the interdependent way in which all things exist. As his wisdom became more and more penetrating, he achieved more expansive states of insight and awareness, and thereby removed subtler and subtler layers of obscuration veiling the pure, clear light nature of his mind. Finally at dawn the following morning, having removed the last obscuration preventing omniscience, he arose as a fully awakened one, a complete and perfect buddha.

Now in his thirty-fifth year, Siddhartha had transformed himself into Shakyamuni Buddha, the Fully Awakened Sage (Able One) of the Shakya Clan. For the next seven weeks he remained in the vicinity of the Bodhi Tree, enjoying the unlimited, blissful consciousness only a fully enlightened being experiences. During this time he refrained from teaching others, expressing the doubt that few if any would have the strength and determination required to travel the path to enlightenment as he had done. Eventually, however, in response to a request made by the worldly gods Indra and Brahma on behalf of all suffering beings, he gave full rein to the compassionate intention that had motivated him from the beginning and began to reveal what he had experienced to others. Realizing that the five ascetics who had shared the six years of austerities with him were the most qualified to benefit from what he could teach, he traveled to the Deer Park in Sarnath where he delivered his first discourse, or sutra. This sutra marked Shakyamuni's first turning of the wheel of *dharma*, the spiritual truths he had discovered. In it he set forth the *four noble truths* of suffering, the origin of suffering, its cessation, and the path leading to this cessation. These four were to occupy a central place in all his subsequent teachings.[5]

Throughout the remaining forty-five years of his life, the sole purpose of Buddha's spontaneously compassionate activity was to help alleviate the ignorantly created and self-imposed suffering of others. Yet as he himself said, a buddha does not remove suffering in the same way that one might pluck a thorn from the flesh of another. Thus despite the fact that Shakyamuni was an immensely inspiring and charismatic figure who had a profound, healing effect on those who met him, his main method of benefiting others was not through exercising his miraculous powers. Instead, his major activity was to reveal the teachings known as the buddhadharma, and one of the most outstanding qualities of these teachings was, and still is, their appropriateness to each individual's capacity and situation in life. To the highly educated, for instance, he might expound subtle lines of philosophical reasoning capable of cutting through the most deeply entrenched misconceptions about reality and the nature of existence.[6] At other times he might relate fables to the simple and unschooled, skillfully illustrating some moral truth in an easily understood fashion.[7] But no matter what approach he adopted, his purpose was always the same: to show others how, through their own efforts, they could free themselves from destructive and limiting patterns of thought and behavior and achieve lasting happiness through the fulfillment of their highest potential.

While it was Shakyamuni's purpose to reveal the path leading to full enlightenment, the decision whether or not to follow this path has always been left to the individual. Furthermore, Buddha emphasized that spiritual development is not a matter of passively accepting what he said as true; rather, it entails an active investigation of the dharma teachings to see if they are valid, applicable to one's own situation and helpful to one's growth. If upon examination the teachings are indeed seen to be reliable and beneficial, then one can confidently enter the path and begin one's spiritual training in earnest. The gateway into the buddhist path is the formal decision to entrust oneself to the *Three Jewels of Refuge*. These are the *Buddha*, the fully enlightened teacher; the *Dharma*, the teachings that lead one to full enlightenment; and the *Sangha*, the spiritual community intent on putting these teachings into practice.

Because of his compassion and skill in alleviating the suffering of others, Shakyamuni is often referred to as the Great Physician. His treatment, like a physician's, starts with a detailed diagnosis of the ills afflicting all sentient beings. One of his fundamental insights is that all experiences of suffering and happiness without exception are rooted in the individual's own mind. As is written in the *Dhammapada*, one of the most widely quoted collections of Shakyamuni's sayings:

> We are what we think. . . .
> Speak or act with an impure mind
> And trouble will follow you

As the wheel follows the ox that draws the cart. . . .
Speak or act with a pure mind
And happiness will follow you
As your shadow, unshakeable.[8]

If we sincerely wish to overcome dissatisfaction, experience happiness and fulfill our highest potential, it is therefore not enough to change the outer circumstances of our life. Instead, it is necessary to turn inward and cleanse ourselves of the impurities currently contaminating the essentially pure nature of our mind. Only by uprooting our greed, hatred, jealousy and other delusions can we experience true, lasting happiness and fulfill the enlightened potential, or buddha-nature, existing within each of us. Because these contaminating delusions are responsible for all our suffering, we must gain as accurate an understanding as possible of their nature, how they arise,[9] and how they compel us to move involuntarily from one unsatisfactory situation to another. Only then shall we be in a position to know how best to counteract and eventually uproot these inner enemies completely.

A detailed description of the way in which deluded states of mind keep us imprisoned within recurring patterns of suffering and dissatisfaction—i.e. within *cyclic existence* (Skt. *samsara*)—is given in Buddha's various teachings on the subject of *dependent arising* (Skt. *pratityasamutpada*). These profound teachings are vividly depicted in the widely reproduced diagram known as the Wheel of Life (Plate 2). Although at first glance it may appear confusing and alien to our experience, the Wheel of Life is an exact reflection of both our external and internal condition within cyclic existence, and it is as relevant to our present-day situation as it was when it was first revealed over two millennia ago. As long as beings remain unenlightened—as long as their essentially pure buddha-potential is shrouded in ignorance—they will continue to imprison themselves in exactly the same way they have always done. Furthermore, as long as they exert sincere effort to understand the nature of the mind and apply effective methods for uprooting the ignorantly produced delusions afflicting it, they will continue to gain liberation from their self-created prisons and free themselves from this cycle of suffering completely.

Buddha presented three interrelated trainings by means of which total liberation from suffering and dissatisfaction can be won. These three—the trainings in moral discipline, concentration and wisdom[10]—are often explained through the analogy of a woodsman felling a tree. For the woodsman's axe to be able to cut through the trunk of a tree, not only must the axe be sharp, but the woodsman must have a sufficiently steady aim to hit the same spot again and again, as well as sufficient strength to strike a penetrating blow. In a similar fashion, anyone intent on cutting through ignorance—the root of the delusions and source of all suffering—must develop a sharp and penetrating wisdom. But this will be of no use without the steadying effect of deep mental concentration, and there will be no way of developing either concentration or wisdom without the strength that comes from moral self-discipline. It is therefore only on the basis of cultivating all *three trainings* properly and thoroughly that ignorance can be overcome, the delusions defeated and true *liberation* (Skt. *nirvana*) achieved. Any man or woman who gains such an outstanding victory over the mental and emotional afflictions is known as a foe-destroyer (Skt. *arhat*). Among Shakyamuni's circle of disciples there were many who through their own spiritual maturity and perseverance, coupled with the inspiration of Buddha and his teachings, were able to achieve nirvana swiftly. Such is the case of the Arhat Lam-chung (Figure 4).

In his eightieth year, after a lifetime of guiding others by means of his discourses and personal example, Shakyamuni decided it was time to demonstrate to others how to die with the same tranquility and clear awareness that he urged them to cultivate throughout their life. While traveling back towards the place of his birth he paused at Kushinagar. There, after giving his final instructions to his followers—

Now monks, I declare to you: all conditioned things are of a nature to decay; strive on untiringly.[11]

he lay down on his right side, entered increasingly profound states of meditative absorption, and passed away into the state known as *parinirvana* or final liberation.

As he had instructed, his body was cremated and the remains enshrined in reliquary monuments (Skt. *stupa*) erected in the various kingdoms of North India. Over the ensuing centuries monuments such as the Stupa of Enlightenment (Plate 3) and related structures—such as the Ceylonese *dagoba*, the Burmese *pagoda* and the Tibetan *chorten*—have proliferated throughout Asia. Each one embodies in its design the essential elements of the path to complete liberation and enlightenment revealed by Shakyamuni. Stupas are now being constructed in the lands to which the teachings of Buddha have spread, serving to impress upon millions an image of enlightenment demonstrated by Shakyamuni under the Bodhi Tree 2500 years ago and still attainable today.

SHAKYAMUNI BUDDHA

Shakyamuni Buddha—fourth of the one thousand Founding Buddhas predicted to appear during the current eon—is shown seated on a jeweled platform upon which is a variously colored lotus supporting cushions of the sun (of which only the gold-colored edge is visible) as well as the moon. Eight snow lions (two in each corner) symbolizing fearlessness support this specially prepared throne, indicating that whoever sits here possesses the fearlessness[12] of a fully enlightened being. The lotus, sun and moon represent the *three principal aspects* of the path leading to a buddha's enlightenment: namely, *renunciation* of the causes of suffering, penetrative *wisdom* into the nature of reality, and the compassionate, *altruistic motivation* to benefit others. Since these three symbols appear repeatedly in buddhist art, it is helpful to examine them more closely now.

The lotus grows in muddy pools and swamps, but when it opens its beautifully colored petals above the surface of the water they are invariably stainless and immaculate. The ability of the lotus to grow and flower in such muddy conditions without becoming contaminated makes it a potent symbol of the way a spiritually evolved being arises from the world without being stained by any of the pollutants of worldly existence.[13] Here the lotus symbolizes the development of pure renunciation: the bold determination to cut attachment to everything keeping us imprisoned in cyclic existence so that we may experience true liberation. The Buddha is shown seated on a lotus to indicate that, having completely overcome the causes of suffering, he is unstained by ordinary concerns for gain and loss, praise and blame, and so forth. To represent the Buddha in this fashion also serves to encourage the viewer to cultivate a mind similarly directed towards complete liberation from worldly bondage.

The sun and moon symbolize omniscient wisdom (Skt. *prajna*) and compassionate *method* (Skt. *upaya*), the two indispensable qualities that must be cultivated jointly if enlightenment is to be achieved. These two also appear in the upper right- and left-hand corners of all the paintings in this series. Just as the sun banishes darkness as it shines upon the world, the wisdom that realizes the actual way in which things exist eliminates ignorance—the root cause of suffering—as it illuminates the mind. And just as the moon is said to shine with a cool, pacifying light, the compassionate methods employed to benefit others pacify all unwanted suffering. Whoever seeks a buddha's enlightenment must cultivate a union of such wisdom and method for, as it is said, method without wisdom is blind, and wisdom without method is dry and sterile.

Shakyamuni Buddha is shown seated in the full cross-legged posture known as the *vajra position* indicating the firmness and unwavering strength of his concentration. His right hand is in the earth-touching gesture (Skt. *mudra*) symbolizing his victory over all interferences and defeat of Mara, while his left hand rests in his lap in the mudra of deep meditative absorption into the nature of reality. In his left hand he cradles a begging bowl—one of the few personal possessions of a buddhist monk—which is filled with the three nectars of wisdom, long life and freedom from disease. The artist has further decorated the bowl with pieces of a mythical fruit said to possess spiritual and medicinal potency.

Shakyamuni's body has a rich, golden complexion and exhibits other special physical characteristics, such as the crown protrusion (Skt. *ushnisha*) and elongated ear lobes, by which the supreme *emanation body* (Skt. *nirmanakaya*) of a buddha can be recognized.[14] He sits within spherical auras of his own radiant wisdom and is clothed in the traditional robes of a monk. His outermost robe is of patchwork design to indicate that it is composed of many separate pieces of material sewn together. This illustrates the monks' custom of dressing in garments made from discarded pieces of cloth which were then colored with the cheapest and most plentiful dyes available, thereby symbolizing their non-attachment to such worldly concerns as reputation and self-aggrandizement.

As is true of the clothing of all the enlightened beings presented in this series, Shakyamuni's garments do not lie next to his skin but are suspended slightly above it revealing their contrastingly colored underside. This demonstrates the great out-pouring of wise, compassionate energy that radiates unceasingly from the heart of all buddhas. It is related that when King Bimbisara of Magadha wanted to give a friend what was to be the first image made of Shakyamuni, the artists he commissioned found the Buddha's radiance so overpowering that they could not look directly at him. Buddha therefore went to the shore of a lake so that the artists could copy the muted

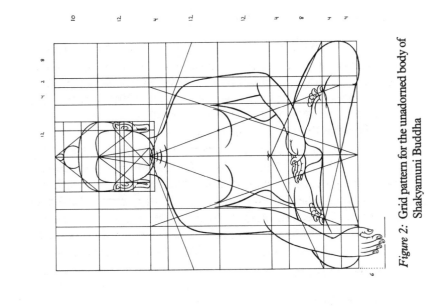

Figure 2: Grid pattern for the unadorned body of Shakyamuni Buddha

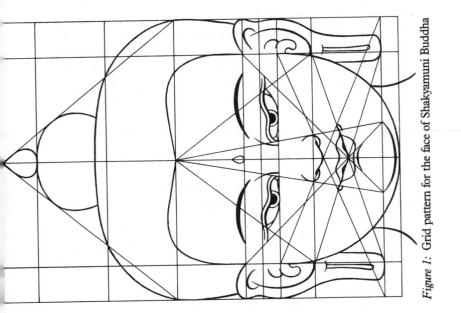

Figure 1: Grid pattern for the face of Shakyamuni Buddha

reflection of his image in the water.[15] This they did, measuring the dimensions of his reflection in finger-widths. These measurements formed the basis of all future representations of the Buddha and have been preserved in grid patterns (see Figures 1 through 3) that are still employed more than two thousand years later by artists of all buddhist traditions.

Before the seated figure of Shakyamuni Buddha the artist has placed an array of beautiful offerings to the transformed senses of the Awakened One. These consist of a flower (offered to the sense of smell), a stringed instrument (sound), a mirror (sight), a selection of different types of food (taste) and a length of cloth (touch). For ordinary, unenlightened beings, it is desirous attachment to such sensory objects that perpetuates the grasping, frustration and disappointment so characteristic of existence conditioned by ignorance. For one who has uprooted all worldly attachment, however, these same objects serve only to enhance the enlightened experience of blissful wisdom. The inclusion of these attractive objects and the care with which the artist has attempted to make them, and indeed the painting as a whole, as beautiful as possible are tokens of respect, gratitude and devotion for the figure depicted, in this case the compassionate Founding Buddha who turned the wheel of dharma for the present world age.

In the meditative practice of visualization an image symbolizing some aspect of the enlightened experience is placed at the focus of one's mind's eye and held there through the power of single-pointed concentration. Then, depending on the type of practice we are doing, we may, for example, visualize rays of light emanating from the imagined deity and bestowing waves of inspiration upon others and ourselves, or we may visualize the image dissolving into us and becoming one with the deepest level of our being. To give an idea how such a creative visualization may be performed, included below are simplified meditative instructions for a practice utilizing the image of Shakyamuni Buddha.[16]

Initial visualization

At the level of your forehead and approximately six feet in front of you is a large golden throne adorned with jewels and supported at each of its corners by a pair of snow lions. Neither the throne, the

Figure 3: Grid pattern for the robed body of Shakyamuni Buddha

lions or any other part of the visualization has even an atom of solid material substance. Instead, the entire visualization is a mere reflection of the mind and made of light—transparent, intangible and radiant.

On the throne is a seat consisting of a large open lotus and cushions of the sun and moon, symbolizing renunciation, wisdom and compassion. Seated upon this is your own personal spiritual guide in the aspect of Shakyamuni Buddha, the embodiment of all enlightened beings.

His body is made of golden light and he wears the saffron robes of a monk; these do not touch his body but are suspended slightly above it. He is seated in the vajra posture with his right hand in the earth-touching mudra signifying his great control and his left hand resting in his lap in the meditation mudra holding a begging bowl filled with three nectars.

Buddha's face is very beautiful. His smiling, compassionate gaze is directed at you and, simultaneously, at every other living being. Feel that this compassionate being is free of all judging, critical thoughts and that he accepts you just as you are.

His eyes are long and narrow. His lips are cherry-red and the lobes of his ears are long. His hair is blue-black and each strand is individually curled to the right. Every feature of his appearance represents an attribute of his omniscient mind.

Rays of light emanate from each pore of Buddha's pure body and reach every corner of the universe. These rays, comprised of countless miniature buddhas, go out and help living beings and then, having finished their work, dissolve back into his body.

Purification

Feel the living presence of the Buddha, understood as one with your spiritual guide, and take heartfelt refuge in him, recalling his excellent qualities and his willingness and ability to help you. Make a request from your heart to become free from all your negative energy, misconceptions and other problems and limitations and to receive all the realizations of the path to enlightenment.

Then feel that your request has been accepted. A stream of purifying white light, which is in the nature of the enlightened mind, flows from Buddha's heart and enters your body through the crown of your head, instantly dispelling the darkness of your negative energy. At the same time recite Shakyamuni's mantra, *OM MUNI MUNI MAHAMUNAYE SVAHA*, and feel that the white light conveys the mantra's enlightened energy from Buddha's heart directly into your own heart. Continue this visualization and mantra recitation until your body feels light and blissful and then concentrate on this feeling for a while.

Receiving inspiring strength

Next visualize that a stream of golden light descends from Buddha's heart and flows into your body through the crown of your head. The essence of this golden light is the Buddha's stainless wisdom. Recite the mantra as before. Your body again feels light and blissful; concentrate on this feeling once more for some time.

Absorption of the visualization

Now visualize that the eight snow lions melt into light and absorb into the throne, the throne dissolves into the lotus and the lotus into the sun and moon. They, in turn, absorb into the Buddha, who now comes to the space above your head, melts into golden light and dissolves into your body.

Your ordinary sense of I—unworthy and burdened with faults—and all your wrong conceptions disappear completely. In that instant you become one with Buddha's blissful, omniscient mind in the aspect of vast empty space.

Concentrate on this spacious experience for as long as possible, allowing no other thoughts to distract you.

Reemergence

Then imagine that from this empty space there appear in the place where you are sitting the lion-supported throne, lotus, sun and moon and upon these your own mind in the aspect of Shakyamuni Buddha. Everything is in the nature of light, exactly as you had visualized it earlier. Feel that you *are* Buddha. Identify with his enlightened wisdom, compassion and power instead of with your usual limited self-image.

Benefiting others

Now visualize that surrounding you in every direction and filling the vastness of space are all living beings. Generate love and compassion for them by recalling that they too want to achieve happiness and freedom from their suffering.

From your heart rays of light emanate and spread in all directions. As you recite the mantra, these rays reach the countless beings surrounding you and fill them with inspiration and strength. Visualize that they are all transformed into buddhas, experiencing great blissful wisdom.

Conclusion

Dedicate all the positive, meritorious energy and whatever insight you may have generated to your eventual attainment of full enlightenment for the benefit of all beings.

When disciples are instructed to practice a visualization such as this one, they are told not to worry that it may be mere pretense, or that they may not have helped even one person by means of it. Such meditations are known as "bringing the future result into the present path" and serve as powerful causes for our own eventual enlightenment, when we shall be able to accomplish what we can now only imagine. Through these meditations we develop a firm conviction in our own innate perfection and begin to peel away the limiting conceptions and deluded habit patterns preventing the fulfillment of this enlightened potential.

THE WHEEL OF LIFE

The diagram known as the Wheel of Life (Plate 2), depicting the various realms of cyclic existence and the beings inhabiting these realms, is primarily a visual aid to help us gain a clear understanding of the workings of our mind. By contemplating it well and studying the teachings it illustrates, we can learn to recognize that the cause of all our unwanted suffering is rooted in the delusions obscuring the essentially pure nature of our mind. We shall then be motivated to eradicate these delusions completely and thereby gain liberation from samsara.

Since the earliest days of Buddhism, such visual aids have played an important part in bringing spiritual teachings to the ordinary person, and they continue to be used for the same purpose today. For example, in modern-day Nepal it is not unusual to see a wandering monk travel from village to village carrying, among other things, a rolled up scroll painting depicting the Wheel of Life or some other teaching. Upon arriving in a village he quickly becomes the focus of attention for the villagers interested in hearing news from the surrounding countryside and distant towns. Then he unrolls his tangka (literally, "written record") and both entertains and instructs by explaining its meaning, sometimes in ordinary prose and sometimes in easily remembered verse or song. As this example illustrates, buddhist art and buddhist teachings have always traveled hand in hand and the spread of one has always involved the spread of the other.

The Wheel of Life diagram is said to have originated as follows.[17] One of Shakyamuni's chief patrons, King Bimbisara of Magadha, had received a precious gift from a neighboring king and could not think of anything suitable to give him in return. Upon learning of Bimbisara's dilemma, Buddha explained how to draw the Wheel of Life and said, "Give this diagram to your friend and he will definitely be satisfied." Bimbisara's friend was so ripe for spiritual instruction and the inspiration of the Buddha was so powerful that, as soon as he had read the stanzas inscribed beneath it, he immediately developed renunciation and a deep insight into reality. When this illustration of the Wheel of Life and the teachings embodied in it were made widely known throughout his kingdom, those who contemplated them well were also greatly benefited.

29

Turning our attention to the center of the wheel we find three animals representing the three root delusions, or mental poisons, responsible for all suffering and dissatisfaction. These are a pig representing ignorance, a pigeon[18] representing desirous attachment and a snake representing anger. In this painting the pigeon and snake are shown coming from the mouth of the pig to indicate that the destructive afflictions of desirous attachment and fearful anger both arise from fundamental ignorance of the way in which things actually exist. In other presentations the three animals are shown forming a ring, indicating the interdependence of all three delusions.

The largest portion of the wheel is divided into six sections illustrating the experiences of those who, under the pervasive influence of fundamental ignorance, are born either as gods, demigods, humans, animals, hungry spirits or hell-beings. These realms are brought into existence, not by a creator god, but through the ripening of potentialities previously generated by our own wholesome or unwholesome actions (Skt. *karma*). Since all such actions of body, speech and mind are initiated by mental intentions, ultimately these *six realms* are all creations of our own mind. These six states of existence can also be understood as states of consciousness we may experience even now as inhabitants of the human realm, as when encountering extremes of mental or physical pleasure and pain.

At the very bottom of the wheel is the *hell realm* (Skt. *narak*) of intense suffering. Shown presiding here is Yama, the Lord of Death, who holds in his right hand a stick which he uses as a pointer, and in his left hand a mirror. Before him kneels a recently deceased person—to be understood as oneself—and the various wholesome and unwholesome deeds of the life just finished are reflected in Yama's mirror and weighed in the scales of the demon standing before him. If unwholesome activities outweigh the wholesome, the unfortunate being is led away to experience the heat, cold, confinement, piercing pain and other torments characteristic of this agonizing state of existence.

It is important to remember that despite what is so vividly and dramatically depicted here, the painful experiences of this and the other realms are not punishments inflicted from without. Nor should these realms be thought of as preexisting places of imprisonment to which the suffering being has been banished by some outside force. As the great Indian master Shantideva wrote:

> Who intentionally created
> All the weapons for those in hell?
> Who created the burning iron ground?
> ...The [Buddha] has said that all such things
> Are [the workings of] an evil mind;
> Hence within the three world spheres
> There is nothing to fear other than my mind.[19]

In the case of hellish suffering, the predominant causes for experiencing such misery are our own uncontrolled mind's poisonous delusion of fearful anger and the extremely harmful actions, such as murder, that we engage in while motivated by such a powerful delusion. Even in the human realm we may experience a measure of this hellish suffering, as when we are boiling with rage or imprisoned in fearful paranoia.

To the left of the hell realm is depicted the realm of the *hungry spirits* (Skt. *preta*). The primary delusion leading one to be born here and experience the miseries shown is miserliness. As a result of negative actions motivated by this delusion, pretas suffer mainly from insatiable hunger and thirst. They are described as having thin necks, which are often tied in knots, and large, cavernous stomachs. They also experience many other hindrances in their quest for food and drink. For example, even when they manage to find something fit to eat, they may be prevented from approaching it by fearsome demons, the projections of their own negativities. And even if they do manage to get some food through their scrawny necks and down into their stomachs, it often turns to acid and brings them nothing but pain.

To the right of the hell realm is that of the *animals*. The main cause for rebirth in this realm is slavishly and stupidly following one's sensory desires, and although experiences within this realm vary enormously, animals in general suffer from limited intelligence. In addition, they must endure being chased and eaten by other animals, hunted and used for heavy labor by humans, exposed to heat and cold and plagued by continual hunger and thirst. We may know or read about people whose situation in life is so debased that it seems they are no longer living a human existence but have been reduced to the level of a beast.

In the upper half of the wheel are pictured the three higher realms of cyclic existence, so-called because compared with the three lower realms they contain less obvious suffering. Yet even in these higher realms there is great disappointment and dissatisfaction to be experienced. On the top and to the right are the interrelated *god* (Skt. *deva*) and *demigod* (Skt. *asura*) realms, sometimes pictured together. Because of their previous performance of sufficient positive actions, beings in the demigod realm enjoy extremely pleasurable surroundings, the company of attractive companions and intense sensory delights. However, the asuras are so consumed by jealousy for the superior devas that, instead of enjoying what they have, they engage in continual warfare with those above them, as depicted.

As for the devas themselves, while some of them are engaged in defending themselves from attacks by the inferior asuras, others live a life of uninterrupted sensory indulgence. Still others, in higher planes, spend their extremely long lifetimes in a sleep-like state of meditative absorption, experiencing neither pleasure nor pain but complete blank-mindedness. Devas easily mistake their experiences for true liberation from suffering but, since they have not uprooted the fundamental delusion of ignorance from their minds, they are not really liberated at all. Eventually, as is true for all the realms, the causes for experiencing life in that realm are exhausted. Because their store of virtuous energy has been depleted, even the most long-lived devas must face death and, what is worse, an inevitable descent to one of the lower realms. It is said that the mental anguish of a once fortunate deva foreseeing such a descent is even more excruciating than the physical torments of the most unfortunate hell-being.

Finally, to the left of the devas is the familiar realm of *human beings*. Life here, as Prince Siddhartha so painfully realized, is filled with the sufferings of birth, sickness, old age and death as well as uncertainty, dissatisfaction, frustration, boredom and the like. Furthermore, the pleasures available here are ephemeral and can easily turn sour, as when over-indulgent eating leads to indigestion. Despite their wishes to experience happiness and avoid suffering, humans are continually misled by their ignorance and must encounter unwanted miseries again and again.

In terms of providing an opportunity for spiritual growth, however, the human realm is considered the most fortunate realm of all. This is because, in general, humans enjoy an amount of freedom that neither the lower realm beings—who are preoccupied with pain— nor the higher gods—who are intoxicated by pleasure—possess. Motivated by the suffering and dissatisfaction they do experience, and endowed with varying degrees of discriminative intelligence, humans are particularly well-placed to do something of consequence with their lives. Specifically, they can learn how to cultivate the moral self-control, concentration and insightful wisdom necessary to uproot the causes of suffering and gain freedom from repeated rebirth in the realms of cyclic existence altogether.

None of the experiences in any of these six samsaric realms is permanent or everlasting; our situation is totally dependent upon changing causes and circumstances. Psychologically speaking, we can be elevated from a dissatisfied preta mentality to a blissful deva state and then thrust down into an agonizing hell all in a matter of a few moments. Furthermore, no matter which realm of cyclic existence we may currently inhabit, sooner or later our stay there must come to an end. Impermanence pervades cyclic existence and this is symbolized by the monstrous Lord of Death who is shown holding the entire Wheel of Life within his fangs and claws.

As Shakyamuni Buddha taught, death is not the final extinction or annihilation some people mistakenly believe it to be. Rather, it merely marks the transition between one life and the next. The mind itself is a beginningless continuum that moves from life to life and from body to body the way a traveler moves from one guest house to another. And just as we move up and down within one lifetime— experiencing alternating pleasure and pain according to changing conditions—so too do we move up and down from one life to the next depending upon the ripening of imprints left on our mind by the positive and negative actions we have committed.[20]

Between the end of one life and the beginning of the next is the *intermediate state* (Tib. *bardo*), illustrated in the half-black and half-white circle located between the hub of the delusions and the section representing the six samsaric realms. The bardo state is like a dream occurring between the sleep of death and the reawakening of the next birth, and in this painting six bardo beings are shown in the forms they will take after they "wake up" in their next rebirth realms.[21] Thus on the left are depicted a future human, asura and deva going upwards towards the higher realms, while on the right a future animal, preta and hell-being are shown descending to the lower realms.

The precise mechanism whereby beings are compelled by their ignorance to move up and down from one realm to the next is illustrated in the outer rim of the Wheel of Life. This rim is divided into twelve segments and each one corresponds to a link in the chain of dependent arising. Starting at the top right these twelve and their symbolic images are:

 (1) *ignorance*: an old, blind person
 (2) *compositional actions*: a potter making pots
 (3) *consciousness*: a monkey climbing up and down a tree
 (4) *name and form*: a man rowing a boat
 (5) *six sources*: an empty house with five windows
 (6) *contact*: a man and woman embracing
 (7) *feeling*: a man shot in the eye with an arrow
 (8) *craving*: a man drinking alcohol
 (9) *grasping*: a monkey grabbing fruit
 (10) *existence*: a pregnant woman about to give birth
 (11) *birth*: a baby being born
 (12) *aging and death*: a man carrying a corpse

A full discussion of these twelve links is beyond the scope of this work, but a very abbreviated explanation couched in terms of taking a human rebirth can be given as follows. (Note that for the sake of simplicity, the order followed in the explanation varies somewhat from the order in the illustration.[22])

In a past life while under the pervasive influence of (1) *ignorance* of the nature of reality, we were driven to preserve and defend our supposedly self-existent ego-identity. We therefore engaged in a wide variety of positive and negative (2) *compositional actions*, thereby planting numerous impressions, or seeds of karmic instinct, upon our (3) *consciousness*. Some of these actions were sufficiently constructive, or virtuous, to leave seeds of a future human rebirth.

As that past life approached its end we experienced great insecurity and an intense fear of dying. With our ego-identity facing the threat of annihilation, we craved and grasped both for the body we were leaving behind as well as for a new body to replace the one we were being forced to relinquish. Through the force of this (8) *craving* and (9) *grasping* at the time of death, certain imprints placed on our consciousness—in this case those for a human rebirth—were selectively ripened, and this ripening process eventually culminated in (10) *existence*, the decisive mental action that ensured our dying consciousness would take rebirth in another human life. (Because this decisive action leads to the coming into existence of another lifetime, it is given the name of its eventual result and called *existence*, or sometimes *becoming*.)

As death was occurring, our consciousness grew more and more subtle and eventually departed the body, whereupon it entered the intermediate state, or bardo. "Blown by the winds of its karma," our mind experienced various dream-like visions of repulsion and attraction until it eventually encountered a human couple having the necessary connection with us to be our parents. Our stream of consciousness again grew more and more subtle and eventually came into contact with the joining sperm and egg of our future parents. Conception marked our (11) *birth* into the human realm, as well as the start of our embryonic development beginning with (4) *name and form*. (*Name* refers to our stream of consciousness bearing various imprints and potentialities from the past, while *form* refers to the basis out of which our physical body will develop—the fertilized egg itself.) While still in the womb there developed (5) the *six sources*— the five sense faculties and the mental sense—leading to (6) *contact* with the appropriate sense objects. This eventually elicited our first (7) *feelings* of pleasure, pain and indifference in relation to these objects as a ripening effect of past positive, negative and neutral actions.

From the moment after conception we begin to grow older, undergoing the various changes and sufferings common to the human condition as we experience (12) *aging* and eventually *death*. While our future death will mark the end of one complete chain of twelve links, we have in the meantime begun forging innumerable new chains by continuing throughout our life to implant additional impressions on our (3) *consciousness* by engaging in further (2) *actions* motivated by (1) *ignorance*. In this way we remain bound to the cycle of recurring, unsatisfactory existence known as *samsara* (literally, "wandering" or "circling").

Until we and all other beings caught up in samsara have eradicated ignorance through the development of penetrating wisdom, we will be condemning ourselves to migrate ceaselessly from one unsatisfactory realm of existence to the next. However, even though this recurring cycle of death, birth and perpetual dissatisfaction has been called the Wheel of Life, there is another type of life we can live that lies outside this vicious circle. This is symbolized in the upper corners of this painting by the figure of a buddha—a being fully awakened from the nightmare of ignorance—who stands pointing to the moon—symbolizing the attainment of nirvana, the complete elimination of all delusion and suffering. Therefore, just as the Wheel of Life represents the first two noble truths of suffering and its cause, the figures outside the Wheel represent the final two truths: the cessation of suffering and the path of spiritual development leading to this cessation.

Finally, mention can be made of the stanzas Shakyamuni affixed to the bottom of the first diagram of the Wheel of Life, which had such a profound effect on King Bimbisara's friend. These read:

> Undertaking this and leaving that,
> Enter into the teaching of the Buddha.
> Like an elephant in a thatch house,
> Destroy the forces of the Lord of Death.
>
> Those who with thorough conscientiousness
> Practice this disciplinary doctrine
> Will forsake the wheel of birth,
> Bringing suffering to an end.[23]

In these lines Buddha indicates that if sufficient effort is exerted in the three trainings of moral discipline, concentration and wisdom as set forth in the dharma, even the heaviest sufferings of samsara can be eliminated completely and for all time. Because the sources of all suffering—ignorance and the other ensuing delusions—are totally devoid of self-existence, the well-trained practitioner can overcome the Lord of Death as easily as a powerful elephant destroys a fragile grass hut.

THE ARHAT LAM-CHUNG

Any being who has uprooted ignorance from his or her mind, thereby eliminating all delusions and extinguishing the source of all contaminated and harmful activity, has attained the complete liberation of nirvana and is consequently given the title of *arhat*. This term, sometimes translated simply as *saint*, literally means "foe-destroyer," for an arhat has overcome the greatest enemy to happiness—the inner poisons polluting the essentially pure nature of the mind.

As the Buddha says in the *Dhammapada*:[24]

> The Arhat's wandering is at an end. He is free from sorrow, completely free. Sorrow no longer exists for the one who has cut all bonds.

> The senses of the Arhat have been calmed, like well-trained horses quieted by a charioteer. The Arhat has abandoned pride and extinguished the passions, so that even the gods wish to be like him.

> The Arhat is as firm as the earth's foundations; firm in his spiritual practice, he is like a blade of tempered steel. Clear and undisturbed as a deep pond, such a being is not bound to the world.

> Quiet is the mind, quiet the body and speech. Completely freed by genuine knowing, such a being is truly at peace.

During the lifetime of Shakyamuni there were many men and women who, owing both to their own efforts and the inspiration and skill of the Buddha, were able to achieve the victory of arhatship. Different artistic traditions within Buddhism depict various groupings of such liberated beings forming the entourage of Shakyamuni. In the Tibetan tradition a group of sixteen arhats[25] is frequently portrayed and one of these is known as Lam-chung—literally, "Small Path" (Figure 4).

As a youth Lam-chung (Skt. *Chuda-panthaka*) gained an unenviable reputation for being dull and stupid. He was expelled from school because his tutors claimed he could never remember any of his lessons, and later the brahmin master to whom he was sent to study the Vedic scriptures dismissed him for similar reasons. Eventually his parents arranged for him to be ordained as a buddhist monk by his older brother Lam-chen ("Great Path"; Skt. *Panthaka*), also one of the sixteen arhats, who took personal responsibility for Lam-chung's education. Lam-chen began by giving his brother just one verse of Buddha's teachings to memorize, but even this proved too difficult for him; whatever he learned in the morning would be forgotten by that evening, and whatever he managed to learn at night would be forgotten by the next day. As a result of Lam-chung's repeated failure, even his patient brother was eventually compelled to dismiss him.

Lam-chung was completely desolate. Utterly depressed and miserable, he began to cry as he thought about his hopeless situation. Through the power of his clairvoyance, Shakyamuni saw all that had taken place and went to meet him. "Why are you crying?" he asked the dejected monk, and Lam-chung answered, "I am so stupid that even my own brother has given up on me."

Buddha comforted him and gave Lam-chung a simple method for purifying the veils that obscured his mind and prevented him from learning anything. He appointed the monk sweeper of the temple and told him merely to recite "Abandon dust; abandon stains" as he went about his duties.

Lam-chung was very happy with his new position and swept the temple floor with great dedication, reciting as he did so the few words Buddha had taught him. He swept and swept for a long time but, owing to the power of the Buddha, he could never get the floor completely clean. Whenever he swept one side of the temple a wind would arise and blow the dust to the other side. Undaunted, Lam-chung continued to sweep and purify just as Buddha had instructed, all the while reciting, "Abandon dust; abandon stains."

The situation remained like this for a long time until one day Lam-chung was struck by a powerful realization: the dust he was so occupied trying to eliminate had no inherent self-existence. He saw that not only the dust but all other phenomena as well, including himself, were completely selfless, lacking even an atom of independent existence. All the heavy, concrete misconceptions obscuring his understanding were obliterated by the strength of his sudden realiza-

Figure 4: The Arhat Lam-chung

tion and he gained direct, intuitive insight into the ultimate nature of reality. By thoroughly familiarizing himself with this insight he was transformed from an ignorant sweeper into a glorious arhat!

Shakyamuni Buddha saw that the purification techniques he had given Lam-chung had proved profoundly successful and decided to proclaim the new arhat's outstanding qualities publicly. He directed his attendant Ananda to inform a certain community of nuns that from then on their new spiritual master was to be Lam-chung. This dismayed the nuns very much, for they thought, "How can we accept being taught by a monk who is so stupid that he could not memorize even one verse of dharma?" Deciding that if they exposed Lam-chung's inadequacies they would not have to accept him as their abbot, they concocted a plan to humiliate him in public. They spread the word in the nearby towns that a monk who was as wise as Buddha himself would be giving teachings in their main hall and that all who attended were assured of gaining realizations. To increase his expected embarrassment they even erected a large, ostentatious throne and purposely failed to provide it with any steps leading up to its elevated seat.

When the day of the scheduled teachings arrived, thousands of people gathered in the main hall, some to listen to the discourse and others to witness Lam-chung's humiliation. When Lam-chung saw the large throne and realized it was designed to make him look foolish, he stretched out his arm like an enormous elephant's trunk and reduced the throne to the size of a tiny speck. Then he returned it to its former grandeur and, to the increased amazement of the gathering, flew up to the top of it! After entering deep meditative absorption and performing further miraculous feats he declared, "Listen carefully. I shall now give a week-long discourse on that same verse of dharma that I could not understand or even remember after months of trying."

When the seven days of teachings were completed, many in the audience attained a direct understanding of reality while others achieved advanced stages of realization up to and including arhatship. And those who had come to see him humiliated experienced a deepening of their faith in the Three Jewels of Refuge—the Buddha, Dharma and Sangha. Afterwards Shakyamuni himself prophesied that of all his disciples, Lam-chung would possess the greatest skill in taming the minds of others.

STUPA OF ENLIGHTENMENT

The state of nirvana, or arhatship, is achieved when all delusions have been completely eradicated from one's mind. When an arhat's fully liberated mind finally departs from his or her body at the time of death, it leaves behind all contamination forever. This is sometimes referred to as final liberation, or parinirvana. In the case of Shakyamuni Buddha, his apparent parinirvana at the age of eighty took place at Kushinagar, which—along with the sites of his birth (Lumbini), enlightenment (Bodh Gaya) and first discourse (Sarnath)—became and remains one of the four major centers of buddhist pilgrimage.[26]

Buddha had instructed his disciples that after his passing his body should be cremated and the remains enshrined in a reliquary monument (Skt. *stupa*) as was the custom with regard to the great leaders of the past in India. Shakyamuni's purpose for having such monuments erected was not self-aggrandizement but, in the words of the late Lama Govinda, "to remind later generations of the great pioneers of humanity and inspire them to follow their example, to encourage them in their own struggle for liberation."[27]

When Shakyamuni's body had been cremated, a dispute arose over whom the remains should belong to and who, therefore, should have the honor of erecting the monument. This quarrel threatened to escalate into serious conflict until a brahmin named Drone interceded. He reminded the would-be combatants that such a violent course of action was completely opposed to the teachings and example of the Compassionate One and suggested that his remains be divided equally among the various contesting parties. This was agreed upon and as a result eight separate stupas were built in different kingdoms of India to house the relics.

This eightfold division is echoed in the eight types of design still used in the Tibetan traditions for the construction of stupas to enshrine the remains of great teachers. These designs commemorate eight major events in the life of Shakyamuni. The type shown in the center of Plate 3 is known as a *stupa of enlightenment* and celebrates his vanquishing the forces of delusion. This and the remaining seven designs, together with the events they commemorate and their places of enactment, are listed below.[28]

41

(1) *The stupa of heaped lotuses*: Shakyamuni's birth at Lumbini

(2) *The stupa of enlightenment*: his defeat of Mara's forces under the Bodhi Tree at Bodh Gaya

(3) *The stupa of many gates*: turning the wheel of dharma at Sarnath

(4) *The stupa of descent from the gods' realm*: descent to earth after teaching his mother at Sankhya

(5) *The stupa of miracles*: his performance of miracles at Shravasti

(6) *The stupa of reconciliation*: his reconciling quarreling factions of the sangha community at the Bamboo grove at Rajagriha

(7) *The stupa of complete victory*: his voluntary prolongation of his life at Vaishali

(8) *The stupa of parinirvana*: his passing at Kushinagar

As suggested earlier, a stupa is more than a mere reliquary monument; it is an abstract image of the state of enlightenment attainable by all beings. As is true for so much of buddhist art, the symbolism of this architectural image operates on several different levels simultaneously. On what we may call the level of archetypes, a stupa incorporates five basic geometric shapes corresponding to the five elements—earth, water, fire, air and space—out of which the world and all the atoms within it are composed. Furthermore, the overall shape of a stupa bears a close resemblance to the image of a seated buddha (see Figure 5). Merely by viewing such harmoniously balanced images we receive subtle benefit, experienced as a feeling of peace, well-being and wholeness. Finally, it should be noted that the various levels of the stupa correspond to the various levels of the spiritual path culminating in full enlightenment.[29]

In addition to their symbolic qualities, stupas serve as focal points for the widely followed practice of circumambulation. At buddhist sites it is common to see pilgrims and other practitioners walking clockwise around a central stupa or shrine while at the same time reciting prayers, mantras and so forth. Such a practice helps to keep the image of enlightenment and all it represents at the center of one's attention and is therefore said to be very beneficial on both a con-

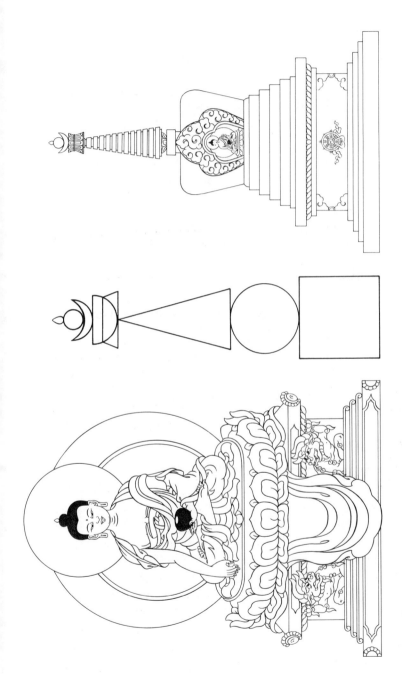

Figure 5: The abstract form of a stupa and corresponding buddha image

scious and sub-conscious level. However, the true value of any ritual activity such as circumambulation depends primarily on the attitude and motivation with which it is undertaken. This is illustrated in the following story[30] involving Dromtönpa, the chief Tibetan disciple of the great Indian master Atisha:

> One day Dromtönpa saw an old man circumambulating the Tibetan monastery of Radreng. Dromtönpa said to him, "Circumambulating is good, but practicing dharma is even better." Thinking this over the old man decided to stop circumambulating and read some buddhist texts instead. When Dromtönpa saw him studying in the temple courtyard he said to him, "Reading texts is good, but practicing dharma is even better."
>
> "Perhaps meditation is what is required," the old man thought and soon afterwards he was found sitting crosslegged on a meditation cushion. Again Dromtönpa approached him and said, "Meditation is good, but practicing dharma is even better."
>
> The old man was now thoroughly confused and asked, "What should I do to practice the dharma?"
>
> Dromtönpa answered, "Give up attachment to the things of this life. Your mind itself must become the practice and for this to happen you must cease being distracted by your habitual worldly concerns. Otherwise, no matter what you do it will not be the practice of dharma."

In conclusion, it should be noted that stupas vary enormously in size. Some, like the Great Stupa of Boudhanath[31] in Nepal, are monumental and attract thousands of pilgrims daily, while others are more modest and may or may not contain a small meditation room. Still others are mere models; these miniature stupas are often placed on a practitioner's altar along with a statue of a buddha and a buddhist text to symbolize, respectively, the purified mind, body and speech of a fully enlightened being.

2 The Bodhisattva Path

Without an acute awareness of our personal suffering and a deep, heartfelt determination to be completely rid of both this suffering and its causes, there is no way to begin the spiritual quest authentically. For just as Prince Siddhartha's sudden and unexpected visions of old age, sickness and death shocked him out of mistaking the world to be a pleasure palace, so too must all spiritual seekers confront the unsatisfactory nature of their lives so directly that they become thoroughly disenchanted with the ordinary human condition. If we do not take a long, hard look at the uncomfortable truths of our impermanent existence, we can easily waste the time between now and our inevitable death in essentially worthless pursuits, never taking advantage of this precious opportunity to do something truly meaningful with our life. Like the foolish prisoner who becomes so accustomed to the confines of his cell that he turns a blind eye to all chances of escape, we shall be condemning ourselves to spiritual stagnation and the endlessly recurring miseries of cyclic existence.

Yet it is not enough merely to become discontent with our present condition; everyone experiences discontent at one time or another but very few do anything of real significance about it. In fact, the usual ways of dealing with problems and disappointment—blaming them on someone else or drowning them in forgetfulness—only bind us tighter to the wheel of suffering. What we must do is recognize that the true causes of all our misery lie rooted in our own ignorant misconceptions and that these can only be eradicated through the development of a clear, penetrating insight into the nature of reality. Only through the continued cultivation of such penetrating wisdom will it eventually be possible to attain liberation from all states of existence conditioned by ignorance and be forever free of suffering.

As necessary as it is to develop the strong determination to win unconditioned release from suffering, eventually we must expand our horizons beyond concern merely for our own liberation. If we are to fulfill our enlightened potential to the maximum extent possible and achieve a goal even beyond self-liberation, our concern must become universal and encompass the welfare of *all* beings without exception.

The situation is dramatically conveyed through the following analogy. Suppose that together with our family we were caught inside a burning building; would it be enough for us to escape knowing that the rest of our family remained trapped and in danger? Obviously not. Because we hold our loved ones as dear and most precious and because we feel their suffering as acutely as we do our own, we could not rest comfortably until we had freed both them and ourselves from danger. Similarly, anyone who recognizes that the pervasive and recurring miseries of cyclic existence affect others as deeply as they do oneself—and who also recognizes the kinship that unites all beings into one family—will never be content with mere self-liberation. Instead, this high-minded being will be moved to emulate Shakyamuni Buddha himself and achieve full and complete enlightenment: the awakening of universal wisdom, compassion and skillful means far surpassing those of an arhat. Motivated by the precious *bodhichitta*—the thought (Skt. *chitta*) to win this full enlightenment (Skt. *bodhi*) for the sake of benefiting others—the altruistically motivated being (Skt. *sattva*) transcends all self-centered impulses and is transformed into a bodhisattva—an enlightenment-bound spiritual seeker and a true son or daughter of the Awakened Ones.

The Mahayana, or Great Vehicle, teachings in which Shakyamuni presented the bodhisattva path were originally delivered at Rajagriha in northern India and are known collectively as the Perfection of Wisdom sutras. In these discourses the path to buddhahood is shown to have two interrelated aspects: method and wisdom. Method here signifies the practices and activities that arise from the compassionate bodhichitta motivation to benefit others, and these are summarized as the five perfections (Skt. *paramita*) of generosity, discipline, patience, effort and meditative concentration. The sixth perfection is wisdom itself: the unmistaken understanding of how things exist devoid of projections and misconceptions rooted in ignorance. Compassionate method alone, unguided by the eye of wisdom, is blind and cannot cut the root of suffering; wisdom alone, unsupported by compassionate method, lacks the strength needed to achieve full enlightenment. It is only through the unified practice of both compassionate method and penetrative wisdom—embodied as the female deity Prajnaparamita (Plate 4)—that the bodhisattva can remove all the obscurations[1] preventing the attainment of complete awakening and thereby fulfill the deepest desires of both self and others.

For this precious bodhichitta motivation—the very heart of Mahayana Buddhism—to be developed it is not enough to mouth pious phrases about wishing to save others. Nor is it enough to look back admiringly to Shakyamuni and the other enlightened masters of the past and invoke their inspiration; this in itself will not bridge the gulf that appears to separate our limited abilities from their boundless attainments. Instead, we must be convinced that enlightenment is an achievable goal and, even more importantly, that we ourselves can attain it.

The state of full and complete enlightenment is characterized by three outstanding qualities—universal compassion, wisdom and power. In Vajrayana imagery these three are symbolized respectively by the meditational deities Avalokiteshvara, Manjushri and Vajrapani (Plates 5 through 8). Although it is said that they had already achieved full enlightenment eons previously, during the lifetime of Shakyamuni these three were among his eight prominent bodhisattva disciples[2] and demonstrated by their example how the bodhisattva path to full enlightenment should be followed.

Just as these three bodhisattvas inspired their contemporaries at the time of Shakyamuni Buddha, so too throughout the history of Buddhism have they continued to inspire others to develop the compassion, wisdom and power of the fully awakened mind. Although statues and paintings of these glorious beings can move us to some extent, it is through the mediation of the guru—a member of the unbroken lineages of transmission going back to Shakyamuni Buddha—that the full transformative effect of their inspiration can be brought to bear upon our innermost being. As is sometimes said by way of analogy, the guru is the magnifying glass that focuses the rays of the sun-like buddhas and bodhisattvas to ignite the flame of inspiration in our own heart.

Through sensitivity to a particular disciple's strengths and weaknesses, the spiritual guide can discern which of the three qualities is most in need of cultivation at any particular stage of development. If, for example, it is compassion, the guru might well introduce the disciple into the practice of Avalokiteshvara. For this practice to be successful, the guru conducts a ceremony of initiation, or empowerment, whereby a deep connection is forged between the disciple's mind and the chosen meditational deity.[3] During such a ceremony the disciple is given permission to practice this deity's *sadhana*, or method of accomplishment, and to recite the deity's mantra, a series of Sanskrit syllables that embody in sound the same enlightened qualities that the deity's image embodies in shape and color. By performing the sadhana every day, reciting the mantra and keeping in mind the fundamental unity of the deity and the guru, the disciple can speedily awaken and cultivate the enlightened qualities embodied by the deity.

PRAJNAPARAMITA

Shakyamuni Buddha gave many different teachings on the perfection of wisdom and these vary greatly in length. The longest is known as the *Perfection of Wisdom Sutra in One Hundred Thousand Verses* while the shortest, intended for those whose minds were particularly ripe for realizations, is merely the syllable *AH*. But whatever their length, their purpose is the same: to show how the bodhisattva should train in the correct view of reality and thereby achieve full awakening from ignorance.

According to these profound wisdom teachings, all our ordinary perceptions of ourselves and the world are mistaken. Why is this? Because to the ordinary, unenlightened mind everything appears to be *inherently* or *truly existent*.[4] As it says in a contemporary commentary to the *Heart Sutra*, the most commonly recited version of the Perfection of Wisdom sutras,

> 'If we are ordinary beings, all objects appear to us to exist inherently. Objects seem to be independent of our mind and independent of other phenomena. The universe appears to consist of discrete objects that have an existence in themselves as stars, planets, mountains, people and so forth, "waiting" to be experienced by conscious beings. Normally it does not occur to us that we are involved in any way in the existence of these phenomena. Instead, each object appears to have an existence completely independent of us and all other objects.[5]

According to Buddha's wisdom teachings, there is a not a single thing in the entire universe that has even one atom of such true, independent self-existence. However, we have become so accustomed to our ordinary view that it is extremely difficult to look at things in any way other than as truly existent. Indeed, it is difficult enough merely to get a clear idea of what our ordinary view is; it is so much a part of our makeup that it is hard to identify precisely.

For all these reasons, training the mind in the perfection of wisdom is not easy. But for those wishing full enlightenment, or even the lesser goal of self-liberation,[6] it is absolutely essential that we recognize our mistaken view, refute it thoroughly and cultivate a profound insight into *emptiness* (Skt. *shunyata*), the absence of all fantasized modes of existence. Only in this way can we soften our overly concrete view of things, let go of our imprisoning misconceptions and gain freedom from suffering and dissatisfaction.

The supreme view to be cultivated is called the *middle way* (Skt. *madhyamika*) because it avoids two dangerous extremes. The first is the extreme of believing that things exist inherently just as they appear to us now, with the result that we remain forever trapped within our present misconceptions. The second is experienced when, realizing that there is something wrong with our ordinary view of reality, we reject too much. We misunderstand what emptiness really means—the mere absence of inherent existence—and wrongly conclude that *nothing* exists. Mistaking emptiness to mean nothingness is a grave error indeed.[7] By rejecting the way in which things actually do exist, we lose whatever faith we may have had in the workings of cause and effect, with the result that our moral discipline—the foundation of all spiritual practice—is abandoned. The challenge, then, is to reject the wrong view of inherent existence while accepting that all phenomena, including ourselves, do have a validly established non-inherent, conventional manner of existence.

Because our mistaken conceptions lie at the root of all our suffering, meditation on the perfection of wisdom is the supreme technique for overcoming fear and averting interferences. As the Seventh Dalai Lama has said:

> Looking at this side, neither the body nor the mind exists
>   as objects to be harmed.
> Looking at that side, the harmer is also like the "snake"
>   projected onto a multicolored rope.
> May I realize decisively that holding merely labeled
>   dependent arisings to be truly existent is the projection
>   of my hallucinating mind.[8]

Concerning the averting of harmful interferences, there is a powerful practice that involves visualizing the deity Prajnaparamita (pictured in Plate 4) and reciting the *Heart Sutra*. We begin by visualizing Shakyamuni Buddha as described earlier. Then,

> At Buddha Shakyamuni's heart we visualize another lotus, moon and sun seat. On this is seated the Great Mother,

Prajnaparamita, who is the embodiment of the wisdom truth body of all the buddhas. She has a body of golden light with one face and four arms. Her first right hand holds a golden vajra with nine prongs at each end. In her first left hand she holds the *Perfection of Wisdom Sutra*. Her remaining two hands rest in her lap in the pose of meditative equipoise. She is adorned with precious jewels and ornaments and wears beautiful garments of thin, heavenly material.[9]

We then proceed with the preliminaries of taking refuge in the Three Jewels, generating the bodhichitta motivation, paying homage, making offerings and requesting blessings. After this comes the main body of the practice: reciting the *Heart Sutra* and the mantra of Prajnaparamita together with performing the appropriate meditations. At this time it is especially important to "contemplate that we and all that offends and harms us are empty of inherent existence."[10] The practice then concludes with making requests, visualizing the complete dissolution of all obstacles into emptiness, and the final dedication:

> May all kinds of interferences, diseases and possessing
>   spirits be pacified.
> May I be separated from unfavorable conditions
> And may I achieve favorable conditions and everything
>   excellent.
> Through this fortune may there be at this time happiness
>   and health.[11]

It is necessary to keep in mind that the effectiveness of this practice is dependent upon how well we understand emptiness and also upon our faith in Shakyamuni Buddha and Prajnaparamita. If our wisdom and faith are strong, it is said that all obstacles can be overcome through this method. One story cited as an example of the effectiveness of this practice relates to the warfare, illustrated in the Wheel of Life, that rages between the gods and demigods:

> There was once a time when the god Indra was in danger
> of losing his life because of an attack by the powerful forces
> of jealous demigods. Indra had previously received teach-

Figure 6: The Tibetan yogini Machig Labdron

ings from Buddha and knew that to kill the demigods would be a serious transgression of those teachings. Wishing, therefore, to overcome his attackers by a peaceful method, Indra contemplated the profound meaning of the *Essence of Wisdom Sutra* [i.e. the *Heart Sutra*] while reciting its words. Through the power of this contemplation and recitation, the demigods ceased their attack; their anger subsided and their minds became peaceful and happy.[12]

There is another practice related to Prajnaparamita that deserves at least brief mention here. This is the *chod,* or cutting off, rite that "teaches how to sever attachment to the concept of an intrinsic personal self."[13] This rite was initiated by the Tibetan yogini Machig Labdron (Figure 6) who is regarded as an incarnation of Guru Rinpoche's consort, Yeshe Tsogyal, and an emanation of the Great Mother, Prajnaparamita herself.[14] Even in her youth Machig Labdron (1055-1152) was well-versed in the Perfection of Wisdom sutras and was often called upon to recite them. Eventually, inspired by the great Indian yogi Padampa Sangye[15], she developed the *chod* rite for gaining insight into emptiness by cutting off attachment to one's body and one's self.

As traditionally practiced, chod is performed in desolate, frightening places such as cremation grounds. The fear that arises in these places provides a powerful opportunity for recognizing the inherently existent "I" that is to be refuted by the wisdom of emptiness, and the practice is designed to overcome ignorance and self-cherishing in the most direct manner imaginable.

Concluding this section on Prajnaparamita—the Great Mother, the Wisdom Gone Beyond—is the following stanza of homage often recited by practitioners when requesting inspiration for the development of enlightening insight:

> Reality is unimaginable and inexpressible,
> Experienced only by the Wisdom Gone Beyond.
> Like the nature of space, it is unborn and unceasing;
> It is an object totally realized
> Only by single-pointed, absolute wisdom itself,
> Which sees the true nature of all phenomena.
> To the Mother of the Buddhas of the three times
> I pay homage.[16]

FOUR-ARMED AVALOKITESHVARA AND
THOUSAND-ARMED AVALOKITESHVARA

Avalokiteshvara—He Who Looks with an Unwavering Eye—is the embodiment of all the buddhas' infinite compassion. He is white in color and is shown in Plate 5 in his four-armed aspect. His first two hands are pressed together at his heart supplicating all buddhas and bodhisattvas to look after sentient beings and protect them from suffering. These hands hold a wish-fulfilling jewel symbolic of Avalokiteshvara's compassionate bodhichitta motivation. His other right hand holds a crystal rosary symbolizing his ability to liberate beings from samsara with ideal means, and reminding the practitioner to recite his six-syllable mantra, *OM MANI PADME HUM*. In his left hand he holds the stem of a blue utpala flower symbolizing his stainless and compassionate bodhichitta motivation. The utpala in full bloom together with two buds stand for the three times and indicate that Avalokiteshvara's compassionate wisdom encompasses past, present and future.

Over his left shoulder is draped the skin of a wild deer, representing the compassionate bodhisattva's kind and gentle nature and his ability to subdue the untamed delusions. As a traditional commentary explains:

> This particular deer is said to live upon mountains in the margins between the snow and rock. It has incomparable physical strength, but is extremely compassionate by nature. One of the hunters' tactics is to enter its territory and pretend to fight among themselves with swords. Seeing this, the deer becomes impatient with compassion and emerges to mediate between them, which provides the hunters the opportunity to kill it. Merely touching its skin with one's feet calms the mind and endows it with bliss.[17]

The deer skin also serves as a reminder of the importance of a spiritual practitioner's developing strong and stable meditative concentration. Ancient Indian traditions going back at least to the Upanishads recommend that yogis—those devoting themselves wholeheartedly to the practice of meditation—sit on such skins as a way of insulating themselves from disruptive, earth-transmitted energies, and this advice is still followed today. Successful meditation depends very much on being able to control and direct one's mental and physical energies, which is difficult if not impossible to do if we are continually distracted by outside forces. This is also why the full cross-legged position is recommended; together with other aspects of the meditation posture it helps center our energies and focus them inward. Even though our main intention is to reach out and help others, it is still vitally important to keep our own inner resources protected. We cannot realistically hope to benefit others if we ourselves are buffeted back and forth by the shifting currents of worldly energy.

As was the custom with ancient Indian royalty, Avalokiteshvara is dressed in silken robes and adorned with various jeweled ornaments, such as bracelets, necklaces and the like, symbolizing his mastery of the perfections of generosity, morality and so forth. In the manner of a prince he wears his black hair long, some of it piled high on his head and the rest flowing down to his shoulders. This indicates that just as a prince is the son of and heir to a royal king, this bodhisattva is the spiritual son and heir to the king-like buddhas. Upon his head is a crown adorned with five variously colored jewels[18] representing the five buddha families, about which more will be said in Chapter Three. He is seated within a transparent aura and the artist has placed him in a peaceful scene of hills and lakes.

With his compassionate gaze Avalokiteshvara looks upon the beings in all realms of cyclic existence with the heartfelt wish that they be separated from whatever mental and physical suffering they may be experiencing. Each syllable of his mantra is directed towards a specific realm and is visualized, according to some practices, in the color that corresponds to that realm, as follows:

OM	white	gods
MA	green	demigods
NI	yellow	humans
PAD	blue	animals
ME	red	pretas
HUM	black	hell-beings

6 syllables = 6 heads

When the practitioner of Avalokiteshvara recites the mantra, he or she visualizes that appropriately colored light radiates to the beings in each realm and, after pacifying their particular suffering, guides them along the path to liberation and full enlightenment.[19]

Like visual images, mantras work on several different levels simultaneously. On the most basic vibrational level they derive their power from their very sound. Having arisen from the deep experiences of enlightened beings, these "words of power" are imbued with enlightening inspiration and blessings.[20] Reciting *OM MANI PADME HUM* with strong faith is therefore extraordinarily effective in countering the negative forces dragging us down into the recurring miseries of the six samsaric realms.

In addition to the sheer power of its sound, a mantra is also effective in terms of the various ways its meaning can be understood. In the case of *OM MANI PADME HUM*, all of the 84,000 teachings traditionally ascribed to Shakyamuni Buddha can be explained in terms of these six syllables. One of the many ways of understanding their meaning follows.[21]

Because the syllable *OM*, which appears at the opening of nearly all mantras, is composed of three elements in the original Sanskrit, it stands for the three doors of our present body, speech and mind. *MANI* literally means "jewel" and stands for an enlightened being's compassionate method; just as the legendary wish-fulfilling jewel has the power to satisfy our desire for wealth, compassion fulfills the desire of all beings to be separated from suffering. *PADME* is derived from "padma," meaning "lotus," and here symbolizes the wisdom of ultimate reality; just as a lotus is unstained by the mud out of which it grows, wisdom is unstained by all hindering conceptions of inherent self-existence. Finally, the syllable *HUM* is made up of five elements representing the five families of buddhas into which our ordinary mental and physical constituents, or *aggregates*, are transformed when full enlightenment is achieved (see Plate 9).

The mantra *OM MANI PADME HUM* can therefore be interpreted as follows: through the blessings of Guru Avalokiteshvara and the combined practice of method and wisdom, our ordinary body, speech and mind are transformed and we attain the full enlightenment of the five buddha families.

During the lifetime of Shakyamuni Buddha, Avalokiteshvara manifested as one of his major bodhisattva disciples. In this capacity he plays an important role in many of Buddha's discourses, especially in the often-recited and much-studied *Heart Sutra*. There he is the main speaker, inspired by Buddha to explain to the arhat Shariputra and a large gathering of lay and ordained disciples how a bodhisattva gains direct insight into the ultimate nature of reality:

> . . . Shariputra, whatever son or daughter of the lineage wishes to engage in the profound perfection of wisdom should look perfectly like this: subsequently looking perfectly and correctly at the emptiness also of the five aggregates. Form is empty; emptiness is form. Emptiness is not other than form; form also is not other than emptiness. Likewise, feeling, discrimination, compositional factors and consciousness are empty. Shariputra, like this all phenomena are merely empty, having no characteristics. They are not produced and do not cease. They have no defilement and no separation from defilement. They have no decrease and no increase. . . .
>
> Therefore, Shariputra. . ., bodhisattvas rely on and abide in the perfection of wisdom; their minds have no obstructions and no fear. Passing utterly beyond perversity, they attain the final nirvana. Also, all the buddhas who reside perfectly in the three times having relied upon the perfection of wisdom became manifest and complete buddhas in the state of unsurpassed, perfect and complete enlightenment.[22]

In another sutra Shakyamuni himself declared that for many ages Avalokiteshvara had a special relationship with the snowy land of Tibet, and prophesied that in future he would subdue its barbarous inhabitants and lead them along the path to enlightenment. All this would be the result of the vow that Avalokiteshvara had made long ago in the presence of the thousand buddhas of this fortunate eon. In that vow he stated his compassionate intention: "May I be able to establish in emancipation all the living beings in the barbaric Land of Snow, where beings are so hard to discipline and none of the buddhas of the three times has stepped. . . . May I be able to mature and emancipate them, each according to his own way. May that gloomy, barbaric country become bright, like an island of precious jewels."[23] Shakyamuni also related how Avalokiteshvara took mirac-

ulous birth from a shaft of light that emanated from the heart of
Amitabha Buddha (Plate 10), lord of the Joyous Pure Land of the
West, and transformed into a radiant lotus. Within this lotus the four-
armed incarnation of Avalokiteshvara was discovered, and Amitabha
predicted that this would be the aspect to subdue the Tibetans.

In front of Amitabha, his spiritual father, Avalokiteshvara repeated
his vow to work unceasingly for the welfare of all beings. So strong
was his compassionate motivation that he declared, "Until I relieve
all living beings, may I never, even for a moment, feel like giving
up the purpose of others for my own peace and happiness. If I should
ever think about my own happiness, may my head be cracked into
ten pieces. . .and may my body be split into a thousand pieces, like
the petals of a lotus."[24] Thereafter he entered a profound state of
meditative absorption in which he remained uninterruptedly for a
very long time. Single-pointedly he recited the six-syllable mantra,
directing his compassionate intention to each and every sentient being, wishing that all of them would be free of their suffering.

When he finally arose from his deep absorption and surveyed the
Land of Snow, he was bitterly disappointed to realize that he had
in fact helped only a minute number of beings out of their misery;
the vast majority remained trapped within their delusions as before.
In desperation he called out, "What is the use? I can do nothing for
them. It is better for me to be happy and peaceful myself." No sooner
had these words passed his lips than, by the power of his previous
vow, his head split into ten pieces and his body into a thousand, filling
the dejected bodhisattva with unbearable pain.

Avalokiteshvara cried out to Amitabha, who immediately appeared
before him. The Buddha of the West looked lovingly at his son and
told him not to despair:

> All circumstances come from cooperative causes
> Conditioned at the moment of intent.
> Every fortune which arises to anyone
> Results from his own former wish.
> Your powerful expression of supplication
> Was praised by all the buddhas;
> In a moment of time
> The truth will certainly appear.[25]

Then Amitabha restored Avalokiteshvara's broken body, transfiguring his torn flesh into a thousand hands, each with its own wisdom eye. Similarly he transformed the shattered pieces of his head into ten faces, nine of them peaceful and one wrathful, so that he could look in all directions simultaneously and reach out compassionately and forcefully to all beings. Finally, to show how pleased he was with his heart-son, he crowned the bodhisattva's ten faces with a replica of his own. In this way the eleven-faced, one-thousand armed aspect of Avalokiteshvara that is so widely loved by the Tibetan people came into being. This deity is represented in Plate 6 where, in addition to the jewel, rosary and lotus of the four-armed version, he is shown holding a vase, bow and wheel and making the mudra of bestowing realizations. (It should be noted that in some illustrations, for the sake of clarity, only eight of Avalokiteshvara's one thousand hands are shown; in more detailed renderings, the remaining 992 hands are in the mudra of bestowing realizations and reach out in all directions, forming a circular design.) It is this aspect of Avalokiteshvara that is the central figure in the fasting and purification practice known as *nyung-nay*, whose lineage is traced back to the fully ordained Indian nun known in Tibet as Gelongma Palmo.

Avalokiteshvara became and remains the patron deity of Tibet and his practice was among the very first introduced there when Buddhism initially entered the Land of Snow from India. The Tibetan people even claim descent from Avalokiteshvara, who, in the form of a monkey, is said to have sired the original inhabitants of the Roof of the World. Throughout subsequent Tibetan history the bodhisattva of compassion has appeared in numerous forms to propagate and defend the buddhist teachings and its practitioners. He has been identified with, among others, the first of Tibet's great religious kings, Songtsen Gampo (617-698); Guru Rinpoche or Padmasambhava, the great Indian master who first brought the Vajrayana teachings to Tibet; Atisha's renowned disciple Dromtonpa (1004-1064); and His Holiness Gyalwa Karmapa, the head of the Kagyu tradition of Tibetan Buddhism.

Most especially it has been through the lineage of successive Dalai Lamas that Avalokiteshvara's compassionate influence has poured into Tibet. And now, with the widespread activities of His Holiness the Fourteenth Dalai Lama, Tenzin Gyatso, this influence is radiating out far beyond the boundaries of occupied Tibet to all corners of this strife-torn world. To request the long life of this eminently compassionate being so that the world may continue to benefit from his enlightened presence, it has been the custom for Tibetans to recite daily the following four-line prayer, a prayer now recited by an ever-growing number of devotees from other lands as well:

> In the heavenly realm of the snowy mountains,
> The source of all happiness and help for beings
> Is Tenzin Gyatso: Avalokiteshvara in person.
> May his life be secure for hundreds of eons.[26]

To conclude, the following stanzas of request are taken from a popular practice centered upon this figure of universal compassion:

> Noble Avalokiteshvara, treasure of compassion,
> Together with your retinue, please listen to me.
> May you quickly rescue me and my fathers and mothers,
> The six kinds of beings, from drowning in samsara's ocean.
>
> I request that we may quickly attain
> The profound and vast bodhichitta.
> May all our karma and delusion
> Accumulated since beginningless time
> Be purified by the nectar of your compassion.
>
> With your outstretched hands
> Please lead us to the Blissful Land.
> I request that you and Amitabha
> Become our spiritual masters in all future lifetimes.
> Guide us along the noble and flawless path
> And quickly lead us to buddhahood.[27]

Avalokiteshvara prayer

MANJUSHRI

Manjushri—Smooth, Glorious, Melodious—is the embodiment of all the buddhas' infinite wisdom. He is golden orange[28] in color and holds the flaming sword of wisdom in his right hand and in his left the stem of a lotus flower upon which rests a volume of the Perfection of Wisdom sutras (Plate 7). The artist has depicted Manjushri as manifesting in the sphere of limitless space as a way of symbolizing the clear, unobstructed nature of this deity's omniscient mind.

All the attributes of Manjushri point to the wisdom that he personifies. His double-edged sword cuts through obscuring layers of misconception and discriminates accurately between the independent way things mistakenly appear to exist and the interdependent way they actually do exist. The *Perfection of Wisdom Sutra* he holds, treasured as Buddha's most profound statement on the ultimate nature of reality, is a further indication that Manjushri's penetrating insight is of the highest order. It is said that the two most powerful ways of developing wisdom oneself are to study these profound sutras and to meditate upon Manjushri. It is the custom of Tibetan school children, and also of monks and nuns, to recite the mantra of Manjushri the first thing each morning and to repeat over and over the seed-syllable *DHIH* that embodies the essence of his wisdom.

As in the case of Avalokiteshvara, Manjushri has been identified with many of the important patrons and gurus instrumental in spreading and preserving the buddhist dharma in Tibet. King Trisong Detsen (742-798), who invited Padmasambhava (Plate 27) from India to establish Vajrayana Buddhism in Tibet, is considered to have been an incarnation of Manjushri, as were the great Nyingma lama Longchen Rabjampa, the Sakya Pandita (Plate 28) and the Geluk master Je Tsong Khapa (Plate 31).

Manjushri not only plays an important role in many of Shakyamuni Buddha's philosophical discourses, but he figures prominently in myths and legends that originated in Buddha's time and are still widely known today. One of the most famous of these relates how Manjushri drained the Kathmandu Valley of Nepal and made it suitable for human habitation and the spread of the buddhadharma.

Ages ago, seated in meditation on the Five-Peaked Mountain in China that is his home,[29] the bodhisattva Manjushri became aware of the Nepal Valley and the lake of pure water which filled it. It was in this lake that a previous buddha had planted the root of a lotus which eventually grew into an enormous thousand-petaled blossom, and it was upon this lotus that the dazzling light known as Svayambhu Dharmadhatu—the Self-created Sphere of Ultimate Reality—miraculously appeared.

Sword

Arising from his meditation, Manjushri came to the valley, taking with him his sword Chanda Hasa, "the Dreadful Laugh." At a place called Turtle Mountain, he cleft the earth with his powerful sword, thereby allowing the water of the lake to drain away to the south. Then, in order to make amends to Turtle Mountain for carving into it in this way, he established a shrine there in honor of Avalokiteshvara so that in the future the site would become a place of homage.

As the water drained out of the valley a hill known as Diamond Peak appeared bearing the lotus and light of Svayambhu. In a later epoch this miraculous light was enshrined in a stupa to preserve it for increasingly degenerate future generations. The Svayambhu Stupa is still one of the main pilgrimage centers in Asia and the site has been visited by a succession of outstanding buddhist masters beginning with Shakyamuni himself. When the great Indian mahasiddha Nagarjuna later went there, he recovered the *Perfection of Wisdom Sutra* that had been entrusted to the *naga* king living beneath Diamond Peak; thereafter he disseminated these precious Mahayana teachings widely, bringing about a renaissance of buddhist thought and practice throughout the Indian subcontinent and beyond.

Another popular story set during Shakyamuni's lifetime tells of Manjushri's encounter with a group of Buddha's disciples who were on the verge of achieving nirvana, the self-liberation of arhatship. Confronting them he declared his belief that there was something far more worthy to strive after than mere self-liberation, namely the full awakening of buddhahood. Then he told them about the compassionate bodhichitta motivation and taught them the path leading to enlightenment for the sake of others. The disciples were very upset to hear the goal of their intense practice, nirvana, relegated to an inferior status and retaliated by maligning the bodhisattva path Manjushri had just revealed to them. As a result of the anger they generated towards this exalted teaching, their previous realizations degenerated and, not only did they fail to achieve arhatship, but after their deaths they were reborn in a suffering lower realm!

The bodhisattva Vajrapani (Plate 8), astounded by what he had witnessed, went directly to Shakyamuni Buddha and asked the Omniscient One to explain the meaning of Manjushri's actions. Shakyamuni answered him by saying, "What you saw was an example of Manjushri's great compassionate wisdom. Had those disciples achieved nirvana it would have taken eons to awaken them from the bliss of their self-liberation so that they could work for the benefit of others. Because of Manjushri's intervention, however, when these disciples emerge from their suffering rebirth—having burnt up and purified the harmful effects of their anger and narrow-mindedness—the impression of the bodhisattva path placed on their consciousnesses will arise strongly in their minds. Following this path they will achieve full enlightenment swiftly, thereby bringing supreme benefit not only to themselves but to countless others as well."[30]

These stories help illustrate the ways in which Manjushri's enlightened wisdom offers protection from what are often referred to as the "two fears," those of samsara and nirvana. Concerning the former, all the frightening mental and physical sufferings in the six realms of cyclic existence are the result of negative karma—those destructive, non-virtuous actions that propel us involuntarily from one unsatisfactory state to another. As illustrated in the Wheel of Life, all such negative actions are motivated by the delusions—greed, hatred, jealousy and the like—which are themselves rooted in our ignorance of the way things exist. Manjushri's sword of wisdom destroys the false and misleading conceptions fabricated by this root ignorance, thereby offering ultimate protection from the fears of cyclic existence.

As for the second of the two fears—those of nirvana, or solitary peace—at first sight this appears to involve a serious contradiction in terms. After all, what is there to fear when the root cause of all personal suffering has been eliminated forever? As the story of Manjushri and the would-be arhats shows, what is fearful about the peace of self-liberation is not one's own suffering—for this has been totally eradicated—but rather the way this blissful liberation breeds complacency and indifference to the suffering of others. Such indifference is the very antithesis of the compassionate bodhichitta motivation to gain enlightenment for the sake of benefiting others. Manjushri's insightful attitude, imbued as it is with this compassionate motivation, never loses sight of the welfare of those who, like ourselves, wish only to be happy and to escape from suffering. This altruistic attitude guards us from the "fear" of striving for our own release to the neglect of all other self-imprisoned beings.

To conclude, the following are verses of praise to Manjushri often recited at the beginning of dharma teachings to invoke the inspiration of enlightened wisdom:

Salutations to my guru and protector Manjushri,
Who holds to his breast a scriptural text
Symbolic of his knowledge of all things to be known;
Whose understanding shines forth as the sun,
Unclouded by defilements or traces of ignorance;
Who teaches in sixty ways,
With the patient love of a father for his only child,
All creatures caught in the prison of samsara,
Confused in the darkness of their ignorance,
Overwhelmed by their suffering.

You, whose dragon thunder arouses us from the stupor of
    our defilements
And frees us from the chains of our karma;
Whose powerful sword of wisdom hews down suffering
    wherever it appears and clears away the darkness of all
    ignorance;
I entreat you, O Manjushri,
Whose princely body is adorned with all 112 signs of a
    buddha;
Who has completed the ten stages
Achieving the highest perfection of a bodhisattva;
Who has been pure from the beginning:

I entreat you to remove the darkness from my mind.
Illuminate the darkness enclosing my mind.
Enable me to receive sure insights into the texts.
Enlighten me with the brilliance of your wisdom,
O Manjushri, all-loving one![31]

VAJRAPANI

Vajrapani—He with a Diamond Scepter in Hand—is the embodiment of all the buddhas' infinite power and is the first meditational deity in this series to be represented in wrathful form. As befits a figure symbolizing enlightened power or energy, Vajrapani is shown in Plate 8 in a standing, active posture rather than in the accustomed seated meditation pose. He is deep-blue in color and wears a tiger-skin cloth, emblematic of fearlessness, wrapped around his waist. Both his hands are in the threatening mudra used for overcoming hindrances, and in his right hand he holds a vajra, or diamond-hard scepter. Just as the Olympian Zeus brandishes a thunderbolt as a symbol of his might, Vajrapani wields a vajra symbolic of the enlightened power of full spiritual awakening.

He is adorned not only with jeweled ornaments but also with snakes of anger, which he controls by the superior force of his compassion. He strides atop a sun disc and displays a wrathful expression, baring four fangs. His eyebrows, mustache and beard are shaped like flames and his long, flowing hair streams upwards violently. Vajrapani is endowed with a third eye of wisdom in the center of his brow and is surrounded by flames of wisdom-energy emanating from all the pores of his powerful body. The artist has set off this fierce-looking figure dramatically by placing him in a Himalayan setting amidst snow mountains.

In front of Vajrapani is an eight-spoked wheel of dharma standing for the *eightfold path* of Buddha's teachings. The wheel also indicates that the dharma of enlightened beings is not static but moves from one culture to another, skillfully adopting new forms to express the eternal truths of the suffering nature of cyclic existence and the paths leading from recurring misery to true liberation and enlightenment.

Buddhahood brings to fruition the three essential qualities of compassion, wisdom and power, the last of which is also referred to as skillful means. The necessity of cultivating all three to fulfill one's altruistic intention to benefit others is illustrated by the following analogy. Suppose that we were to witness an accident in which a young boy falls into a river and is in danger of drowning. Even if the child is not ours it is very easy to develop compassion for him be-

65

cause there effortlessly arises in us the heartfelt wish that he be rescued as quickly as possible. We may also have a clear understanding of what caused the danger and what must be done to save the
boy from it, and this understanding itself is a form of wisdom. But
if we are crippled or weakened by disease or hindered in any other
way, all our compassion and wisdom will be to no avail; there is no
way we can be of any real help to the boy.

In a similar fashion, if we are to be of true benefit to all beings we
need more than compassion for their suffering and the clear wisdom
that penetrates the cause of that suffering; we need to be endowed
with the skill and ability required to put our compassion and wisdom into action. This entails, among other things, knowing the
predispositions of those we are to help and having an intuitive understanding of which approach will bring about the intended benefit most effectively. If we are unskillful, then despite our good intentions, it is easy to make matters worse than they already are.
Therefore, along with the compassion and wisdom personified by
Avalokiteshvara and Manjushri, the bodhisattva practitioner must
cultivate the power and skillful means of Vajrapani.

Because each individual has his or her own predispositions, karmic
obscurations and so forth, no one method—no matter how profound—
will work best for everyone. The truly skillful guide, therefore, sometimes has to resort to unorthodox means to tame the minds of others,
as when Shakyamuni gave Lam-chung the menial task of sweeping
the temple floor as his sole spiritual practice. In another example,
Buddha once told a monk who was having trouble with his practices that, instead of sitting in the traditional cross-legged position,
he should lie down when meditating. With his clairvoyance he saw
that this particular disciple still had strong imprints left over from
previous lives as a cow and that a reclining position would therefore
be more suitable for him. Finally, mention can be made of a contemporary master who was asked why he told some of his disciples
to do one thing while he told others to do exactly the opposite. He
replied, "When I see someone going too far over to the left I say,
'Go to the right.' And when I see someone too far over to the right
I say, 'Go to the left.' Whether I say 'left' or 'right' I am in fact trying to guide all of them down the center of the same path."[32] All
of these examples demonstrate the skillful means Vajrapani represents.

As for the bodhisattva disciple of Shakyamuni Buddha named Vajrapani, many stories are told of the powerful means he used to promote and protect the teachings. On one famous occasion Shakyamuni was seated at Vultures' Peak near Rajagriha, the site where he delivered the Perfection of Wisdom sutras. At that time his jealous cousin Devadatta rolled a large boulder down the hill in an attempt to assassinate him. Just as the huge stone was about to crush Buddha, Vajrapani used his immense powers to split it in two so that pieces of the boulder fell harmlessly to either side. In recognition of Vajrapani's powerful abilities, Shakyamuni entrusted him with the protection of the tantras, those powerful Vajrayana teachings capable of guiding qualified disciples to full enlightenment in even one short lifetime. As protector of these precious and esoteric tantric teachings, Vajrapani is sometimes referred to by the title "Lord of the Secret."

It should be noted that Vajrapani is not always represented in wrathful form. His peaceful form may be found, for example, in certain practices centering on the female long-life deity Ushnisha Vijaya (Figure 8), in which she is visualized as flanked on her right by a two-armed Avalokiteshvara and on her left by a peaceful emanation of Vajrapani. Just as we worldly beings cloak our essentially pure nature in a vast number of different emanations, so too does the enlightened impulse take on different manifestations in order to reach out to beings most effectively. Thus the very richness and variety of Vajrayana images are themselves examples of the skillful means that Vajrapani embodies.

As was the case for both Avalokiteshvara and Manjushri, certain important figures in the religious history of Tibet have been recognized as emanations of Vajrapani. Among these is the ninth-century dharma king Ralpachen who greatly furthered the cause of Buddhism by standardizing the Tibetan terms used to translate the original Sanskrit dharma texts. The great Sakya lama Drogon Chagna Dragpa is also considered an emanation of Vajrapani, as is Je Tsong Khapa's famous disciple Khedrub Je, who is often depicted with a slightly wrathful expression demonstrating his kinship with the fierce Lord of the Secret.

The superior qualities of Vajrapani are summarized in the following verses of prostration taken from the daily practice of this fierce meditational deity:

> The unified power of all Supreme Beings
> Has appeared as Vajrapani, Lord of the Secret.
> The mere remembrance of his glorious name awakens
>   the pure, indestructible energy
> And eliminates completely all negative karma,
> Delusion, harm and every obstruction.
> To the holder of the Secret Treasure I prostrate.[33]

The essence of the bodhisattva path emerges through the following verses by the Thirteenth Dalai Lama in which the seeker of enlightenment is likened to a warrior, a fit image for the spiritual aspirant, whose Avalokiteshvara-like compassion and Manjushri-like wisdom must be complemented by the development of Vajrapani-like power and skill:

> Bodhisattvas are like the mightiest of warriors;
> But their enemies are not common foes of flesh and bone.
> Their fight is with the inner delusions,
> The afflictions of self-cherishing and ego-grasping,
> Those most terrible of demons
> That catch living beings in the snare of confusion
> And cause them forever to wander in pain, frustration
>   and sorrow.
> Their mission is to harm ignorance and delusion, never
>   living beings.
> These they look upon with kindness, patience and
>   empathy,
> Cherishing them as a mother cherishes her only child.
> They are the real heroes, calmly facing any hardship
> In order to bring peace, happiness and liberation to the
>   world.[34]

3   The Five Buddha Families

The attainment of a buddha's enlightenment involves a most profound transformation: an alchemical transmutation of our base,
egocentric limitations into the golden radiance of universal love and
understanding. But how is such a dramatic transformation to come
about? According to the advanced teachings of the Vajrayana, the
answer lies within the very delusions that are presently keeping us
imprisoned and unfulfilled. As the system symbolized by the buddhas of the five families reveals, the same knotted energy that feeds
the poisonous delusions, when unknotted, empowers the various
transcendent wisdoms of the enlightened mind.

The Vajrayana system of spiritual transformation as illustrated by
the Five Buddha Families (Figure 7 and Plate 9) makes us aware of
the profound differences between the egocentric and thoroughly unsatisfactory state of our ordinary consciousness and the open, fully
evolved state of enlightened consciousness. Paradoxically, it also
makes us aware that beneath the superficial obscurations veiling our
mind there exists an essential nature that is in no way different from
the essential nature of the Awakened Ones.

Figure 7: Nirmanakaya aspects of the buddhas of the five families[1]

Table 1: Attributes of the five buddha families

family	head	consort	direction	color	hand gesture
vajra (diamond scepter)	Vairochana	Lochana	east (bottom)	white	teaching
ratna (jewel)	Ratnasam-bhava	Vajradhat-vishvari	south (left)	yellow	giving
padma (lotus)	Amitabha	Pandara-vasin	west (top)	red	meditation
karma (action)	Amogha-siddha	Tara	north (right)	green	protection
buddha	Akshobhya	Mamaki	center	blue	earth-touching

The link between the limiting delusions and the enlightened wisdom-energy into which they are transformed can be illustrated most directly through the medium and experience of color.[2] It is well known that color influences our moods and that changing the color of our surroundings can have a profound effect on our state of mind. Color also expresses our emotions, as when we say that we are green with envy or feeling blue. What is also true, but not always immediately apparent, is that our moods affect how we experience color. For example, the blue sky that appears bright and sparkling when we are happy may seem dull or harsh when we are depressed.

Vajrayana art and the practices of creative visualization in which it is used are very much concerned with this intimate relationship between color and states of mind. It is not by chance or artistic whim, for example, that the figures presented in this volume are all depicted in pure, bright colors. To have toned them down or mixed them might have brought these paintings more in line with certain western aesthetic conventions, but this would have inevitably deprived these images of their characteristic power. And it is precisely in their power—their ability to assist and embody the transformation from conditioned existence to enlightened wisdom—that their special value lies.

SAMBHOGAKAYA ASPECTS OF
THE BUDDHAS OF THE FIVE FAMILIES

Vajra Family = top / Akor's energy / For awakening = Vairochana

The colors of the five buddha families provide a valuable key for understanding on a direct, intuitive level what is involved in the process of spiritual transformation (see Plate 9). Vairochana (the Illuminator), for example, is white, which in the Vajrayana is the color associated with both the element of water and the delusion of anger. Just as the color white can be either cloudy or bright, and just as water can be muddy or clear, so too can the energy underlying anger be expressed destructively or beneficially. The practices associated with Vairochana and the deities of the vajra family are designed to tap anger's energy and redirect it in the most beneficial manner possible—along the path to full awakening.

Ordinarily we become angry in response to disappointment, insult, aggression and the like; an aspect of our supposedly solid ego-structure is threatened in some way and suddenly we experience a great upsurge of energy directed against that threat. The results are generally very destructive—screaming, fighting, even killing—but the aroused energy itself is not negative. If it is released from feeding the neurotic syndrome of anger, its enormous power is free to work a dramatic change on our state of consciousness. Our mind, which previously might have been as cloudy and listless as stagnant water or as turbulent as a whirlpool, suddenly becomes remarkably clear and concentrated, its mirror-like quality enhanced so that things previously hidden from it are now reflected vividly and distinctly. This increase in our level of awareness is brought about not by denying or suppressing anything essential to our nature. On the contrary, it results from gaining control over our mind's fundamental energies and using them to break through the limiting and self-destructive habit patterns born from ignorance and insecurity.

The transformational practices of the remaining four families of buddhas can also be understood as untying the egocentrically knotted habit patterns of their respective delusions and freeing their underlying energies for constructive purposes. Ratnasambhava (the Jewel-born) works on our miserliness and arrogant pride, the defensive attitude that tries to cloak its insecurity within the imposing disguise of self-aggrandizement or haughty aloofness. Such pride cuts us off

Usual energy of Anger For Transformation

from others and it is the function of the jewel family to turn this sickly yellow attitude inside out so that the rich golden light of open-hearted generosity is allowed to radiate evenly to all.

Table 2: Transformation and the five buddhas

buddha	element	aggregate	delusion	transcendent wisdom[3]
Vairochana	water	form	anger	mirror-like
Ratnasambhava	earth	feeling	pride, miserliness	equanimity
Amitabha	fire	discernment	attachment	discriminating
Amoghasiddha	wind	compositional factors	jealousy	all-accomplishing
Akshobhya	space	consciousness	stupidity	all-encompassing

In a similar fashion the lotus family of Amitabha (Infinite Light) works with the energy of deluded attachment. The color red represents the burning passion we feel for desirable objects, whether people or things, and this intense passion is often so all-consuming that we are blinded by it. Through the agency of Amitabha and the deities of his family, this blinding passion is transmuted into the clear-sighted warmth of true loving compassion as we escape from the selfish demands of ego and turn our concern towards the welfare of others. Such altruism is exemplified by Avalokiteshvara, one of the foremost members of Amitabha's lotus family and the very personification of enlightened compassion.

As for jealousy, when this extremely destructive emotion arises, it eats away at our insides and we feel as if we were turning green. We become so obsessed with the object of our jealousy that our attention involuntarily focuses on it narrowly, scrutinizing it in every detail. While our jealousy lasts, nothing else seems to exist. But green is also the color of abundant growth, the selfless outpouring of Mother Nature, the continual replenishment of life in all its myriad forms. This same inexhaustible energy resides at the core of our being but to release it we must first direct our attention away from the gnaw-

Amoghasiddha
= unobstructed
accomplishment

ing concerns of our petty ego. This we can do by relying on the practices of the action family of Amoghasiddha (Unobstructed Accomplishment), enabling us to accomplish whatever is necessary to bring
about benefit for others.

Finally there is the family of Akshobhya (the Immovable) whose
blue color symbolizes spaciousness and the all-encompassing wisdom that directly comprehends the ultimate reality of all phenomena.
Just as apparently substantial clouds are observed to arise from and
eventually dissolve back into the clear blue sky, so too our supposedly concrete conceptions of "this" and "that" arise from and dissolve back into the clear, unobstructed nature of the mind itself. In
the open, spacious view of wisdom all notions of separate selfhood
are seen as illusory. But to the mind conditioned by ignorance this
spaciousness poses a grave threat. We become terrified that we shall
be swallowed up and annihilated in a vast, amorphous nothingness,
and in fear of this we cling to our individual ego-identity more and
more desperately. Seeking to protect ourself, we turn away from
everything that might be a threat to our fragile ego and sink into a
dull-blue state of narrow-minded stupidity. For enlightenment to be
achieved, the energy supporting this frightened stupidity must be
liberated and allowed to radiate outward until it becomes as expansive as space itself. This is accomplished through the practices of
Akshobhya, the buddha of the all-encompassing center.[4]

AMITABHA

Of the five buddhas just mentioned, arguably the most popular is Amitabha, head of the lotus family (Plate 10). His name means "infinite light" and he is the principal buddha of Sukhavati, the Blissful Pure Land of the West. (In another context he is the embodiment of the enlightened speech of all the buddhas, with Vairochana representing enlightened form and Akshobhya enlightened mind.) Amitabha's body is the color of the setting sun and he sits in meditation posture, his hands resting in his lap holding a begging bowl filled with nectar. He is shown here wearing the robes of a monk and appearing within a sphere of rainbow light supported by clouds.

As visitors to the Orient or to galleries of Far Eastern art will attest, Amitabha is one of the most widely venerated figures in the Buddhism of China, Korea and Japan. The main reason for this is the popularity in these countries of a form of worship and practice known as Pure Land Buddhism, of which Amitabha is the focus. Followers of this system center their devotion upon Amitabha in the belief that after death they will be born in his presence in Sukhavati. This pure land is outside the suffering realms of ordinary cyclic existence and all conditions there are conducive for one's eventual attainment of enlightenment. As is stated in the sutras upon which this devotional form of buddhist practice is based,[5] even the sound of the wind and the songs of the birds in Sukhavati proclaim the dharma for the benefit of those fortunate enough to be born there.

Shakyamuni Buddha revealed that the pure land of Sukhavati came into existence as the result of the stainless motivation and pure practices of Amitabha when, long ago, he was known as the bodhisattva Dharmakara. This was at the time of Buddha Lokeshvararaja, in the presence of whom Dharmakara declared:

> When I have attained buddhahood, if those beings who are in the ten quarters, after they have heard my name, should direct their thoughts to my country and should plant their roots of merit and should bring them to maturity with their serene thoughts, and wish to be born in my country—if they should not accomplish [their desire], may I not obtain the perfect knowledge.[6]

75

Having made this vow on behalf of all beings, Dharmakara performed the duties of a bodhisattva for many eons. So great was his accumulation of merit that wherever he was born he gave forth the pleasing fragrance of incense, was surrounded by riches and was able to emanate food and drink miraculously from his body. When eventually he achieved full enlightenment as Amitabha his surroundings spontaneously transformed into Sukhavati, the western paradise, a land of unimaginable radiance and beauty.

It is into this pure land that, after their death in this world, the faithful devotees of Amitabha are born. Seated upon lotus blossoms they receive teachings from Amitabha himself and from the countless other buddhas inhabiting this realm. Experiencing none of the sufferings of cyclic existence and forever freed from having to take lower rebirth, these fortunate beings progress irreversibly towards enlightenment and eventually attain buddhahood.

One of the main sutras studied by followers of Pure Land Buddhism gives instructions on how to visualize Amitabha, his entourage, Sukhavati and all the splendors of that realm in preparation for death. Along with other sutras it also recommends the recitation of the mantra of Amitabha, which according to some schools is itself sufficient to bring about rebirth in Sukhavati.

Generally speaking, the main requirement for successful practice is faith in and devotion to Amitabha and this accounts for the tremendous popularity of pure land practices among lay people in the Far East. There are temples in Japan, for instance, where the priests themselves follow the more rigorous and demanding path of Zen meditation while teaching devotion to Amitabha to those who come for worship.

It would be a mistake to infer from this that pure land practices are somehow inferior, or only fit for the simple- minded multitudes. Even authorities on more austere forms of practice have stated that a greater number of people benefit from the path of devotion than from more intellectually demanding disciplines. Furthermore, as with other buddhist teachings, there are many levels on which the pure land practices can be followed. The story is told of a learned monk who encountered an old woman reciting the mantra of Amitabha as she walked along. "Where are you going?" he asked her. "To Sukhavati" was the reply. "Then tell me, Granny," the monk inquired in a mocking tone full of condescension, "where is this Sukhavati?" The old woman pointed to her heart and the monk, impressed by this simple woman's understanding, bowed to her in respect.

Practices leading to a pure land rebirth are not exclusive to the Far East, nor do they all center upon Amitabha. They are, in fact, a usual feature of many of the Vajrayana methods that evolved in India and spread to Nepal, Tibet and elsewhere. The most advanced of these methods are capable of leading the qualified and determined practitioner to full enlightenment within this very lifetime. However, it is recognized that of those engaging in these profound techniques, only a few will be able to bring them to completion before they die. Spiritual trainees are therefore taught how to transfer their consciousness at the time of death into a pure land state so that they can continue their practices without interruption. For example, the following prayer for a pure land rebirth is found at the end of a text dealing with Heruka Chakrasamvara (Plate 22), one of the major deities of highest yoga tantra:

> If in this lifetime I should not achieve the supreme goal,
> May I be met at my death by the Lord and his Lady.
> Having passed through the clear light of death,
> May I be led to Dakini land,
> The pure realm of tantric practitioners,
> And there may I quickly complete this profound path.[7]

We can see then that there is a strong link between the devotion to Amitabha in Far Eastern Pure Land Buddhism and the practice of *transference of consciousness* (Tib. *po-wa*) found in the Vajrayana Buddhism of Tibet. And although in the Tibetan traditions po-wa is not practiced exclusively in relation to Amitabha, he is still of major importance—although it must be said that Avalokiteshvara and Tara (Plates 5 and 11), his spiritual son and daughter, are even more popular. One commonly recited prayer of the Tibetans, the *Great King of Prayers*, concludes with the following stanzas:

> When the moment of my death arrives
> May I remain free from spiritual obscurations;
> May I perceive the face of Amitabha
> And transmigrate to Sukhavati, the pure land of joy.

Having arrived there may I fulfill
All aims of this prayer of aspirations
And benefit the countless living beings
Residing throughout the ten directions.

In the joyous mandala of Amitabha Buddha
May I be reborn from a beautiful lotus
And may I there have the pleasure of gaining
A pure prophesy from Amitabha himself.

Having won this word of prophesy
By the power of mind may I fill all directions
With many millions of mystical emanations
And bring limitless benefits to the world.

If by reciting this prayer of the sublime ways
I have amassed a tiny fragment of goodness
May it work immediately to fulfill
All dharmic hopes of the living beings.[8]

4 Enlightened Activity

As the discussion of the five buddha families illustrates, the bodhisattva's path involves profound inner transformation. Our clouded delusions must give way to clear-sighted wisdom and our imprisoning egocentricity to heartfelt concern for others. Concerning the latter, the tantric text *Offering to the Spiritual Master* contains the following prayer to the guru:

> In brief, infantile beings labor for their own gain only
> While buddhas work solely for others:
> Understanding the distinctions between the faults of the
> former and the virtues of the latter,
> May I be inspired to be able to exchange myself for others.[1]

This prayer, based on a similar stanza in Shantideva's eighth-century masterpiece, *A Guide to the Bodhisattva's Way of Life*, underscores the necessity of replacing our narrow, "infantile" selfishness with an all-encompassing, sympathetic interest in the welfare of others. Otherwise it will be impossible to awaken and fulfill our enlightened potential. If we do nothing to vanquish the inner demon of self-cherishing—the egoistic concern that places our own welfare above all else—we shall, in effect, be condemning ourselves to remain forever imprisoned within the fearful cycle of frustration and dissatisfaction. Thus again we are faced with a paradox: the only way to achieve our own true happiness is to cease being so obsessed with it and instead channel our concern towards the happiness of others.

It is not enough merely to wish others to be happy, or even to wish that we ourselves may someday be able to bring them the happiness they desire. Although such compassionate aspirations are of inestimable importance, it is essential that we translate our intentions into effective action. Not only should our activities be appropriate to the needs of others and suitable to their situation, they should also suit our own capabilities as well. The bodhisattva is therefore urged to cultivate the thought, "May I do for others all that I am able to do now, and in the future may I be able to do whatever is beyond my ability at the moment." Ultimately, the aim is to benefit others in the spontaneous, effortless and supremely skillful manner of those who have achieved full enlightenment.

The relationship between the wish to help others and the activity that puts this wish into effect is illustrated by a famous legend concerning Avalokiteshvara, the embodiment of compassion. Once, while he was looking down at the pitiable condition of the beings in the six realms of cyclic existence and wishing that they could be separated from their recurring misery, he began to weep. His tears of compassion were so copious that soon a lake formed in front of him, and from the depths of this lake the goddess Tara suddenly appeared.[2] Turning to Avalokiteshvara she said, "Do not cry, for I vow to work continuously to remove all beings from their suffering." From then on, in a multiplicity of forms, Tara put Avalokiteshvara's compassionate wish into practice, caring for each and every being as a mother does for her only child.

Tara thus represents the enlightened and liberating activity of all the buddhas. Of her many forms, the two most widely venerated are Green Tara (Plate 11) and White Tara (Plate 12). The Tibetans have a special fondness for these two goddesses and identify them with the two wives of Songtsen Gampo, their great religious king, who himself is considered to have been an emanation of Avalokiteshvara. These two queens, one Nepalese and the other Chinese, were instrumental in establishing Buddhism in the Tibetan court during the seventh century and also in introducing Vajrayana art to the Land of Snow. Eventually, largely through the work of the Indian buddhist master Atisha in the eleventh century, Tara became one of the most widely venerated deities in the vast pantheon of Vajrayana Buddhism.

Just as children call upon their mother for many different kinds of assistance, devotees of Tara invoke her aid in all aspects of life— love affairs, childbirth, business ventures, building projects, and so on without limit. The practices related to White Tara are especially effective for lengthening one's lifespan and are therefore widely employed when one's own life or someone else's is felt to be in danger. *Tara*

Methods for increasing one's lifespan—ideally to allow more time for completing the spiritual path—are also found in the practices of Ushnisha Vijaya (Figure 8) and Amitayus (Plate 13), the Buddha of Infinite Life. Amitayus is an emanation of Amitabha, the spiritual father of both Avalokiteshvara and Tara, and there are certain practices in which the methods of Ushnisha Vijaya, Amitayus and Tara are combined into one. In general, the decision as to which practice or combination of practices is to be followed is made by one's spiritual guide, the guru who is well acquainted with one's needs and tendencies and can see which approach will prove most effective. Sometimes the guru will even suggest to a sick person which doctor to consult, for the ability to heal depends not only upon the doctor's skill but on the prior establishment of the necessary karmic relationship between doctor and patient, and this is something that the guru can discern through his or her heightened awareness.

The desire for a long life is related to the universal wish to be free of illness of every sort, and one of the most powerful ways of overcoming disease is through the practice of the Medicine Buddhas, chief of which is Bhaishajyaguru Vaiduryaprabha (Plate 14), the Healing Master of Lapis Lazuli Radiance. Whether practiced separately or in the company of the seven other buddhas of healing—one of whom is Shakyamuni himself—the Lapis Medicine Buddha is greatly relied upon by Tibetan doctors, many of whom are highly qualified spiritual masters as well.

In addition to long life and freedom from disease, one of the main wishes of all beings, whether they are spiritual practitioners or not, is for wealth. Ordinarily the craving for money and possessions only serves to perpetuate dissatisfaction and unhappiness, keeping us trapped in a cycle of unfulfilled desire. As Shakyamuni Buddha and later masters have pointed out, such craving is like drinking salt water:

the more we indulge, the thirstier we become. However, there is nothing intrinsically evil about wealth, possessions or the like; it is the *motivation* to obtain these things that is either harmful or helpful, destructive or beneficial. Among the many positive impulses that could motivate the wish for wealth are, for example, the intention to help the needy, sponsor the publication of dharma texts, make donations to monasteries and further one's own or others' spiritual practice. It is for these and similar aims that there exist practices such as those associated with Vaishravana (Plate 15), the Deity of Wealth.

Even if the ability to extend life, overcome disease, attract wealth and so forth seems far beyond us now, through the blessings of the guru and our own dedicated practice it is possible to become a conduit allowing such enlightened power to flow through us and out to others. As our motivation to help others deepens so does the scope of our abilities increase. No matter how ordinary our present situation may be, there need be no limit to our altruistic intentions. We can follow the example of the Tibetan lama who made it his practice to transform all the means of livelihood he encountered into enlightened activity. Whenever he met a farmer, blacksmith, merchant and so forth he would take hold of the implements of their trade and declare, "In the future may I be able to use these very tools to lead all beings to the happiness of full enlightenment." The beneficial effect of such a widespread, compassionate motivation is beyond measure. As it says in the *Great King of Prayers* quoted earlier:

> May my deeds never reach a limit;
> May my qualities of excellence become boundless;
> And by abiding in immeasurable activity
> May I find buddhahood, the state of limitless manifestation.

> Limitless is the extent of space.
> Limitless is the number of sentient beings.
> And limitless are the karma and delusions of beings.
> Such are the limits of my aspirations.

GREEN TARA

Green Tara—the Swift Liberator—is seated upon a lotus arising from the waters of a lake (Plate 11), just as Tara is said to have arisen from the compassionate tears of Avalokiteshvara. Her right hand is in the boon-granting mudra indicating her ability to provide beings with whatever they desire. Her left hand at her heart is in the mudra of bestowing refuge: her thumb and ring finger are pressed together to symbolize the united practice of method and wisdom, and the three remaining fingers are raised to symbolize the Three Jewels of Refuge—Buddha, Dharma and Sangha. In each hand she holds the stem of a blue utpala flower and the three blossoms of each indicate that Tara, the embodiment of enlightened activity, is the mother of the buddhas of the past, present and future.

Tara is dressed in the silken robes of royalty. She wears rainbow-colored stockings, a white half-blouse and various jeweled ornaments. The tiara fastened in her black hair is adorned with jewels, the central one a red ruby symbolic of Amitabha, her spiritual father and the head of her buddha family. She is seated in a distinctive posture, her left leg withdrawn to symbolize her renunciation of worldly passion and her right leg extended to show that she is always ready to arise and come to the aid of those who need her help. With a warm, compassionate gaze she looks down upon each sentient being as a mother regards her only child. Her emerald-green color—related to the wind element and hence to movement—signifies that Tara is the active principle of compassion, capable of bringing to fruition all activities, mundane or supramundane, that bring benefit to others. As the embodiment of the purity of the wind element, the medium without which the buddhas would be unable to perform their virtuous deeds, Tara assumes her role as the consort of Amoghasiddha, the buddha of all-accomplishing wisdom (see Plate 9 and Table 1).

Tara is the principal female manifestation of enlightenment in the buddhist tradition. According to her legend, many eons ago as the Princess Jnanachandra (Wisdom Moon) she devoted herself to the teachings of Buddha Dundubhisvara (Drum Sound) and made copious offerings to that buddha and his entourage. Eventually, as the result of her untiring practice, she generated the pure, altruistic bodhichitta motivation for the first time and thereby became a glorious bodhisattva. At that time some monks, recognizing her great potential, urged the princess to pray for a transformation that would allow her to complete her spiritual training as a male. But she rejected this advice, saying,

Tara

> Here there is no man, there is no woman,
> No self, no person, and no consciousness.
> Labeling "male" or "female" has no essence,
> But deceives the evil-minded world.[3]

Still, knowing how rare advanced female practitioners were, she made the following adamantine vow: "Until samsara is empty, I shall work for the benefit of sentient beings in a woman's body."

From that time onwards the princess dedicated herself to winning full and complete enlightenment. By mastering extremely profound states of meditative absorption she developed great skills in liberating others and hence her name was changed to Tara, the Savioress. From her spiritual master she received the prophecy, "As long as you manifest the unsurpassed enlightenment, you will be known only by the name of Goddess Tara."

Swiftness

One attribute of Tara that makes her a favorite of so many devotees is her swiftness in responding to the calls of those who invoke her. In paintings and poetry she is often depicted as coming to the immediate aid of those in danger. Because of the widespread protection she grants, Tara is often referred to as the One Who Rescues from the Eight Great Fears. These eight are traditionally listed as the fear of lions, elephants, fire, snakes, robbers, imprisonment, water and demons, and a typical story relating to Tara's ability to overcome danger without causing harm to anyone is the following:

> In a part of Gujarat called Bharukaccha there lived an extremely wealthy merchant. Loading his baggage on some thousand camels and five hundred bulls, he set out for the country of Maru. On the way, he came to a wilderness where there lived as many as a thousand bandits. The whole place was full of the flesh, blood and bones of all the merchants who had come before and had been killed. So the merchant was very afraid and, as he had no other protector, prayed to Tara. Thereupon appeared a measure-

less army of heroes, wielding weapons, who were emanations of Tara, and drove the bandits a long way away, but
without killing any. Thus the bandits were dispersed, while
the merchant went on his way and got back to Bharukac-
cha safely.[4]

Such traditional tales may seem very removed from our modern-
day reality but even nowadays there are many people who tell of being
rescued by this compassionate goddess. Not long ago, in fact, a vessel
full of Asian fishermen was in danger of sinking in a fierce storm.
In response to their cries the merciful goddess Kuan Yin—a Far Eastern deity who combines attributes of Tara with those of local
divinities[5]—appeared and calmed the waves. This magical appari-
tion was seen by many people and a painted version of the incident
has become well known in the East.

The divine intervention in human affairs of a nurturing Mother
Goddess is a recurring feature in cultures both inside and outside
the buddhist tradition.[6] Throughout European history, for example, the repeated appearances of the Holy Virgin, the Mother of God,
have had a profound effect on the lives of believers and non-believers
alike, and these appearances have continued right up until the present
day. Some of the sites where visions of the Virgin Mary have occurred
became and still remain places of healing, attracting pilgrims from
all over the world. In some cases statues of the Virgin have
miraculously appeared and there are many accounts of their having moved, spoken or shed tears.

These accounts do not differ in any essential detail from the many
reports of similar spontaneous appearances of Tara in various Asian
cultures. For example, just to the south of the Kathmandu Valley
in Nepal, not far from the gorge where Manjushri is said to have
drained the waters of the primordial lake, is the pilgrimage site of
Parping. On the side of a hill containing a meditation cave used by
Guru Rinpoche (Plate 27) and close to a famous shrine of Vajrayogini (Plate 24), there is a rock face out of which a small image of Tara
is gradually emerging. This image has grown decidedly more distinct and detailed over recent years without any apparent assistance
from a sculptor.[7] In the center of Kathmandu itself there is another
shrine containing three differently colored images of Tara. Accord-

ing to the priest maintaining this shrine, one of these images flew by itself from Tibet to Nepal while another has on occasion spoken to him!

As these and many other stories help demonstrate, the deity known here as Tara is not limited to appearing in any one form; like all fully enlightened beings, she manifests in whatever guise is most appropriate to the situation. Her ability to assume a variety of forms to answer a variety of needs is illustrated in the commonly depicted assembly of twenty-one Taras, some of whom are white or yellow and peaceful while others are dark red or black and extremely wrathful. The following two stanzas of homage, addressed respectively to the eighth and fifteenth of these twenty-one goddesses, illustrate the vastly different ways in which Tara can manifest herself:

> Homage to *TURE*, extremely fearsome one,
> Who completely destroys the chief of demons.
> With the wrathful expression on your lotus face
> You slay all foes without exception.

> Homage to you who are happy, virtuous and peaceful,
> Within the sphere of the peace of nirvana.
> Fully endowed with *SVAHA* and *OM*,
> You completely destroy heavy evil actions.[8]

Tara's ability to assume a wide variety of forms depending upon the deeds and circumstances of those to be helped is also illustrated in the following relatively recent story from Tibet:

> There was once a lone traveler making his perilous way across the forbidding plateau of Tibet. Exhausted and without food he was in immediate danger of losing his life when he came upon a young girl tending a herd of yaks. She took the weary man into her tent, nursed him back to health and fed him until his strength returned.
>
> As the man was recovering he observed that the young girl was alone. Single-handedly she was doing the work that even a number of strong men would have found difficult. Eventually he was fit enough to travel again and the girl sent him on his way with a bag of provisions. Although it was a long journey the man discovered that the food she

had given him never ran out until he was back in his own valley again. Marveling at all that had happened he thought, "Perhaps that girl was actually Tara." When he went to his lama and told him the story, the lama upbraided him saying, "Of course she was Tara, you blockhead! How stupid of you not to recognize her. You must have a strong connection with her, but if you ever want to see her again you had better purify your delusions and practice harder."[9]

The assembly of twenty-one Taras is generally visualized surrounding a Green Tara and prayers incorporating homages to these goddesses are commonly recited by Tibetans as a way of invoking their aid. Dromtönpa, Atisha's main disciple in Tibet, had a disciple of his own who was suffering from a very serious disease. With his heightened awareness Dromtönpa realized that if this man recited the homages to the twenty-one Taras ten thousand times he could be cured. However the sick man was in no condition to do such a lengthy and demanding practice, so Dromtönpa consulted Atisha to see what could be done. Atisha in turn consulted Tara directly and from her received a five-line prayer incorporating the essence of all twenty-one homages and the mantra of Tara as well:

> *OM*, I prostrate to the Liberator, the Noble Blessed Mother.
> I prostrate to the glorious Mother who liberates with *TARE*,
> Who eliminates all fears with *TUTTARE*,
> Who grants all success with *TURE*.
> To *SVAHA* and the other syllables we offer greatest homage.[10]

This proved effective in healing Dromtönpa's disciple and is still recited today by Tara's devotees.

Although Tara is invoked by the faithful to answer even their most mundane prayers, her supreme benefit lies in guiding practitioners along the path to full awakening. The obstacles encountered on this path are mainly internal and thus the eight great fears mentioned earlier against which Tara offers protection can also be understood as the delusions obscuring the clear nature of the mind itself. Interpreted in this way these eight fears are our own pride (lion), ignorance (elephant), anger (fire), envy (snake), wrong views (robbers), avarice (chains), attachment (flood) and doubt (demons). The relation between the outer dangers and these inner obstacles is brought out clearly in a hymn of praise to Tara written by the First Dalai Lama and entitled *A Crown Ornament for the Wise*, one stanza of which reads:

> Protect us from the terrifying lion of pride
> Which dwells on the mountain of wrongly held views,
> An inflated mentality holding itself as superior
> And wielding a claw to belittle the world.[11]

The First Dalai Lama was only one of a long line of Indian and Tibetan masters who devoted themselves to the practice of Tara. Atisha and Taranatha (whose very name means "Son of Tara") were two masters largely responsible for introducing her practice to Tibet, and other famous Indian practitioners who received guidance directly from her include Nagarjuna, Chandrakirti and Chandragomin. Because of the efforts of these and other adepts, a multitude of methods are now available for achieving the transcendent state of Tara oneself. These methods encompass both the initial and most advanced forms of tantric practice,[12] and through them it is possible to achieve everything from temporal happiness and well-being to the full enlightenment of buddhahood. There are even special po-wa, or transference of consciousness, practices associated with Green Tara. One such practice includes the following verses of request concluding this section on the divine savioress:

> To you, the Noble Guru Mother,
> The synthesis of all my gurus,
> I make requests for the destruction
> Of obstacles, outer and inner.
> Oh, please transform me with your blessings
> So that I may complete the training
> Of the profound path of transference;
> Lead me to the supreme pure land![13]

WHITE TARA

7 eyes

White Tara (Plate 12) is seated cross-legged on a lotus and moon seat and holds her hands in the same pose as Green Tara. Her special attributes are her seven eyes—the "third eye" located on her forehead and the other four on the palms of her hands and soles of her feet. Like those of the eleven-faced Avalokiteshvara, these eyes allow her to look upon beings in every realm of existence with clear-sighted wisdom and heartfelt compassion.

White Tara is specifically associated with practices designed to lengthen one's lifespan and overcome life-threatening hindrances. In one such practice she is referred to as Yeshin Khorlo, the Wish-Granting Wheel, and the practitioner strives to identify him- or herself with this deity and thereby purify all obstacles to longevity:

> When I see the signs of untimely death,
> May I clearly behold the body of the Wish-Granting
> Wheel;
> May this destroy the boldness of the Lord of Death
> And may I quickly become a deathless Knowledge
> Holder.[14]

This method can also be employed on behalf of someone else whose life is in danger, in which case the practitioner identifies with Tara and visualizes the afflicted person in one's own divine heart, bathed in purifying white light.

Among the Tibetans it is common for a person who is gravely ill not only to consult a doctor but also to call in someone to recite White Tara's mantra and perform a related offering ritual (Skt. *puja*). In certain severe cases a lama—who himself may be a doctor—will recommend that the afflicted person sponsor a special one-day puja. During that time there are a specified number of mantras to be recited and the patient is also instructed to commission the painting of a White Tara image—or one of the other long-life deities—which must be completed within twenty-four hours. Such an intense one-day practice accumulates a great store of constructive, meritorious energy (Skt. *punya*) which, depending on many other factors, can counterbalance and even overcome the destructive and deluded forces at the source of the disease. In this way it is sometimes possible to bring about a cure even when conventional medical treatment has proved ineffective.

The remarkable ability of a mere image to work such a powerful, beneficial effect is illustrated in the legend that tells how the first painting came to be.[15] In ancient India there was a benevolent king and one day one of his subjects, a member of the priestly brahmin caste, appeared before him grief-stricken. He explained that his young son had died before his time and implored the king to help bring him back to life. The king then went before Yama, the Lord of Death, and after paying his respects asked for the life of the brahmin's son. Yama explained, "His death was not of my doing, but the result of the exhaustion of his own karma." The king insisted, but Yama could only reply, "I am sorry; there is nothing I can do." Suddenly Brahma, the wise and powerful Lord of Creation, appeared and said to the king, "Do not blame Yama. Instead, draw a likeness of the brahmin's son and bring it to me." When this was done Brahma blessed the painting and the boy immediately came back to life. The king who painted this image has, since that time, been honored as the forerunner of all artists.

From the point of view of the buddhist teachings, the main purpose for wishing to have a long life is to enable one to progress further along the path to spiritual fulfillment. As the great Tibetan lama Marpa the Translator said, if the only thing people are doing with their lives is giving harm to others and creating negative karma for themselves, then it would be better if they died sooner rather than later. The situation for those bringing benefit to themselves and others is, of course, just the opposite. Especially in the case of spiritual guides, the longer they remain alive, the more they are able to lead others along the path to enlightenment. For this reason disciples in the Tibetan tradition often present their lamas with a painting of White Tara or one of the other long-life deities, together with a request that these spiritual mentors have an uninterrupted lifespan and continue to turn the wheel of dharma for the sake of all unenlightened beings. In the case of His Holiness the Dalai Lama, the spiritual and temporal guide of the Tibetan people as a whole, the Tibetan government has at times commissioned the state artist to paint one such image every month as one way of creating the necessary conditions for His Holiness' enlightened presence to remain in this world.

It should be noted that there are certain occasions when an extended lifespan, even for a highly qualified guru, is not of paramount importance. When the great Indian master Atisha was invited to go to Tibet to help revitalize the buddhist teachings there, he consulted Tara—his special deity—to see if he should leave for the Land of Snow or not. Tara told him that if he stayed in India he would live until the age of ninety-two, but that if he went to Tibet his lifespan would be shortened by twenty years. Then Atisha asked whether he would be of more benefit to others if he stayed in India or went to Tibet, and Tara replied that there was no comparison: he would be of far greater benefit and service to the dharma if he accepted the invitation and went to Tibet. Without any hesitation Atisha decided to go, gladly willing to give up twenty years of his life to bring the benefit of the buddhadharma to others.

Atisha's
20 years
of lost
life

USHNISHA VIJAYA

Ushnisha Vijaya—Victorious Crown Protrusion—is an emanation of Vairochana Buddha and, along with White Tara and Amitayus, one of the three major longevity deities in the Tibetan buddhist pantheon (see Figure 8). Her practice is considered to be extremely effective not only for eliminating obstacles to long life but also for purifying the negative results of unwholesome actions of body, speech and mind motivated by the poisonous delusions.

Ushnisha Vijaya's ability to purify negativity is illustrated in the following story.[16] A god residing in the Heaven of the Thirty-three was on the threshold of death and saw with his clairvoyance that he was going to be reborn in a lower realm as a pig. Greatly agitated, he went to Indra, king of the gods, and begged to be protected from this horrible fate. Indra responded by saying that there was nothing he could do to help him and suggested the god consult Shakyamuni Buddha. The Awakened One then taught him to recite the mantra of Ushnisha Vijaya; this ripened his latent good karma sufficiently for him to take rebirth, not as a lowly pig, but as an exalted celestial being once again.

The great Indian master Vasubandhu, possessor of peerless scriptural knowledge, was said to have had such a special relationship with Ushnisha Vijaya that she was like a mother to him. According to traditional accounts,[17] Vasubandhu wanted to achieve a direct vision of Maitreya, the Future Buddha (Plate 32), just as his half-brother Asanga had done (described below in Chapter Seven). But because he had been skeptical of the validity of the Mahayana teachings and had denigrated them when he was younger, Vasubandhu was told by Asanga—who was in direct communication with Maitreya—that he would not be able to see this buddha until his next lifetime. "Then whom should I rely upon now?" asked Vasubandhu. After consulting Maitreya, Asanga answered, "You have a close connection with Ushnisha Vijaya; you should rely upon her." Vasubandhu did so and had a direct vision of her from then on.

In one popular practice centered upon Ushnisha Vijaya, she is visualized seated within the dome of a stupa indicating that she is the emanation of the mind of all enlightened beings. In this practice she is described as follows:

Figure 8: Ushnisha Vijaya

[She has] a white-colored body, three faces and eight arms. The central face is white, the right yellow; the left is blue and slightly wrathful. Each face has three eyes.

The first right hand holds a crossed vajra at the heart. The second holds a lotus on top of which sits Amitabha. The third holds an arrow. The fourth is in the gesture of supreme generosity.

The first left hand is in the threatening mudra, holding a vajra noose. The second holds a bow. The third is in the gesture of giving refuge. The fourth is in the meditation gesture, holding a precious vase filled with nectar.[18]

As in other sadhanas, the practitioner dissolves his or her self-identity into emptiness and then arises in the form of the chosen meditational deity, in this case cultivating the divine pride and vivid appearance of being the actual Ushnisha Vijaya. Then the meditator continues as follows:

I am clothed with upper and lower garments made of silk and decorated with various jewels. I am surrounded by a garland of white light.

On my right side, on a moon disc, is white Avalokiteshvara, holding a yak-tail fan in his right hand and a lotus in his left. At my left side, on a sun disc, is blue Vajrapani, holding a yak-tail fan in his right hand and, in his left hand, an utpala flower with a vajra on top of it.

Both have peaceful expressions. Both are decorated with jeweled ornaments and are dressed in silken garments. They are both standing in the same posture.[19]

The practice then proceeds with a visualization of four surrounding guardian protectors, two offering deities and other details. Later, when all these figures receive purifying ablution, each deity is crowned by the head of the buddha family with which he or she is associated; thus Ushnisha Vijaya is crowned by Vairochana, Avalokiteshvara by Amitabha, Vajrapani and the four guardians by Akshobhya, and the offering gods by Ratnasambhava.

For the main part of the practice, one visualizes one's guru, parents, disciples, relatives, friends, attendants and so forth all seated at the center of one's heart. Then, while one recites various mantras, light rays are visualized purifying all adverse conditions and invoking the blessings and inspiration of all the buddhas and bodhisattvas throughout the universe. In this way the lifespan, meritorious energy and wisdom of oneself and all others are increased.

The practice is then concluded with verses of prayer, dedication and praise such as the following:

> I prostrate at the feet of Ushnisha Vijaya,
> Glorious goddess with the color of the autumn moon,
> Having an extremely beautiful and peaceful body with
>   three faces and eight arms,
> And who bestows boundless wisdom and the best of lives.[20]

AMITAYUS

Amitayus—the Buddha of Infinite Life—is depicted here in the same red color and cross-legged pose as Amitabha. But whereas Amitabha was given the attributes of a monk, Amitayus is shown here in his glorified aspect, adorned in the silken garments and jeweled ornaments of royalty (Plate 13).[21] Like Green Tara he wears a white half-blouse and, as his distinguishing feature, holds in his lap a vase filled with the nectar of immortality. On top of this vase is a wish-fulfilling tree; if the size of the painting permits, this tree is often shown supporting a miniature image of Amitabha.

Amitayus and Amitabha are essentially identical, being reflective images of one another. Sutras in which Shakyamuni expounds the glories of Sukhavati, the Joyous Pure Land, speak of the presiding buddha of this western paradise sometimes as Amitabha—Infinite Light—and sometimes as Amitayus—Infinite Life. In Far Eastern Buddhism he is simply called Amida ("the Infinite") indicating his existence beyond time, space and all other limitations of conceptual thought.

The practice of Amitayus has been one of the most popular among the Tibetans and many different lineages of his life-extending methods still survive today. It is common for the laity to invite monks to their homes to perform religious ceremonies and two of the most requested services are those centering upon Amitayus, for achieving a long life, and Vaishravana (Plate 15), for gaining wealth. Furthermore, qualified gurus are often called upon to give tantric empowerment into the practice of Amitayus and these are generally attended by great numbers of people wishing to receive the blessings of an extended lifespan.

As stated earlier, certain long-life deities are commonly practiced in combination with one another, and tangkas depicting Amitayus, White Tara and Ushnisha Vijaya grouped together are especially popular. In particular, when a young *incarnate lama*, or *tulku*, is recognized, his or her family, attendants or monastery often commissions a large painting of these three deities to ward off harmful influences that may interfere with the life of the sensitive and vulnerable child. Such paintings are also useful to those, ordained and lay alike, who use these long-life deities as part of their daily practices for their own and others' sakes.

Whether these and similar practices are successful in extending life or not depends on many different factors, including the wisdom, faith and concentration of the practitioner and the type of connection existing between the practitioner and those he or she is trying to help. But whatever the short-term benefit, these open-hearted and compassionately motivated methods plant seeds for successful practice in the future. And, perhaps more importantly, they serve to enhance one's compassionate bodhichitta motivation and thus help direct all of one's energy and effort towards achieving enlightenment for the welfare of others.

The following excerpts from the sadhana of Amitayus paint an expressive portrait of the Buddha of Infinite Life while listing various benefits of his practice.

> O Protector Amitayus, born from *HRIH*
> On a moon seat upon a thousand-petaled lotus,
> Like the vermilion color of the young rising sun
> Covered with a pleasing red-yellow veil.
> I prostrate to you whose body is completely beautified
> With various garments and many jeweled ornaments like
>   a ruby mountain
> Completely covered by the rays of the sun.
> I prostrate to you who grant the attainment of life
> From a bowl filled to the brim with the nectar of
>   deathlessness
> Which you hold in the center of your two hands,
> Supple as the branches of a young sapling.
>
> I prostrate to you for all time,
> By calling just your name untimely death is destroyed.
> By mentally recalling you we are protected from the fears
>   of cyclic existence and peace
> And by relying on you as refuge a lasting happiness is
>   conferred.
> With devotion I rely on you who are free from faults.
> Temporarily may all undesired dangers be pacified
> And ultimately may I be born spontaneously
> From a lotus in Sukhavati and do what pleases you.

Having revered you in this way with a pure mind,
Through the power of requesting with a single-pointed
    devotion,
May all sickness, spirits and hindrances be pacified
And ultimately may I enjoy the attainment of life without
    death.

Bestow on me swiftly the increasing attainment
Of the good qualities of the three trainings,
The stainless wisdom of hearing, contemplating and
    meditating,
Unobservable compassion, merit and life.
When I see signs of untimely death
May I immediately see clearly the body of Protector
    Amitayus
And having destroyed the Lord of Death
May I quickly attain the deathless state.[22]

MEDICINE BUDDHA

The full name of the Medicine Buddha depicted here (Plate 14) is Bhaishajyaguru Vaiduryaprabha, the Healing Master of Lapis Lazuli Radiance. Like Shakyamuni and Amitabha he wears the robes of a monk and is seated in the full cross-legged posture. His left hand is in the meditation mudra, resting in his lap and holding a begging bowl filled with medicinal nectar and fruit. His right hand rests upon his knee with palm facing outward in the mudra of granting blessings and holds a stem of a myrobalan plant (*Terminalia chebula*), renowned as the king among medicines because of its effectiveness in treating both mental and physical diseases.

In traditional Tibetan tangkas, the Lapis Healing Master is often shown in the company of seven other Medicine Buddhas,[23] one of whom is Shakyamuni himself. And in depictions of his eastern buddha realm known as Pure Lapis Lazuli, the Healing Master is generally flanked by the two leading bodhisattvas of that pure land, Suryaprabha and Chandraprabha, respectively All-pervading Solar and Lunar Radiance. In keeping with the clear and direct style of this series of paintings, however, the Lapis Healing Master has been presented without any entourage and is shown seated within a transparent aura of blue light.

The most distinctive feature of this Medicine Buddha is his color, the deep blue of lapis lazuli. This precious stone has been greatly prized by Asian and European cultures for more than six thousand years and, until relatively recently, its ornamental value was on a par with, or even exceeded, that of the diamond. An aura of mystery surrounds this gemstone, perhaps because its principal mines are located in the remote Badakshan region of north-east Afghanistan, an all-but-inaccessible area located beyond the Hindu Kush. One commentator has written, "The finest specimens of lapis, intensely blue with speckled waves and swirls of...shining gold-colored pyrite, resemble the night aglow with myriads of stars."[24] Traditionally this beautiful stone was used to symbolize that which is pure or rare. It is said to have a curative or strengthening effect on those who wear it, and its natural smoothness allows it to be polished to a high degree of reflectivity. For all these reasons—plus the fact that deep blue light has a demonstrable healing effect on those who use it in visualization practices—lapis is the color of the principal Medicine Buddha. ✓

The Lapis Healing Master is one of the most honored figures in the buddhist pantheon. The sutras in which he appears compare his eastern pure land with the western paradise of Amitabha, and rebirth there is said to be as conducive to enlightenment as is rebirth in Sukhavati.[25] Recitation of his mantra, or even the mere repetition of his holy name, is said to be sufficient to grant release from the lower realms, protection from worldly dangers and freedom from untimely death. In one of the main sutras concerning the Medicine Buddha, Shakyamuni tells his close disciple and attendant Ananda:

> If these sentient beings [those plunged into the depths of samsara's sufferings] hear the name of the Lord Master of Healing, the Lapis Lazuli Radiance Tathagata, and with utmost sincerity accept it and hold on to it, and no doubts arise, then they will not fall into a woesome path.[26]

In Tibet the Medicine Buddha is revered as the source of the healing arts for it is through him that the teachings embodied in the *Four Medical Tantras*, the basis of Tibetan medicine, came into being. As explained in the first of these *Four Tantras*,[27] the Lapis Lazuli Healing Master was once seated in meditation surrounded by an assembly of four circles of disciples including divine physicians, great sages, non-buddhist gods and bodhisattvas, all of whom wished to learn the art of healing. Rendered speechless by the radiant glory of his countenance, they were unable to request the desired teachings. To accommodate their unspoken wishes, the Medicine Buddha manifested two emanations, one to request the teachings and the other to deliver them. In this way, then, the buddhist explanation of the various mental and physical ailments, their causes, diagnoses and treatment and the maintenance of health is said to have originated.

Cause of Disease

According to the *Four Tantras*, the fundamental cause of every disease is to be found in the three poisonous delusions—ignorant bewilderment, attachment and hatred—occupying the hub of the wheel of samsaric existence. These three root delusions lead to imbalances in the three so-called humors (phlegm, wind and bile), the various bodily constituents (blood, flesh, bone, etc.) and waste products, or impurities (excrement, urine and perspiration), all of which are analyzed in twenty-five divisions. The *Root Tantra* says:

> Thus if all these twenty-five are in balance and the three
> factors of the (1) tastes and (2) inherent qualities of one's
> food and (3) one's behavior are wholesome, one's health
> and life will flourish. If they are not, one's health and life
> will be harmed.[28]

And further on:

> Attachment, hatred and bewilderment are the three causes
> producing imbalances of wind, bile and phlegm. Along
> with these, the four contributing circumstances of time,
> spirits, food and behavior cause the humors to increase and
> decrease. The imbalance then spreads over the skin, in-
> creases in the flesh, moves along the vessels, meets the
> bones and descends upon the solid and hollow organs.[29]

Treatment of disease and the maintenance of health are therefore
primarily a matter of bringing the various elements of the body back
into balance and this is accomplished through four progressive types
of treatment. The first two involve changes in the type of food we
eat and behavior we engage in. Only when these prove ineffective
is the physician advised to prescribe medicine and only when this
also fails is he or she to resort to external forms of treatment such
as cauterization and the like. However, none of these types of treatment will have a lasting effect unless they are accompanied by
spiritual transformation. If ignorance and its associated delusions
remain festering inside, sooner or later they will give rise to disease
and the recurring miseries of cyclic existence.[30] Thus buddhas such
as Shakyamuni and the Lapis Healing Master are referred to as great
physicians not because of their medical abilities—as great as these
are—but because they have the compassion, wisdom and skillful
means to diagnose and treat the root delusions underlying all mental and physical malaise.

The following prayer of request is addressed to the Lapis Healing Master:

> I beseech you, Blessed Medicine Guru,
> Whose sky-colored, holy body of lapis lazuli
> Signifies omniscient wisdom and compassion

As vast as limitless space,
Please grant me your blessings.

I beseech you, compassionate Medicine Guru,
Holding in your right hand the king of medicines
Symbolizing your vow to help all the pitiful sentient beings
Plagued by the four hundred and twenty-four diseases,
Please grant me your blessings.

I beseech you, compassionate Medicine Guru,
Holding in your left hand a bowl of nectar
Symbolizing your vow to give the glorious undying nectar
   of the dharma
Which eliminates the degenerations of sickness, old age
   and death,
Please grant me your blessings.[31]

VAISHRAVANA

Vaishravana—the God of Wealth—is seated upon a white snow lion (see Plate 15). His large, rounded body is golden-yellow in color and his expression stern. In his right hand he holds a banner of victory and in his left a mongoose, an animal associated with good fortune, which is shown vomiting jewels. Vaishravana is also known as Jambhala and in addition to being a god of wealth is also the Guardian King of the North. In this aspect he is often depicted on the outer walls of monasteries and temples, together with the three other protectors of the cardinal directions, as a safeguard against harmful interferences.[32]

Mention has already been made of the popularity of this wealth deity and of the beneficial uses to which wealth can be put. But it is important to emphasize that even when one's wealth and possesions are being used for noble purposes, it is still the underlying motivation that determines whether such acts of generosity are truly meritorious or not. This point is illustrated in the following story:

A rich man once invited Shakyamuni and a number of his monks to his house to do them honor. For days beforehand he made preparations and when the time of the great feast arrived, villagers from far and wide crowded near to catch a glimpse of the Awakened One and the marvelous reception being planned for him. The rich man was very pleased with himself and thought, "Now my reputation for generous hospitality is assured."

Among those witnessing this splendid occasion was a poor beggar. As he looked in through the doorway he pressed his palms together in reverence and thought, "How wonderful to be able to make such a glorious offering to the Blessed One! I rejoice in all the merit that this rich man has gained through his generosity and devotion."

At the conclusion of the feast, when all the offerings had been made, Shakyamuni was requested to speak. Tradition dictated that he mention the name of the meal's benefactor, but knowing exactly what was going on in the minds of all who were present and aware of the pride and attachment to worldly fame polluting the motivation of his

103

host, he avoided citing the rich man's name and mentioned that of the impoverished beggar instead!³³

Below and to either side of Vaishravana the artist has arranged the eight auspicious symbols—the golden fish, conch shell, treasure vase, lotus, wheel, banner of victory, knot of eternity and umbrella—said to represent the celestial offerings presented to Shakyamuni after he had gained enlightenment under the Bodhi Tree. These symbols, reproduced at the ends of various chapters throughout this book, are very popular among Tibetans and can be found not only in monasteries but in most people's homes as well. There they may be painted on the walls, carved out of wood or even fashioned from precious metals. Apart from their obvious decorative function, these eight are thought to be auspicious omens of spiritual and material well-being. Because of their auspicious nature, these eight symbols are also drawn in flour on the path leading to a monastery or temple to welcome a highly respected lama. The meaning of these eight can be expressed as follows:

The two golden fish (page 20) represent release from the ocean of samsara. Just as fish are not bothered by the turbulence of water when they swim through the deepest oceans, so too is it possible for spiritual seekers to follow the path without being distracted or impeded by the vicissitudes of life.

The white conch shell that spirals to the right (page 102) is blown to announce a buddha's enlightenment to the entire world. The conch therefore symbolizes the ability of all beings to awaken from the sleep of ignorance in response to the call of the dharma.

From the treasure vase (page 119) pours forth an endless rain of long life, health and prosperity available to all beings who follow the dharma purely.

The lotus (page 105) represents spiritual purity and compassion and symbolizes the stainless actions of body, speech and mind leading to happiness and enlightenment.

The eight-spoked golden wheel (page 132) is known as the wheel of dharma and its spokes symbolize the buddhist eightfold path consisting of right view, right thought, right speech, right action, right livelihood, right effort, right mindfulness and right concentration. The wheel represents the movement of the dharma from one land to another as it awakens the buddha-potential present within all beings.

The banner of victory (page 106), which is planted on the summit of Mt. Meru at the center of the universe, proclaims the victory of the dharma over the forces of ignorance.

The knot of eternity, also known as the lucky diagram (page 173), is variously interpreted as representing the beginningless round of existence, the inextricable link between wisdom and compassionate method in a buddha's enlightenment, and the unending love and harmony of full awakening.

Lastly the umbrella (page 192) is a symbol of royalty and represents the protection from evil influences provided by the compassionate buddhas.

5 The Path of Bliss and Emptiness

The images presented so far in this work have corresponded quite closely to the general impression of Buddhism as a spiritual path emphasizing moral self-discipline, clear-minded tranquility and compassion. The figures have a balance, purity and gentleness of expression well in keeping with buddhist ideals; even the powerfully depicted Vajrapani and stern-faced Vaishravana can be understood as representations of forces fundamentally rooted in compassion and generosity.

It can therefore be unsettling and even shocking when we encounter for the first time the images treated in this chapter, replete as they are with violent and sensuous imagery. What are we to make of deities brandishing an array of fierce weapons, wearing garlands of human skulls, standing naked or seated in sexual embrace? How are we to reconcile these images of passion and rage with the teachings of the fully renounced and compassionate Buddha? Or are they, as some of the first influential Western writers on Tibet maintained, evidence that the Tibetan Vajrayana is a corrupt, morally bankrupt and degenerate form of Buddhism in which black magic and devil worship have supplanted and obscured the purity of Shakyamuni's original teachings?[1]

To answer these questions and allay any qualms we may feel when first introduced to these startling images, we have to be prepared to look more deeply not only at the images themselves but, more uncomfortably, into the blood-and-guts reality of our own existence. Passion and rage, whether outwardly expressed or not, figure prominently in our lives while desirous attachment colors and motivates our behavior to an enormous extent. Shakyamuni Buddha referred to our current state of existence as the realm of desire (Skt. *kamadhatu*). The very fact that we have the type of body and mind we do means that we are continuously influenced by mental and physical urges and desires of great depth and complexity, whether we are consciously aware of them or not.

It does no good to deny these uncomfortable aspects of our makeup or reject them because they do not fit neatly into our image of what a religious or spiritual person should be like. As contemporary psychologists have pointed out, pretending that these darker elements do not exist and banishing them into the shadows of our consciousness only serves to give them more power to haunt us in the future.[2] The only effective course of action is to become as aware as possible of whatever is going on inside ourselves, whether agreeable or not, and confront it directly with the discerning eye of wisdom.

Within Vajrayana Buddhism the most profound methods for delving deep into ourselves and rechanneling or transforming the energies we discover are set forth in the system known as highest yoga tantra (Skt. *anuttarayogatantra*). "Highest," or "unequaled," indicates that this system is supreme, beyond the scope of the three other "lower" levels of tantra.[3] *Yoga* is related to its English cognate *yoke* and here refers to the various spiritual disciplines to which we yoke ourselves so that our potential for enlightenment can be most effectively realized. *Tantra* literally means "thread," "continuity" or "stream" and can denote a web or network of interwoven strands. One way of understanding highest yoga tantra, therefore, is as an unparalleled system of spiritual disciplines through which we can make contact with and gain conscious control over the entire range of interwoven energies making up not only ourselves but the universe in which we live. This most advanced branch of Vajrayana practice is capable of unleashing extraordinary power. Understandably then, the meditational deities who embody and symbolize this potent transformational path reflect its enormous power in their overwhelmingly vivid and sometimes violent visual imagery.

Because the techniques of highest yoga tantra utilize the tremendous energy abiding within the interwoven threads of our internal and external universe, it is of the utmost importance that we approach these techniques with a respectful appreciation of their immense power. If we are not properly prepared then these powerful methods, instead of leading to enlightened buddhahood, will only serve to inflate our imprisoning ego-hood, with predictably disastrous results. What saves the aspiring tantric practitioner from this and related dangers is reliance on a fully qualified master. In fact, the very root and foundation of the tantric path is the cultivation of a proper relationship with such a trustworthy guide. Thinking that we can proceed on our own by following whatever tantric instructions we may have read in a book is foolhardy in the extreme and more dangerous than playing with radioactive material. Furthermore, without the blessings of a master of the Vajrayana lineage we shall be cut off from the inspiration of that lineage and therefore unable to complete our practices successfully.

One of the most important aspects in the cultivation of a proper attitude towards one's guru is to recognize and focus upon his or her enlightened qualities. As is often said, "If you want to receive the blessings of a buddha, you must see your guru as a buddha." Thus it is a fundamental tantric practice to visualize one's guru as inseparable from Vajradhara (Plate 16), the manifestation in which Shakyamuni Buddha revealed his tantric teachings. This is especially important at the time of initiation or empowerment when we are introduced to the specific meditational deity upon whom our subsequent practice will center. Without recognizing the underlying identity of our guru, Buddha Vajradhara and the deity into whose practices we are being initiated, we shall never receive the seeds of insight and inspiration necessary for spiritual growth. And without such seeds or imprints upon our mindstream, even the most strenuous practice will be in vain. Like the foolish farmer who watered and fertilized his field zealously but had neglected to sow any seeds beforehand, we shall reap nothing from our efforts but disappointment.

The image of our mind being like a farmer's field and the fulfillment of our enlightened potential as the intended crop is a useful one to pursue. It reminds us that in addition to receiving the necessary seeds from the tantric guru we must cultivate our mind in such a way that these seeds have the chance to germinate. This is accomplished in two ways. First we must rid the field of our mind of the rocks and weeds presently clogging it—these are the unwanted residue of all the unskillful and harmful actions we have engaged in under the influence of ignorance and the other delusions. And second, we must enhance our mind's nutrient level so that the seeds implanted there will have the nourishment required for them to grow— we need to amass a store of positive or meritorious energy by engaging in actions which are especially skillful and wholesome. The dual task of cleansing defilements and collecting meritorious energy is accomplished through conscientious performance of the so-called *preliminaries* to tantric practice.[4]

The preliminaries, or preparatory trainings (Tib. *ngon-dro*), can be divided into two groups: the common and uncommon. Chief among the common preliminaries are the three principal aspects of the sutra path to enlightenment: renunciation, the altruistic bodhichitta motivation and the correct view of reality. It is on the basis of these three that we cultivate the detachment from ordinary sense gratification, freedom from self-cherishing and liberation from concrete conceptualization so necessary if the intended tantric transformations are ever to be achieved. The so-called uncommon preliminaries consist of a number of powerful techniques designed to cleanse and strengthen our three doors of body, speech and mind. Of these various techniques, the methods for purification associated with the meditational deity Vajrasattva (Plates 17 and 18) are of fundamental importance.

As for the actual highest yoga tantra deities themselves, there is an overwhelming variety of forms—both male and female, wrathful and peaceful—to take as the basis for one's practice. The choice is not an arbitrary one, nor is it made as if one were shopping in a supermarket. Ideally, it is our personal guru—well acquainted with our character and sensitive to our needs and capabilities—who selects the specific deity for us to practice. This choice can also be influenced by such factors as the repeated appearance of a particular deity in a disciple's dreams, a strong feeling of familiarity with a certain image, and so forth.

In this chapter there is room to present only a few of these deities and the ones chosen have been selected primarily because through them the major aspects of the Vajrayana path can be clearly outlined. Guhyasamaja (Plate 19) incorporates the five buddha lineages discussed in Chapter Three and presents the two main divisions of highest yoga tantra practice: the generation and completion stages. The fierce Yamantaka (Plate 20) and his protector Dharmaraja (Plate 21) indicate how the delusion of anger may be transformed into the spiritual path, while Heruka Chakrasamvara (Plates 22 and 23) deals mainly with desirous attachment. Vajrayogini (Plate 24) derives from the *Chakrasamvara Tantra* and like Chakrasamvara himself is mainly concerned with transforming the energy of passionate desire into the path of full awakening. Also pictured is Vajradharma (Plate 25), who serves as the focus of the all-important guru-yoga practice in the sadhana of Vajrayogini.

The chapter concludes with a major *dharma protector* (Skt. *dharmapala*), the extremely wrathful Mahakala (Plate 26). Despite his ferocious appearance, Mahakala is in fact an emanation of the gentle and supremely compassionate Avalokiteshvara. Why is there need of such a violent-looking protector? Engaging in the practice of highest yoga tantra means opening ourselves up to deeply rooted energies of great destructive potential. Hindrances and interferences from both inside and outside ourselves can easily arise when we stir up these energies, making it difficult if not impossible for us to proceed. The particularly unskillful practitioner, especially one who flagrantly disregards the precepts of the guru and attempts practices beyond his or her ability, risks the dangers of madness and even death. To guard against all these dangers and hindrances the tantric practitioner is directed by his or her spiritual guide to rely upon a powerful protector, such as Mahakala, who can divert these interferences and safeguard one's practice against possible degeneration.

VAJRADHARA

To receive the blessings and inspiration necessary for the success-ful practice of highest yoga tantra, the qualified disciple is instructed to visualize his or her spiritual master as inseparable from Vajradhara, Holder of the Diamond Scepter (Plate 16), as described in the fol-lowing verses from the *Six-Session Yoga*:

> In the sky before me, on a breath-taking throne of jewels,
> On a mandala seat of a lotus, a sun and full moon,
> Sits my root guru, the all-pervading Vajradhara,
> With a blue-colored body, one face and two arms.
> Holding vajra and bell, and embracing his duplicate consort,
> He shines resplendent with all the marks of a buddha,
> Adorned with many dazzling jeweled ornaments,
> Draped with fine garments of enchanting, heavenly scarves.
> Even the mere remembrance of him dispels all my torment.
> With a nature encompassing every supreme refuge,
> He sits cross-legged in the vajra position,
> The three spots of his body marked with three letters.[5]

This description of Vajradhara contains succinct references to the most important features of Vajrayana practice in general and guru-yoga in particular. The opening phrase, "In the sky," indicates that nothing within the subsequent visualization has even one atom of concrete, inherent self-existence but arises instead from the unob-structed space of emptiness. Out of this space-like emptiness of in-herent existence appears the seat of lotus, sun and moon symboliz-ing the three principles upon which the Vajrayana practice is founded: renunciation, wisdom and the altruistic motivation of bodhichitta. And enthroned on this special seat is one's root guru—the spiritual guide who has directed one's mind to the path—visualized not in his ordinary form but as indistinguishable from the buddha of the tantras, the glorious Vajradhara himself.

Guru Vajradhara's body is deep blue in color, indicating the pro-found and boundless nature of his omniscient mind. His two hands are in the embracing mudra to show that he has mastered the union of method and wisdom characteristic of the path leading to the full enlightenment of buddhahood. The powerful diamond scepter (Skt. *vajra*; Tib. *dorje*) in his right hand is the symbol for compassionate method—the supremely effective means Vajradhara employs to fulfill the wishes of others—while the bell in his left hand stands for his penetrative wisdom into the ultimate nature of reality.

The symbolism of the bell is sometimes explained as follows. When a bell is struck it produces a sound which, like all other phenomena appearing to our senses, seems to be inherently existent. In other words, to an unenlightened being this sound appears to exist solely from its own side, in its own right, as an independent something "out there" waiting to be perceived. But when we search to find such an independently existing sound, we cannot find it anywhere. We cannot locate it in the clapper, in the rim of the bell, in our ear or anywhere else. But although we cannot find it in this way, it still exists. As analysis reveals, sound is a phenomenon that arises totally in dependence upon the interaction of other phenomena, e.g. the striking of the clapper against the rim. It is a dependent-arising and, as such, lacks even one atom of inherent self-existence. Sound, therefore, serves as a clear example of a phenomenon that is totally empty of inherent existence, and the bell is used to remind us of the wisdom that directly perceives this emptiness and cuts through our imprisoning ignorance of the way things exist.

Vajradhara's consort, who possesses the same enlightened attributes as himself, is Vajradhatu Ishvari: Powerful Goddess of the Diamond Sphere. They are shown sitting together in *father-mother* (Tib. *yab-yum*) embrace. The ecstatic expressions on their faces symbolize profound absorption into the clear light nature of the mind, devoid of limitations and pervaded by inconceivable bliss. The brilliantly colored aura of rainbow light radiating from them both is a further expression of this blissful state of meditative absorption into ultimate reality.

Buddhas such as Vajradhara have fulfilled two types of purpose through their attainment of two types of body (Skt. *kaya*). They have fulfilled their own purpose through the attainment of a completely unobstructed mind—the so-called *dharmakaya*, or *truth-body*—and they benefit others through their attainment of *rupakaya*, the innumerable *form bodies* through which the dharmakaya mind spontaneously manifests. For example, to some a buddha may appear as a fully renounced monk and teach the graded paths of the sutra vehicle, while to others he may appear as glorious Vajradhara and reveal the lightning path of Vajrayana. To achieve a buddha's enlightenment ourselves, we also have to attain these two kayas, and this is accomplished by the joint practice of wisdom and compassionate method, the former being the primary cause of a buddha's truth body and the latter the cause of the various form bodies.

Highest yoga tantra is distinguished from all other paths to enlightenment in that it alone contains techniques whereby wisdom and method can be generated simultaneously as two aspects of a single moment of consciousness.[6] The practitioner is taught how to gain control over the elements of his or her *vajra body* and thereby awaken the very subtlest level of consciousness residing at the heart. This subtle and extremely blissful mind of clear light can be used as the most powerful tool for gaining a direct insight into ultimate reality, or emptiness. Without abandoning this wisdom, the practitioner's blissful consciousness can manifest in the form of the chosen meditational deity. This combination of the appearance of the deity and the understanding of the deity's ultimate nature is the highest yoga tantra union of method and wisdom, a union that surpasses all others and serves as the direct cause for the unified rupakaya-dharmakaya experience of enlightenment.

This explanation of the distinguishing characteristics of highest yoga tantra practice, although greatly abbreviated, allows us to understand the symbolic meaning of the *yab-yum* embrace more fully (see Table 3). The father, Vajradhara, stands for method, which in this context is the very subtlest level of consciousness pervaded by inconceivable bliss. The mother, Vajradhatu Ishvari, stands for wisdom, the clear light penetration into emptiness, the ultimate nature of reality. The image of Vajradhara and his consort in embrace, therefore, has nothing to do with ordinary sense gratification. Rather, it is a potent symbol of the blissful, simultaneous union of method and wisdom: the priceless treasure of highest yoga tantra and the quickest and most powerful means for achieving enlightenment within this very lifetime.

Table 3: Symbolism of the *yab-yum* embrace

yab (father)	*yum* (mother)
method	wisdom
bliss	emptiness
vajra	bell
right	left
attainment of form body (rupakaya)	attainment of truth body (dharmakaya)
fulfilling the purpose of others	fulfilling the purpose of oneself

Guru Vajradhara, visualized in *yab-yum* embrace, has not only achieved enlightenment himself but has the unsurpassed ability to lead us along the spiritual path in the quickest manner possible. The description of Vajradhara quoted at the beginning of this section concludes by stating, "The three spots of his body [are] marked with three letters." These spots are the crown, throat and heart—the centers of body, speech and mind—and the letters marking them are a white *OM*, a red *AH* and a blue *HUM*. At various points in the initiation as well as the daily sadhana of tantric deities, colored lights are visualized as emanating from and dissolving back into the three centers not only of the guru-deity but of ourselves as well. These light rays purify the defilements of our three doors and confer the blessings and inspiration of the fully enlightened experience upon the deepest level of our being. The wish to bring to fruition this ultimate benefit of guru-yoga practice is reflected in the closing lines of the *Six-Session Yoga*:

Throughout all my lives may I never be parted from perfect gurus.
By making good use of the glorious dharma
To fulfill the good features of the stages and paths,
May I quickly achieve Vajradhara-Enlightenment.[7]

VAJRASATTVA

Vajrasattva—the Diamond, or Adamantine, Being—is the main deity employed for purification by practitioners of all levels of tantra. Depending on which type of practice is being followed, he can be visualized either alone (Plate 17) or with consort (Plate 18).

Vajrasattva is white in color, signifying his immaculate purity. Like Vajradhara, of whom he is an emanation, he holds a vajra symbolizing method in his right hand and the bell of wisdom in his left. Although the solo Vajrasattva is sometimes depicted as sitting with his leg partially outstretched, here he is in the unshakeable full vajra posture. Again, Vajrasattva wears the beautiful silken garments and jeweled ornaments of ancient Indian royalty.

The techniques of tantric transformation will not be able to produce their profound results as long as our present body, speech and mind remain contaminated by the impurities accumulated from our past unwholesome physical, verbal and mental actions. For our practices to succeed we must not only avoid such unskillful and destructive activities now and in the future, but we must cleanse ourselves of those negative imprints still with us from the past. Vajrasattva meditation is the chief method recommended by the various traditions of Vajrayana Buddhism to accomplish this cleansing, or purification. Furthermore, it is extremely effective for rectifying transgressions of the sacred pledges made by the disciple to the tantric master at the time of empowerment and for restoring whatever tantric commitments we may have broken.

Although a full explanation of the Vajrasattva practice is beyond the scope of this book, a brief indication of what it involves can be given as follows. Above the crown of our head we visualize our root guru in the form of Vajrasattva, having a transparent body of light. At the crown of his head is Akshobhya, the head of the buddha family to which Vajrasattva belongs. At Vajrasattva's heart we visualize the letters of his hundred-syllable mantra standing upright around the edge of a moon disc, in the center of which is the seed-syllable *HUM*.

Having stabilized this visualization, and entreating our root guru from the depths of our heart to purify all our negative karmic imprints, we recite Vajrasattva's mantra with undistracted concentra-

116

tion. As we do so we visualize cleansing rays of light descending from the *HUM* and mantra at Vajrasattva's heart, entering us through the crown of our head, purifying us of all defilements and transforming our body into light. At the conclusion of our meditation session we generate the strong feeling that all stains and obscurations have been completely removed. Vajrasattva then dissolves into light and descends into us, becoming indistinguishable from our own body, speech and mind, and we remain for a time in a state of clear awareness without conceptualization.

For this practice to be effective, it is not enough to generate a clear image of the deity and follow the succeeding stages of the visualization practice in their proper order. Without employing what are known as the four powerful opponents,[8] even the clearest visualization will be of little use. First we must generate an honest sense of regret for our past unwholesome actions and transgressions of our sacred word of honor, recognizing their destructive potential. Then we must vow to turn away from committing all such negativities in the future. Thirdly, we invoke the power of reliance by bringing to mind both our refuge in the Three Jewels of Buddha, Dharma and Sangha and our altruistic bodhichitta motivation. Finally we engage in those remedial actions—in this case the recitation of Vajrasattva's mantra and so forth—that counterbalance, uproot and purify our accumulated obscurations. Only if these four powers of regret, vow, reliance and remedy are strong is it definite that purification will take place.

There are various signs that indicate successful purification of negativities. A number of these occur while we are dreaming, such as fighting and overcoming a person dressed in black, vomiting noxious substances, drinking milk, meeting gurus, receiving visions of meditational deities and the like. If we have such dreams repeatedly, not just once or twice, this is an indication that our practices have been fruitful. But there are more definite signs of success that occur while we are awake. Our physical body may come to feel light and buoyant, we find that our need for sleep has decreased, our thinking will be clearer than before and, most importantly, we gain insight into areas of the spiritual path that had previously been obscure. In connection with this last point a contemporary Tibetan master has stated that if we had only an hour in which to study the profound teachings on the Perfection of Wisdom sutras and were to spend the first forty-five minutes engaged in such "collecting and cleansing" techniques as Vajrasattva meditation, we would not be wasting our time in the slightest. Instead, we would be ensuring that whatever study we did in the remainder of the hour would be of maximum benefit.

Although there is a great purpose in performing such preparatory practices as Vajrasattva visualization as part of a daily spiritual routine, Tibetan lamas highly recommend that the serious practitioner engage in prolonged meditational retreats during which the deep experience of these practices can be cultivated. Certain lamas will not give disciples the empowerment of highest yoga tantra deities until they have completed an extensive retreat on all the preliminary practices. In addition to Vajrasattva these include taking refuge and generating bodhichitta, making mandala offerings, cultivating guru-yoga, performing prostrations, and so forth. In one such retreat the disciple may recite the hundred-syllable mantra of Vajrasattva more than one hundred thousand times, and this may be repeated many times during his or her training.

The stipulation that the advanced teachings of highest yoga tantra will not be given unless and until the disciple completes these extensive preliminary practices serves several purposes. It not only weeds out all those whose interest in pursuing tantra is superficial and those who are easily discouraged by hardships, but most importantly it provides those who have the perseverance and dedication to complete these preliminaries with the necessary foundation for their future spiritual growth. It has even been said that for a disciple with the proper qualifications, the goal of enlightenment can be achieved through the practice of these preliminaries alone.

Those who have completed an extensive retreat of Vajrasattva purification testify from their own experience that their perception of the phenomenal world undergoes a profound change. It is not that the world itself has been transformed but that the meditator's view of it has been purified. It is as if the doors of perception have been opened wider and subtly obscuring curtains have been drawn back from the windows of the mind. Beings and phenomena take on a pure appearance—a reflection of the practitioner's own newly revealed purity—and the gravitational field keeping us anchored in ordinary mundane reality is relaxed. Although this exhilarating vision of a world filled with infinite possibilities may fade, it provides a great incentive for pursuing the higher practices and a conviction that full enlightenment, though still a distant goal, is actually attainable.

GUHYASAMAJA

Guhyasamaja—the Secret Assembly—is one of the main deities of the highest yoga tantra class, and the scriptures to which his practice is traced are the oldest known texts of buddhist tantra, going back at least to the fourth century C.E.[9] Guhyasamaja is known as the King of Tantras not only because his texts are so ancient but because they and their commentaries provide the key for understanding the vast range of tantric literature, which is generally cryptic and hard to penetrate. Among the Indian mahasiddhas who wrote extensively about the *Guhyasamaja Tantra* were Nagarjuna, Aryadeva and Chandrakirti, and one of the great accomplishments of the eleventh-century Tibetan master Marpa the Translator (Plate 29) was to carry teachings on this supremely important tantra from India to the Land of Snow.[10]

The high regard in which this tantra is held by the Tibetans can be judged by the extensive commentaries to it written by such masters as Je Tsong Khapa, who devoted several texts to elucidating its meaning. Concerning Guhyasamaja, Tsong Khapa wrote:

> The *anuttara yoga* tantras are
> The highest teachings given by the Buddha.
> From amongst these the most profound is
> That of glorious Guhyasamaja, the king of all tantras.
> ...Understanding the sublime path of Guhyasamaja
> Bestows fearless, confident understanding
> Of all the teachings of the Buddha.[11]

The *Guhyasamaja Tantra* was given by Shakyamuni Buddha to King Indrabhuti, who had asked the Blessed One, "By what means can people like myself, who are not yet detached from the world of the senses, attain liberation?"[12] In response, Shakyamuni manifested as Guhyasamaja and taught Indrabhuti this profound system of highest yoga tantra. These teachings were later most fully transmitted through two main lineages, the Arya and Jnanapada, named after Aryadeva and Buddhashri Jnanapada.[13]

The central deity of the *Guhyasamaja Tantra* (Plate 19) is dark blue in color and has three faces and six arms, and embraces a consort whose attributes are identical to his own. Guhyasamaja has a semi-peaceful, semi-wrathful expression. His central face is blue, the right is white, the left is red and each face is adorned with a third eye of wisdom. These three faces are variously interpreted as symbolizing the transmuted delusions of anger, ignorance and attachment; the three major channels of the so-called vajra body; the purified minds of white appearance, red increase and black near-attainment (see page 130); and the experience of illusory body, clear light and union.

As for his six arms, the first two are in the embracing mudra and hold vajra and bell, symbolizing the union of method and wisdom. The remaining two right hands hold a wheel and lotus while the left hands hold a jewel and sword. Guhyasamaja and his implements represent the various buddha families, or lineages, as shown in Table 4.

Table 4: Guhyasamaja and the buddha families

symbol	head of buddha family
Guhyasamaja himself	Akshobhya
wheel	Vairochana
jewel	Ratnasambhava
lotus	Amitabha
sword	Amoghasiddha
vajra and bell	Vajradhara

In Chapter Three we spoke of five buddha families, while here six are mentioned. In the *Guhyasamaja Tantra*, Vajradhara—the head of the sixth family—is considered an amalgam of the other five. Furthermore, in other contexts the tantras speak of *one* buddha family headed by Vajradhara as Lord of All Buddhas, *three* families, and so forth. While the enumerations vary, the reality indicated is the same: the state of full enlightenment experienced when all coverings obscuring the mind's fundamentally pure nature have been removed forever.

The Vajrayana offers many methods for clearing away the obscurations of the mind, and some of the most profound are employed during the ceremony of tantric initiation, or empowerment, itself. During such a ceremony the initiate is led in meditation to various points within the divine abode (Skt. *mandala*) of the main deity and introduced to the buddhas—Vairochana and so forth—through whom the desired enlightened transformation can be effected.

Highest yoga tantra is the supreme system for achieving enlightenment and the *Guhyasamaja Tantra* provides the key for understanding its unique transformative methods. These methods are contained in the two divisions of highest yoga tantra practice, namely the *generation stage* (Tib. *kye-rim*) and the *completion stage* (Tib. *dzog-rim*). On the generation stage the practitioner overcomes the ordinary appearances and conceptions tying him or her to the wheel of recurring suffering and dissatisfaction. This is accomplished first of all by dissolving the ordinary, limited and concrete view, or image, of oneself into the clear and unobstructed space of emptiness, and then by arising in the form of one's chosen meditational deity, or *yidam*. Thus the generation stage can be described as a combination of *emptiness yoga* and *deity yoga*, and involves cultivating the *clear* or *vivid appearance* of oneself as having the form of the meditational deity together with the *divine pride* of actually being such a deity.[14]

By recognizing one's own innate buddha-potential, receiving the inspiration of the guru, and putting into practice the transformative techniques employed at this stage, the yogi learns to regard all appearances as the manifestation of the deity, all sounds as the mantra of the deity and all thoughts as arising from the unobstructed wisdom of the deity. These techniques not only affect the way practitioners view themselves, they also help transform their environment, sensory experiences and activities into the mandala, resources and enlightened behavior of the deity.

The purpose of these generation stage practices is to replace one's limited self-identity—which, when analyzed, is seen to be the product of ignorance and the source of suffering[15]—with the expansive and enlightened identity represented by the deity. However, at this stage such profound transformation takes place largely on the level of imagination alone. Although one develops great powers of concentration and meditative absorption that have a profound effect on one's entire being, the practices of the generation stage are mainly a rehearsal for the enlightened transformation that actually takes place during the completion stage.

At this second, more advanced stage, the main emphasis is on gaining full conscious control over what is known as the vajra body, an entity that exists on a subtler level than our gross physical form and is intimately connected with increasingly subtle levels of consciousness.[16] The vajra body is pervaded by *channels* (Skt. *nadi*) through which flow currents of *energy-wind* (Skt. *prana*) and in which are found *drops* (Skt. *bindu*) of varying degrees of purity. By engaging in such practices as the vajra recitation (Tib. *dor-lay*) and *inner heat* (Tib. *tum-mo*), the practitioner learns how to manipulate these channels, winds and drops in such a way that the very subtlest level of consciousness—the blissful mind of clear light—is aroused and activated.[17]

Through constant and progressive practice under the eye of a fully qualified tantric master, the disciple merges this subtle clear light consciousness with the understanding of ultimate reality, and by means of its extraordinary power eradicates the various levels of delusion obscuring the mind. These practices give birth to the so-called *illusory body*, and eventually to the *union* (Skt. *yuganadda*) of clear light and illusory body that leads directly to the experience of full enlightenment. The transformation that was merely imagined in the generation stage is actually brought about in the completion stage, and the goal of buddhahood is attained.

No brief outline like this can begin to do justice to the profundity and complexity of these generation and completion stage yogas. Although practices connected with the clear light and illusory body are present in nearly all highest yoga tantras, there are differences of emphasis among them. Guhyasamaja's system stresses the illusory body and since such a subtle body is associated with method and method itself is characterized as male in the Vajrayana, Guhyasamaja is regarded as the chief of the *father tantras*. Similarly, because Chakrasamvara emphasizes the generation of clear light, which is associated with wisdom and characterized as female, that deity is said to belong to the *mother tantras*. But no matter how they are classified, all these highest yoga tantra systems present complete paths to full enlightenment and are capable of leading the properly qualified and motivated disciple to the supreme goal as swiftly as possible.

YAMANTAKA AND DHARMARAJA

Of all the images illustrated in this work, perhaps none is more startling than that of the terrifying Yamantaka (Plate 20). To introduce this deity we relate the legend of how such a wrathful figure came into being.[18]

There was once a powerful yogi who went into a cave to pursue his practices of deep meditative absorption. He sat down in the unshakeable vajra position and soon his consciousness was soaring to elevated planes far beyond this ordinary worldly existence. Night fell and into the apparently abandoned cave hurried a band of poachers driving before them a water buffalo they had stolen. They immediately slaughtered the beast and set about devouring their ill-gotten prey. Suddenly, by the light of their fire they caught sight of the yogi's silent form seated in the shadows. Fearful of what would happen to them if this witness to their misdeeds were left alive, they leapt up, cut off his head, and returned to their feast.

Soon thereafter the meditator's consciousness returned from its travels and reentered his body, only to discover that it was headless! Frantically he felt around the floor of the cave, searching for something to place upon his shoulders, but all he could find was the buffalo's severed head, so he put that on. Then, wild with anger at what had befallen him, he set out to wreak his revenge on the poachers who had so cruelly disfigured him. With his psychic powers he not only destroyed them but vented his boundless fury on whomever he met. Soon he became the scourge of the countryside, a hideous monster who left behind him a ghastly trail of destruction—a veritable Lord of Death.

In hopes of putting an end to this carnage a group of holy men set about making prayers and offerings to Manjushri, beseeching his aid to protect them all from the deformed yogi's rage. Out of his great compassion Manjushri responded to their entreaties. Realizing that only an extremely wrathful emanation would be suitable for overcoming such a powerful force, he manifested himself as Vajrabhairava, the Diamond Terrifier, otherwise known as Yamantaka, Destroyer of the Lord of Death. The central face of this terrifying emanation took on the aspect of an enraged buffalo to match the fury of the yogi, but it was crowned with the head of Manjushri himself as a sign of

Yamantaka's fully enlightened nature. In this form, then, Manjushri subdued the yogi so completely that he was converted from a malevolent force into a protector of dharma practitioners. As such he is invoked by followers of Yamantaka's tantric path and given the name Dharmaraja, King of the Dharma (Plate 21).

This legend gives us insight into the meaning and purpose not only of Yamantaka but, by extension, the other wrathful meditational deities as well. Their terrifying appearance is not, as some naive viewers may believe, a sign of their supposedly demonic nature; on the contrary, it is an expression of the powerful and skillful means the compassionate buddhas employ to transform destructive forces into aids along the spiritual path. Thus the apparent anger and hatred of these deities are not directed at other beings, but at the deluded forces that interfere with the happiness of other beings. In the case of Yamantaka, his practice utilizes enlightened wrath specifically to overcome and transmute the poisonous delusion of anger itself. His Holiness the Dalai Lama explains the effectiveness of such practices as follows:

> With compassion as the causal motivation. . .the practitioner utilizes hatred or wrath for a specific purpose. This technique is based on the fact that when we become angry, a very energetic and powerful mind is generated. When trying to achieve a fierce activity [for beneficial purposes], the energy and power make a difference. Thus it is because of the usage of hatred in the path in this way that there come to be wrathful deities.[19]

A particularly noteworthy example of Yamantaka's wrath being invoked to combat the forces of delusion is found in the text *Wheel of Sharp Weapons* written in the tenth century by Dharmarakshita, one of Atisha's main gurus. This work belongs to a class of teachings known as Mahayana thought transformation (Tib. *lo-jong*), whose purpose is to help us overcome obstacles to the full development of the compassionate bodhichitta motivation.[20] In this work we read:

> This sly, deadly villain—the selfishness in us
> Deceiving ourselves and all others as well—
> Capture him, capture him, fierce Yamantaka,

> Summon this enemy, bring him forth now!
> Batter him, batter him, rip out the heart
> Of our grasping for ego, our love for ourselves![21]

And in the verses repeated as a refrain:

> Trample him, trample him, dance on the head
> Of this treacherous concept of selfish concern!
> Tear out the heart of this self-centered butcher
> Who slaughters our chance to gain final release![22]

Further on in the same work we read:

> O mighty destroyer of selfishness-demons,
> With Body of Wisdom unchained from all bonds,
> Yamantaka come brandish your skull-headed bludgeon
> Of egoless wisdom of Voidness and Bliss.
> Without any misgivings now wield your fierce weapon
> And wrathfully swing it three times 'round your head.[23]

As a traditional commentary explains,[24] Yamantaka's bludgeon represents the wisdom of emptiness common to both sutra and tantra, as well as the non-dual wisdom of emptiness and bliss cultivated on the two stages of highest yoga tantra. As Yamantaka swings this weapon three times around his head he destroys (a) the ignorance of ego-grasping keeping us trapped in recurring misery, (b) the self-cherishing attitude preventing us from generating the compassionate bodhichitta and achieving enlightenment, and (c) all the defilements, including those of our presently deluded form, arising from these two "demons."

The enlightened and fiercely subjugating attributes of Yamantaka are reflected in the numerous details of his image, a few of which can be mentioned here. Yamantaka is deep blue in color—representing unobstructed wisdom as boundless as space—and has nine faces, thirty-four arms and sixteen legs. His belly is large and he stands naked upon a sun disc within an aura of flames, his erect sexual organ symbolizing great bliss. His main face is that of a black buffalo, extremely fearsome, with eyebrows, eye-lashes and beard all ablaze and the hair on his head bristling upwards. In place of the five crown jewels and shining ornaments of the peaceful deities, Yamantaka's head is adorned with five dried skulls symbolizing the five buddha families and he wears a garland of fifty freshly severed human heads.

Above his main head and between its two horns is an extremely fierce red face, and above that the youthful and slightly wrathful face of Manjushri. On his right are three faces—blue, red and yellow; on his left are three more—white, smoke-colored and black. Each of these faces has three eyes. His uppermost right and left hands hold the freshly severed skin of an elephant, stretched open by its left fore- and hind-legs. The next two right and left hands at his heart hold a curved knife and skull-cup filled with blood. The remaining thirty hands hold various weapons—such as axe, spear, bludgeon and sword —to destroy delusions and obstacles, and ritual implements—such as hand-drum and bell—with which to make and enjoy offerings.

His eight right feet trample upon a human being, buffalo, bullock, donkey, camel, dog, sheep and fox; his left feet stand upon a vulture, owl, raven, parrot, hawk, kite, mynah bird and swan. Also being trampled upon are eight celestial devas, or gods—Brahma, Indra, Vishnu, Rudra, Six-headed Kumara, Ganesh and the gods of the Sun and Moon.

Within the sadhana and commentaries to the Yamantaka practice, the symbolism of all these various elements is explained. In brief, Yamantaka's nine faces stand for the nine traditional categories of buddhist scriptures[25] and his hair standing on end symbolizes his attainment of nirvana. The garland of fifty heads represents the purity of Yamantaka's holy speech, fifty being the number of vowels and consonants in the Sanskrit alphabet. His two horns are the two levels of truth; the thirty-four arms together with Yamantaka's body, speech and mind are the thirty-seven Limbs of Enlightenment[26] and the sixteen legs are the sixteen emptinesses.[27] The man and animals under his right feet represent the eight great accomplishments; the eight birds under his left feet represent the eight powers[28]; and the eight gods, four on each side, show that Yamantaka surpasses the glory of the heavenly beings. Finally, the fact that Yamantaka is standing naked shows that his mind is not covered by any obscurations. When the practitioner visualizes him- or herself as Yamantaka and recalls the meaning of all these symbols, this greatly enhances the divine pride so important for self-transformation on the generation stage.

In addition to the traditional representation of the deity, the artist has placed Yamantaka in the setting of a charnel ground. In front of him are skull-cups containing the five sense organs, while scattered around are the bleached bones of human skeletons, and corpses being eaten by vultures and jackals. On one side, next to the stupa containing the relics of a deceased guru, sits a monk meditating upon death and impermanence. On the other side, behind the feasting jackals, is a yogi playing a hand-drum as part of the chod rite, using the terror-provoking scene before him to cut off the related fears of ego-grasping and self-cherishing.

There are many levels of meaning behind these abundant symbols of death and decay. Yamantaka is the one who destroys or overcomes Yama, the Lord of Death. As the wrathful emanation of Manjushri's enlightened wisdom, Yamantaka represents the penetrative insight that fully comprehends the transient character of all impermanent phenomena as well as their ultimately selfless, or empty, nature. With this direct, intuitive understanding, all fears of death are overcome. The great yogi Jetsun Milarepa (Plate 30) said:

> I fled to the mountains
> Because I feared death;
> I have realized emptiness,
> The mind's primordial mode of existence.
> Even if I were to die now
> It would be no pity.[29]

But there is another reason why Yamantaka is characterized as the destroyer of death, and this relates directly to the highest yoga tantra practices of the generation and completion stages. As the Wheel of Life illustrates, as long as we remain under the influence of ignorance and the delusions we not only move through this life uncontrollably—chasing after elusive happiness and encountering unwanted suffering—but we are also forced to pass uncontrollably from one life to the next and from one unsatisfactory realm to another. We die without conscious control, enter the intermediate state without control and are reborn without control, forced to experience suffering and dissatisfaction again and again. From the point of view of highest yoga tantra, it is the uncontrolled experience of these three times—death, the intermediate state and rebirth—that is the main obstacle preventing the fulfillment of our innate buddha-potential. A distinguishing feature of highest yoga tantra is its ability to give us such complete control over these three critical experiences that we can transform them into an incomparably powerful path of spiritual development.

To understand what this transformation entails, we have to become familiar with the natural unfolding of the death process.[30] Death is the separation of the stream of consciousness from the body it is currently inhabiting. This does not happen all at once but takes place in successive stages (listed in Table 5). At each stage different energy-winds lose their ability to support consciousness as they enter, abide and dissolve into the *central channel* (Skt. *shushumna* or *avadhuti*) of the vajra body. As this happens the mind becomes more and more subtle until eventually the very subtlest level of consciousness—the clear light mind of death—is reached.

Even for those who have not developed the extraordinary control of a tantric adept, it is possible to stay in the clear light of death experience for up to three days. Eventually, however, the very subtle red and white drops constituting the indestructible drop at one's heart open. When this happens the very subtle mind, together with the very subtle energy-wind upon which it is mounted, departs from the body. Death has now finally taken place.

The eight visions of the death process—from the mirage to the clear light—also occur as we fall asleep, though most people have not developed the mindfulness to be aware of them. And for a well-trained practitioner of highest yoga tantra—one who has gained control over the various energy-winds and can cause them to enter the central channel—these very same visions occur as a result of meditative training. The advantage of having this experience in meditation is that the yogi can remain completely aware of what is happening while the mind is growing subtler and subtler. Eventually, as a result of fully integrated practice, the yogi learns to focus the extremely subtle and blissful mind of clear light directly upon the ultimate truth of emptiness. This extraordinary accomplishment puts the skillful tantric practitioner in possession of a penetrating wisdom consciousness unmatched in its ability to cut through delusions and eradicate the stains of ignorance.

Table 5: Stages in the death process

stage	description	inner vision
first	the earth element dissolves[31]; the body grows weak and thinner; vision becomes unclear	shimmering mirage
second	the water element dissolves; liquids of the body begin to dry up; perception of external sound ceases	smoke
third	the fire element dissolves; heat absorbs from limbs to the heart; detection of odors ceases; inhalation becomes weak and shallow while exhalation becomes long and strong	sparks
fourth	the air, or wind, element dissolves; all signs of breathing stop; the tongue becomes thick and can no longer move	dying candle flame
fifth	white drops descend from the crown of the head to the heart	"white appearance": a clear empty sky pervaded by moonlight
sixth	red drops ascend from the navel to the heart	"red increase": an even clearer empty sky pervaded by sunlight
seventh	both drops encircle the indestructible drop at the heart center	"black near-attainment": a very dark and completely empty sky
eighth	the sphere enclosing the indestructible drop opens	"clear light": like the autumn sky at dawn

By developing the ability to remain fully conscious and in control during the death process, we are transforming the ordinary experience of death into the clear light experience of an enlightened being's unobscured truth body (Skt. *dharmakaya*). Similarly, the intermediate state and rebirth experiences can be transformed respectively into the two aspects of an enlightened being's form body (Skt. *rupakaya*), namely the enjoyment body (Skt. *sambhogakaya*) and *emanation body* (Skt. *nirmanakaya*) (see Table 6). In this way, then, the uncontrolled experience of death, the intermediate state and rebirth is transmuted into the enlightened experience of the three buddha bodies as we overcome the Lord of Death and transform our most feared enemy into our greatest protector.

It is often pointed out that sincere practitioners of the buddha-dharma, depending upon their level of achievement, have three different attitudes towards death. The most excellent practitioners—such as those who have mastered the methods of highest yoga tantra just mentioned—look forward to it the way ordinary beings look forward to going on a picnic. They are confident in their ability to negotiate the death experience with full, conscious control and hence determine their future. Those of lesser ability may not view death with such joy, but they have no fear of it, having gained familiarity with the process through repeated training. As for those of least ability, they can die without regrets, knowing that they have done everything within their capacity and have mended all broken vows and breaches of commitment made to their gurus.

Table 6: Correspondences between death, sleep and the three buddha bodies

death	sleep	truth body (dharmakaya)	
intermediate state	dream	enjoyment body (sambhogakaya)	form bodies (rupakaya)
rebirth	reawakening	emanation body (nirmanakaya)	

This section on the fierce Opponent of the Lord of Death concludes with a stanza from the verses of auspiciousness recited at the close of Yamantaka's sadhana:

> The vast space and this mother earth
> Are entirely filled, with neither let nor hindrance,
> By the hosts of deities related to the Opponent of Yama,
> The mere recollection of whom subdues all demons and
>   interferers and effortlessly fulfills all wishes of the mind.
> By this practice which releases a rain of flowers that
>   pervades the sky
> With the sound of a song endowed with the fidelity of
>   Brahma,
> You are maintained in everlasting glory.
> As ecstatic joy arises in you through knowing this,
> We shall proclaim this melodious song of good fortune.[32]

HERUKA CHAKRASAMVARA

Heruka Chakrasamvara—the Wrathful Lord of the Wheel of Supreme Bliss—is one of the major meditational deities of the mother tantras, the principal sources explaining the methods for realizing the clear light.[33] This deity is sometimes referred to as Samvara and sometimes merely as Heruka, though this latter term can be applied in general to all wrathful male deities of highest yoga tantra. In this section two forms of Heruka Chakrasamvara are presented: one having one face and two arms (Plate 22) and the other four faces and twelve arms (Plate 23).

In his simpler form, Chakrasamvara is blue-black in color and stands on a sun disc surrounded by a flaming aura of his own radiant wisdom. His hands are crossed in the embracing mudra and hold the vajra and bell symbolic of unified bliss and emptiness. He wears a tigerskin loin cloth in the manner of an ascetic yogi and is adorned with both bone and jeweled ornaments and a garland of fifty freshly severed human heads. On his forehead is a third eye of wisdom and the expression on his face is a mixture of wrath and passion.

Chakrasamvara embraces his red consort, Vajrayogini (see Plate 24), who holds a curved knife in her right hand to cut off ego interferences and in her left a skull-cup (not shown) symbolizing blissful wisdom. The artist has portrayed this divine couple as appearing in the clear, empty space of the limitless dharmakaya, and the radiant light shining from their place of union symbolizes the enlightened transformation of sensual desire through the union of bliss and emptiness.

Chakrasamvara's right leg is extended and stands on the back of the worldly deity wrathful Ishvara (also known as Bhairava), while his left leg is bent and tramples on the breast of Bhairava's consort, the goddess Kalarati. This stance symbolizes the ability of Chakrasamvara to overcome the forces of ignorant hatred and desirous attachment respectively. It is also directly related to the legendary origins of the *Chakrasamvara Tantra*, which can be briefly related as follows.[34]

At one time this world was under the control of Bhairava. Worship of this fierce deity, most notably in the twenty-four places sacred to him and his consort Kalarati, often took the form of ritual

133

sacrifice at which thousands of animals were slaughtered. On occasion human sacrifice was also practiced in the belief that such offerings would move these powerful worldly deities to grant divine assistance in both temporal and spiritual matters. Degenerate practices of aggression and licentiousness became so widespread that countless beings, thinking they were performing virtuous actions, were in fact led away from the path to liberation.

Unable to tolerate this situation any longer, Vajrapani and the buddhas of the five lineages implored Buddha Vajradhara to help. Moved by their request, Vajradhara manifested in the form of Heruka Chakrasamvara and subdued Bhairava through the power of his enlightened inspiration and blessings. In those places where the divine abodes, or mandalas, of Bhairava and his consort had been, Chakrasamvara manifested his own enlightened mandalas and left them there without reabsorbing them. This is said to be an auspicious sign that when the times become more degenerate and the poisons of anger and lust become even more powerful than they are now, while other tantric systems will suffer a decline, that of Chakrasamvara will become even stronger, fueled by the deluded energies his practices so effectively transform.

This story indicates that a principal characteristic of Chakrasamvara is his ability to enter even the most unpromising worldly situations and transform them instantly through the power of insightful wisdom. Many of the most famous practitioners of Chakrasamvara were men and women who, in their outward appearance and behavior, were highly unorthodox but who had nevertheless mastered the esoteric science of spiritual transformation completely. Often, for the sake of cutting through the stultifying conceptions of conventional society, they manifested their spiritual mastery in the most dramatic fashion imaginable. Reference has already been made to a few of these mahasiddhas; in the traditional list of eighty-four such celebrated yogis and yoginis, two practitioners of Chakrasamvara, Luipa and Ghantapa, figure prominently.[35]

Luipa was a prince who, despite his contempt for wealth and power, was compelled to ascend the throne of his father. Eventually, like Shakyamuni before him, he made his escape from the royal life. Traveling to another land he exchanged his golden throne for a simple deer-skin and his couch of silks and satin for a bed of ashes. In this way he adopted the manner of a fully renounced wandering yogi and took to begging for his daily food.

Eventually his travels took him to Bodh Gaya, the site of Shakyamuni's enlightenment some thirteen centuries earlier, and then to Pataliputra, the capital of the local kingdom. At a brothel there he met a courtesan who was in reality a *dakini*, a female embodiment of enlightened wisdom-energy. She looked into the nature of his mind and said, "Your four psychic centers and their energies are quite pure, but there is a pea-sized obscuration of royal pride in your heart."[36] Then she poured some putrid food into his begging bowl and told him to be on his way. When Luipa threw the inedible slop into the gutter, she called after him, "How can you attain nirvana if you are still concerned about the purity of your food?"[37]

The yogi was mortified to realize that his judgmental mind still perceived some things as intrinsically more desirable than others and that this propensity was the chief obstacle to his attainment of full enlightenment. With this realization he went down to the banks of the Ganges and began a twelve-year practice to overcome his discursive thought-patterns, prejudices and preconceptions. During that time he lived on the entrails of fish that the local fishermen discarded, and thus came to be known as Luipa, Eater of Fish-Guts.

Luipa was initiated into the tantra of Chakrasamvara by Shavaripa, who himself was a disciple of the great master Saraha.[38] By assiduous practice of Chakrasamvara's sadhana, Luipa achieved insight into the innately pure nature of his mind, beyond all dualistic discriminations of this and that. This is the profound *mahamudra* (literally, "great seal") experience and through it Luipa attained enlightenment.

One of the greatest practitioners of Luipa's Chakrasamvara lineage was Ghantapa. He had been a monk at the famous Nalanda Monastery and gained a great reputation for his learning. Eventually he met Luipa's disciple Darikapa who initiated him into the Chakrasamvara mandala and its practices and told him to go into the jungles to meditate. There he was initiated again, this time by a female swineherd.

As a result of his ascetic life-style and poor diet, Ghantapa became emaciated and ragged in appearance. When the local ruler came by one day on a hunting expedition and caught sight of this thin man in poor health, he encouraged him to come into the city where he would receive proper food, clothing and shelter. But Ghantapa replied, "Just as a great elephant cannot be led out of the jungle on a thread, I, a monk, cannot be tempted from this forest even by the immense wealth of a king."[39]

This answer humiliated and infuriated the proud ruler. Seeking revenge for the insult he felt he had suffered, he offered a large reward to any woman who could seduce this arrogant monk and force him to break his vow of celibacy. One woman, a low-caste seller of wine, boasted that she could do what the king wished. She found the hut where Ghantapa lived and asked him to keep her on as his servant. Although Ghantapa had no need of such a servant he told the woman she could stay, realizing that there existed a strong karmic relationship between the two of them from previous lives.

Several years went by and Ghantapa decided the time was ripe to help the people in the city develop greater interest in the dharma. He arranged that the woman would go to the king and tell him that she had not only seduced the monk but that their union had produced two children, a son and a daughter. Delighted that his plan had worked so well, the king instructed her to bring Ghantapa to the city on a particular day. Then he issued a proclamation full of disparaging comments about Ghantapa and calling upon his subjects to insult this bogus holy man when he arrived.

On the appointed day, Ghantapa and the woman left the forest accompanied by their children, the boy walking on Ghantapa's right and the girl on his left. Ghantapa himself staggered along as if he were drunk and held a bowl into which the woman poured wine. The people who had gathered shouted insults and jeered, "When our king first invited you to the city, you arrogantly refused him, but now you come drunk with a wine-seller and children! This isn't a very good example for a buddhist monk, is it?"

When Ghantapa heard this he pretended to become angry and threw his bowl on the ground in rage. Where it hit, the earth split open and water gushed out in a flood. Then, to the increased amazement of the assembled witnesses, his son transformed into a vajra, his daughter into a bell and his consort into Vajrayogini. Ghantapa himself transformed into Heruka Chakrasamvara and taking the vajra and bell in hand he embraced Vajrayogini, whereupon they both flew up into the sky!

The astonished onlookers, including the king, prayed to the di-

Plate 1 Shakyamuni Buddha

Plate 2 Wheel of Life

Plate 3 Stupa of Enlightenment

Plate 4 Prajnaparamita

Plate 5 Four-armed Avalokiteshvara

Plate 6 Thousand-armed Avalokiteshvara

Plate 7 Manjushri

Plate 8 Vajrapani

Plate 9 Sambhogakaya aspects of the buddhas of the five families

Plate 10 Amitabha

Plate 11 Green Tara

Plate 12 White Tara

Plate 13 Amitayus

Plate 14 Medicine Buddha

Plate 15 Vaishravana

Plate 16 Vajradhara

Plate 17 Vajrasattva

Plate 18 Vajrasattva with Consort

Plate 19 Guhyasamaja

Plate 20 Yamantaka

Plate 21 Dharmaraja

Plate 22 Two-armed Heruka Chakrasamvara

Plate 23 Twelve-armed Heruka Chakrasamvara

Plate 24 Vajrayogini

Plate 25 Vajradharma

Plate 26 Mahakala

Plate 27 Guru Rinpoche, Padmasambhava

Plate 28 Sakya Pandita

Plate 29 Marpa the Translator

Plate 30 Jetsun Milarepa

Plate 31 Je Tsong Khapa

Plate 32 Maitreya

vine couple to return and save them from the water that was now threatening to engulf them. Ghantapa refused, absorbed in the concentration of immutable wrath, but told the people that if they felt regret they should pray to Avalokiteshvara, the embodiment of great compassion. When they did so the benevolent bodhisattva immediately appeared and stopped the flood by pressing his foot on the fissure through which the water had come forth. Before departing to the pure dakini-land, Ghantapa declared:

> Although medicine and poison create contrary effects,
> In their ultimate essence they are one;
> Likewise negative qualities and aids on the path,
> One in essence, should not be differentiated.
> The realized sage rejects nothing whatsoever,
> While the unrealized spiritual child,
> Five times poisoned, is lost in samsara.[40]

As a result of all that had happened, the king and his subjects became extremely devoted in their practice of the dharma and many attained high realizations.

Ghantapa—also known as Vajraghanta, Bearer of the Vajra and Bell—is regarded in Tibet as the founder of the five-deity lineage of the Chakrasamvara teachings in which the central deity is visualized in the two-armed form presented in Plate 22. Eventually the esoteric insights he transmitted reached Naropa and other mahasiddhas who, in turn, formulated them into such practices as the Six Yogas of Naropa[41] and passed them on to their Tibetan and Nepalese disciples. They, in turn, established lineages that preserved these profound practices of highest yoga tantra and transmitted them personally from guru to disciple so that they are still alive and flourishing today.

Another major lineage of Heruka Chakrasamvara visualizes him in the twelve-armed form illustrated in Plate 23. In addition to vajra and bell, this four-faced deity holds the skin of an elephant and a variety of other implements, namely the drum, dagger, curved knife and three-pointed spear in his right hands and the staff, skull-cup, noose and the head of a worldly deity in his left hands.

The symbolism of these various attributes can be explained as follows. Chakrasamvara's four faces stand for the four doors of liberation. [42] His twelve arms signify the purification of the twelve links of dependent arising explained in the Wheel of Life. As before, the vajra and bell held in embracing mudra symbolize the supreme unification of method and wisdom while the elephant skin illustrates the abandonment of ignorance. By playing the hand drum, Chakrasamvara enhances the blissful happiness experienced in the minds of all Fully Enlightened Ones. The dagger and curved knife cut off the three poisons at the hub of the Wheel of Life and eliminate all extreme views while the three-pointed spear pierces through the delusions of the three realms of existence. The staff symbolizes Chakrasamvara's ultimate bodhichitta, his direct insight into the empty nature of all things. The skull-cup filled with blood stands for the blissful wisdom filling Chakrasamvara's holy mind while the noose signifies that this powerful deity binds himself and others to nothing but this experience of bliss beyond all suffering. Finally, by displaying the severed head of a samsaric deity, Chakrasamvara demonstrates his attainment of liberation and enlightenment free of all the obstacles of delusion.

Before concluding this section it is worthwhile mentioning that there exist ways of combining the three major yidams just presented—Guhyasamaja, Yamantaka and Chakrasamvara—into one integrated practice. The Tibetan master Je Tsong Khapa received instructions directly from Manjushri for doing just this and then passed on this profound advice to his disciples. According to one explanation[43] of such integrated practice, Guhyasamaja forms the actual path, Yamantaka serves as the preliminary, and Chakrasamvara activates it. This means that the practitioner takes Guhyasamaja as his or her main deity and chiefly follows the methods contained in this tantric path. To insure a long life and to develop the wisdom necessary for following these methods successfully, the yogi relies on Yamantaka as a preliminary. And when engaging in the part of the completion stage dealing with the so-called "four joys,"[44] where it is necessary to cultivate progressively more intense experiences of bliss, the yogi extracts the relevant portions of the Chakrasamvara practice that activate and strengthen such blissful experiences. By blending these three tantras into a unified whole in this way, the skillful practitioner is greatly increasing his or her chances of success.

VAJRAYOGINI

The great mahasiddha Naropa, mentioned above as a lineage holder of the Chakrasamvara tradition, had once been the foremost scholar at the famous Nalanda monastic university in North India. In honor of his intellectual accomplishments, of which he was very proud, Naropa was appointed gatekeeper of Nalanda's northern entrance. In this position it was his duty to defend the monastery's philosophical traditions against all who came to challenge them. Through the power of his immense learning and stainless logic, he was invariably successful in this demanding task, and thus his fame grew.

One day a withered old hag appeared before him and asked if he had truly mastered all the words of Buddha's teachings. When he confidently answered that he had, the old woman laughed out loud. But when he added, "I also understand their meaning," the old woman began to weep bitterly.

Naropa was confused and asked her why she reacted in this way. "When you said that you knew the words of the teachings, I laughed for joy because this was the truth," she replied. "But I cry when you say you understand their meaning, because this is not so." Naropa was chastened by what this strange old woman—who in reality was a manifestation of Chakrasamvara's consort, the mighty Vajrayogini—had declared. Eventually he received empowerments and advice from this woman and, at her insistence, began a long search to find Tilopa (Figure 10), the guru who would awaken in him an intuitive understanding of the meaning of the dharma, as revealed in the *Chakrasamvara Tantra*. Finally, he received a direct vision of Vajrayogini herself in the form depicted here in Plate 24, a form that has come to be known as Naro Khachoma, or Naropa's Dakini.[45]

This story illustrates several important points about the relationship between the meditational deities of the Vajrayana path and the spiritual seekers who follow it. Although deities such as Vajrayogini can be thought of as the embodied fulfillment of the enlightened potential, or buddha-nature, existing within each one of us, these deities are not merely idealized projections of our own internal universe. They have their own existence and it is therefore possible to

139

make contact with these external entities and receive inspiration, empowerment and even detailed instruction directly from them. How such contact is made and the precise form, or forms, in which these deities appear to us depend on our own state of receptivity and openness. Thus while Naropa's mind was under the strong influence of dry intellectual pride, Vajrayogini appeared as a withered hag; later, when all such obscurations veiling the clear light nature of Naropa's mind had been removed—thanks to a combination of his own efforts and his guru's inspiration—she revealed herself in the fully purified and enchantingly beautiful form shown here.

Ultimately it makes no difference whether we view the various meditational deities as reflections of our own enlightened potential or as externally existing entities, for both approaches, followed with sufficient faith and perseverance, eventually lead to the same realizations. What must be understood is that the way we ordinarily differentiate so sharply between internal and external, self and other, what belongs to me and what does not, is invalid, arising from the habit-patterns of our limited, dualistic, conceptualizing mind. If we are to progress spiritually it is necessary to cut through these dualistic interpretations and discover the essential oneness of the meditational deity, the guru and our own innate clear light nature.

On the most fundamental level Vajrayogini, the Diamond Practitioner, is the wisdom of the inseparability of great bliss and emptiness. Because this wisdom functions to destroy ignorant confusion—symbolized by a pig, as at the hub of the Wheel of Life—this deity is also known as Vajravarahi, the Diamond Sow, and is sometimes adorned with the head of a pig. This is in keeping with a device repeatedly found in Vajrayana imagery whereby the traits overcome by a particular deity appear symbolically as the attributes of that deity.

Of the three major forms of Vajrayogini, the one depicted here accords with the vision of Naropa.[46] She is red in color, has one face and two arms and, like Chakrasamvara, stands upon Bhairava and Kalarati. There are different ways in which these two worldly deities can be understood. According to one, they represent the hatred and attachment that Vajrayogini's wisdom has overcome. According to another, they represent the enlightened attributes of Vajrayogini herself, Bhairava symbolizing her method aspect and Kalarati her wisdom. Since Vajrayogini's right leg is itself a symbol of her method and is standing upon Kalarati, a symbol of her wisdom, and since the reverse is true with respect to her left leg, Vajrayogini's stance doubly reinforces the union of method and wisdom so vital to the practice of highest yoga tantra.

Vajrayogini is sixteen years old, radiantly beautiful with a youthful freshness and vitality, and her face bears an intense expression reflecting her passionate nature. She has three eyes, symbolizing her enlightened ability to see past, present and future simultaneously. Her eyes gaze upwards to the Land of the Dakinis, demonstrating that Vajrayogini has the power to guide serious practitioners directly to her pure land. In her right hand is a curved flaying knife marked by a vajra, and in her left she holds a skull-cup filled with blood as if she were about to drink from it. These implements symbolize respectively the wisdom that cuts through the fabrications of ignorance and the blissful clear light consciousness that has unified with this penetrating wisdom.

Supported on her left shoulder is a staff known as a khatvanga. This represents her consort Heruka Chakrasamvara and indicates that he and Vajrayogini are inseparable, whether he is explicitly visualized together with her or not. It should be borne in mind that the practices of Vajrayogini are derived from the *Chakrasamvara Tantra* and are the distilled essence of that profound meditational system. The symbolism of the khatvanga itself is extremely profound and each detail can be understood as representing different aspects of Chakrasamvara's mandala and the sixty-two deities contained therein.

Vajrayogini has beautifully smooth, freely flowing waist-length black hair. Since black hair cannot be dyed the way lighter hair can, it symbolizes the unchanging nature of Vajrayogini's enlightened dharmakaya, or truth body. Her breasts are full with nipples erect, symbolizing the arousal of desire and indicating that Vajrayogini helps those with strong passion to transform it into the realization of great bliss. Her body is naked, demonstrating Vajrayogini's freedom from ordinary conceptions and appearances. She is adorned with various bone ornaments—crown, bone-apron and so forth—symbolizing the first five perfections making up the method aspect of the path: generosity, discipline, patience, effort and meditative concentration.

Her body itself represents the sixth perfection, wisdom, and so through her wearing of these bone ornaments the union of method and wisdom is indicated yet again. Finally, around Vajrayogini's neck hangs a garland of fifty human skulls symbolizing the purity of her speech. Here, unlike in the images of Yamantaka and Chakrasamvara, these skulls are bleached and dry, indicating the fierce arousal of inner heat (Tib. *tum-mo*) in the Vajrayogini practice.

Below the lotus and sun disc upon which Vajrayogini is standing the artist has painted a red triangular design. This represents the heart of Vajrayogini's mandala abode, the manifestation of her blissful wisdom appearing as a celestial mansion. All meditational deities are visualized within their own three-dimensional mandalas, but Vajrayogini's abode has a unique shape, an inverted pyramid whose "base" is a double triangle. The outer triangular shape principally symbolizes great bliss and the inner one emptiness; together they stand for the wisdom of great bliss indivisibly one with emptiness. This unified structure is often referred to as Vajrayogini's "phenomena source" (Skt. *dharmadaya*). In front of this phenomena source is a skull-cup offering bowl containing the various human sense organs emitting flames. This symbolizes the way our ordinary sensory experiences can be transformed, by the blissful wisdom understanding emptiness, from being factors imprisoning us in samsaric dissatisfaction into the very nourishment fueling our journey along the path.

One of the special features of Vajrayogini's tantric path is that it contains methods for practicing the generation and completion stages of highest yoga tantra simultaneously. And one of the unique results of this unified path is the ability of the supremely successful practitioner to attain Vajrayogini's pure land without having to give up his or her present body. There are many accounts—some of them very recent—of dedicated practitioners who at the end of their lives simply disappeared, leaving nothing behind but their hair, fingernails and the clothes they were wearing; this is a mark of having attained the so-called rainbow body, a sign of successful practice. The shrine at Parping mentioned earlier is the site where the original disciples to whom Naropa taught the tantra of Vajrayogini, the Pamdingpa brothers, gained such supreme success.

The lineage of Vajrayogini and Chakrasamvara practitioners is filled with stories of a miraculous nature. Many of these stories—like the one of Naropa at the beginning of this section—relate how a particular practitioner encountered a living manifestation of Vajrayogini herself. One of the most famous accounts concerns the novice monk Kusali who, when traveling with his guru by the banks of the Ganges, met an old woman with leprosy who wanted to cross the river. His guru ignored the woman but Kusali, overcome with compassion, wrapped her in his shawl and began fording the river with her on his back. When they were halfway across the old woman suddenly transformed into Vajrayogini and transported Kusali directly to her pure land!

As miraculous as these stories sound, it would be a mistake to dismiss them too readily as nothing but products of a fanciful imagination. Recently, among the exiled community of Tibetan refugees, there have been examples of highly accomplished meditators who displayed signs of a decidedly supramundane nature. In the 1970s, for example, the monk Jepa Rinpoche died in Manali, a site in North India called the Valley of the Gods. It had been part of this simple-looking monk's practice to make a daily offering of one thousand water bowls and one thousand butter lamps to Vajrayogini. When he died and his body was cremated, the mantra of Vajrayogini was clearly visible on his bones. Happenings such as this are far from rare and indicate that the methods of highest yoga tantra, if practiced diligently enough, have a transformative power of extraordinary potential. The ultimate purpose of these methods, of course, is to transform limited, self-centered beings like ourselves into fully evolved and effortlessly compassionate Awakened Ones; there can be no greater or more worthwhile transformation than this.

A special prayer of auspiciousness recited regularly by Vajrayogini's devoted practitioners reads:

> May there be the auspiciousness of swiftly receiving the blessings
> Of the hosts of glorious, sacred gurus,
> Vajradhara, Pandit Naropa and so forth,
> The glorious lords of all virtue and excellence.

May there be the auspiciousness of the dakini truth body,
Perfection of wisdom, the supreme Mother of the
   Conquerors,
The natural clear light, free from elaboration from the
   beginning,
The lady who emanates and gathers all things stable and
   moving.

May there be the auspiciousness of the complete enjoyment
   body, simultaneously born,
A body radiant and beautiful, ablaze with the glory of the
   major and minor marks,
A speech proclaiming the supreme vehicle with sixty
   melodies,
And a mind of non-conceptual bliss and clarity, possessing
   the five exalted wisdoms.

May there be the auspiciousness of the emanation body,
   born from the places,
Ladies who with various form bodies, in various places,
Fulfill by various means the aims of various ones to be
   tamed
In accordance with their various wishes.

May there be the auspiciousness of the supreme dakini,
   mantra-born,
A venerable lady with a color similar to that of a ruby
With a smiling, wrathful manner, one face, two hands
   holding curved knife and skull-cup
And two legs in bent and outstretched positions.

May there be the auspiciousness of your countless millions
   of emanations
And the hosts of the seventy-two thousand dakinis
Eliminating all the obstructions of practitioners
And bestowing the attainments that are longed for.[47]

BUDDHA VAJRADHARMA

Every Vajrayana sadhana, or method of accomplishment, contains some form of guru-yoga practice so that the meditator can receive the necessary blessings and inspiration of the lineage. In the sadhana of Vajrayogini this practice is centered upon the figure of Buddha Vajradharma (Plate 25) who is described as follows:

> In the space before me, arising from the appearance of the exalted wisdom of non-dual purity and clarity, is a celestial mansion which is square with four doorways, ornaments and archways, and complete with all the essential features. In the center on a jeweled throne supported by eight great lions, on a seat of a lotus of various colors, a sun and a moon, sits my kind root guru in the aspect of Buddha Vajradharma. He has a red-colored body, one face and two hands which are crossed at the heart and hold a vajra and bell. His hair is tied up in a top knot and he sits with his legs crossed in the vajra posture. He assumes the form of a sixteen-year-old in the prime of his youth, adorned with silks and all the bone and jeweled ornaments.[48]

Around this figure of the root guru as Buddha Vajradharma—recognized as inseparably one with Amitabha—are arranged all the lineage gurus through whom the practice of Vajrayogini has been transmitted up until the present, including Naropa, the Sakya Pandita (Plate 28) and many other supreme masters. These lineage gurus are not visualized in their ordinary form but rather

> ...in the aspect of Hero Vajradharma with red colored bodies, one face and two hands. Their right hands play damarus which reverberate with the sound of bliss and emptiness. Their left hands hold at their hearts skull-cups filled with nectar and their left elbows hold khatvangas.[49]

Keeping the root and lineage gurus firmly in view, the meditator engages in various practices—such as prostration, offering and the like—that align his or her mind with the enlightening influence of these past and present masters. All of this is designed so that the sub-

145

sequent yogas of self-transformation will be as successful as possible.

As we can see from the description just given, there is no one set form in which the guru must be visualized for us to receive his or her inspiration. Sometimes the guru is seen in ordinary form, other times as Buddha Vajradharma, Hero Vajradhara, or Vajrayogini. It is the mark of a fully qualified guru that he or she can take on whatever aspect is appropriate for contacting the minds of those requiring blessings and instruction. In some cases, the guru may manifest as an animal or even as an inanimate object, if this is the most skillful way of bringing benefit.

The qualified tantric disciple also possesses the ability, at least potentially, to manifest in a variety of forms. Some people may feel that a woman practitioner should devote herself to the practices of Vajrayogini, Tara or some other female deity and a man should choose Chakrasamvara, Manjushri or one of the other male yidams. However, it has been pointed out that:

> If a man finds it uncomfortable to see himself as Vajrayogini and if a woman experiences the same difficulty in seeing herself as Heruka, this is only because they have failed to overcome their ordinary appearances. Once this fault has been eliminated, it makes no difference whether you choose to see yourself as a male or female deity.[50]

MAHAKALA

As the previous discussions have shown, the practices of tantra—specifically those of highest yoga tantra—involve the arousal of latent forces, both mental and physical, of enormous power. If these are channeled correctly, their transformative effects can be outstandingly beneficial; but if they are handled improperly, with the wrong motivation or with lack of skill, they can bring the unfortunate practitioner such miseries as disease, insanity and even an untimely death.

There is a story about a practitioner of Yamantaka who became obsessed with the personal power he could acquire through following this advanced tantric system. His meditative concentration was strong and stable, but his motivation was completely devoid of compassion for others; his only interest was in gaining worldly benefit for himself. For a long time he meditated single-pointedly upon himself in the form of Yamantaka, untiringly cultivating the clear appearance and divine pride of being this powerful, wrathful deity. After he died a tantric master with clairvoyant abilities was asked what had become of him. The guru replied that because of his impure, selfish motivation he had not achieved any realizations at all. On the contrary, he had taken rebirth in the lower, suffering realms as a preta, a wandering and perpetually dissatisfied spirit. The only fruit of his previous intense practice was that this preta had the outward form of Yamantaka!

This story points out some of the dangers connected with the practice of tantra. These dangers, or interferences, are of two types: external and internal. The former consist of any outside forces, animate or inanimate, that interfere with or hinder the successful completion of our practices, or that prevent us from accomplishing our worldly aims. It often happens that spiritual practitioners, because of the purity of their intentions, attract hindrances in the same way that a magnet attracts small pieces of metal. The most famous illustration of this is the story of Shakyamuni Buddha who, while seated under the Bodhi Tree, was attacked by demonic spirits intent on disturbing his meditation. One of the reasons why followers of the tantric path are advised to keep their practices hidden and to maintain a humble outward appearance is to avoid attracting such external hindrances, be they human or non-human. As one contemporary lama has put it,[51] exposing our practices to others and boasting about being a tantrika is like letting everyone know that we are carrying around precious jewelry: sooner or later we shall attract thieves intent on stealing our valuables.

Internal interferences arise from the delusions—pride, avarice and so forth—obscuring the essentially pure nature of our mind. As long as we remain in samsara, it is all too easy to be misled by mistaken conceptions, break the vows we have taken, use whatever power we may gain for selfish purposes and the like. The serious dharma practitioner, especially the one engaging in highest yoga tantra, is in need of protection from these external and internal interferences, and there exists a class of wrathful deities known as dharmapalas, or protectors of the teachings, who can be relied upon for assistance. Prominent among these protecting deities is Mahakala, one of whose many forms is depicted in Plate 26.

Mahakala—the Great Black One—is shown in his six-armed manifestation.[52] His body is usually painted dark blue or black to symbolize his changeless dharmakaya nature. His three eyes symbolize his clear comprehension of past, present and future and his crown of five skulls represents the five poisonous delusions—anger, desire, ignorance, jealousy and pride—transformed into the wisdoms of the five buddha families.

Mahakala's six arms signify the completion of the six perfections and hold various implements with which he carries out his protective functions. The curved knife in his first right hand cuts ego-attachment and the skull-cup filled with blood in his left hand shows his subjugation of evil-doers. As we have seen earlier, the knife and cup also represent the inseparability of bliss and emptiness, the tantric union of method and wisdom. His other right hands hold a rosary of skulls, symbolizing his continuous activity for the benefit of beings, and a damaru with which he exerts control over all classes of dakinis. His remaining left hands hold a trident, symbolizing his power over the three spheres of existence—the desire, form and formless realms—and a lasso with which he binds those who would break their vows.

Other ways of interpreting these implements include recognizing the hand-drum as making the sound that arouses us from our ignorance, the trident as representing the destruction of the three root delusions, and the lasso as that which reins in the caprices of the confused mind.

Mahakala's left leg is outstretched and his right is bent to symbolize his accomplishments for the benefit of others and oneself. He tramples on an elephant-headed deity to symbolize his destruction and dispersal of great obstacles. The elephant can also represent the use of wealth for limited, samsaric ends and Mahakala's domination shows the enlightened transformation of such worldly behavior. Mahakala stands upon a sun disc, symbolizing his illumination of the darkness of ignorance, which itself rests upon a lotus, symbolizing his undefiled purity. The blazing fire emanating from all the pores of his body demonstrates his powerful activities in consuming all neurotic states of mind. Finally, he is adorned with a tigerskin loincloth, a snake necklace and holds an elephant skin; these three represent Mahakala's purification of desire, anger and pride. His other ornaments symbolize his possession of the complete qualities of a fully enlightened buddha.

Although Mahakala and the other dharmapalas are sometimes pictured as the central figures in Tibetan tangkas, it is far more common for them to assume a subordinate position. The main figure will often be the particular meditational deity—such as Manjushri, Tara or Chakrasamvara—with which the practitioner is training to identify. Above this central figure will be the lineage gurus who transmitted the practices of that deity, or perhaps the head of the appropriate buddha family. Along the bottom of the painting will be depicted one or more of the various dharma protectors, specifically those relating to the main practice in which the meditator is engaged. It should be remembered, however, that no matter how many figures might appear in a particular tangka, they are all to be understood as manifestations of one's own kind root guru, who in turn is seen as inseparable from the buddhas of the past, present and future.

Despite his ferocious appearance, Mahakala is a manifestation of Avalokiteshvara, the embodiment of universal compassion. It is said that when Avalokiteshvara realized that his peaceful methods were too mild to subdue the degenerate beings in this age of darkness and protect them from the consequences of their misguided behavior, he decided that a wrathful form would be better able to accomplish his compassionate intentions. He therefore emanated the dark blue syllable *HUM* which transformed into the powerful Mahakala. Amitabha and all the buddhas of the ten directions praised Avalokiteshvara's resolve to benefit others by means of this wrathful form and predicted that Mahakala would serve as an invincible dharma protector in all realms where enlightened beings appear and reveal the path to complete spiritual awakening.

Of the eighty-four Indian mahasiddhas, one of the major practitioners of Mahakala was Shavaripa.[53] He was a mighty hunter whom Avalokiteshvara sought to tame by manifesting as a superior marksman. When Shavaripa begged the bodhisattva to teach him to shoot as he did, Avalokiteshvara promised to do so, but only on the condition that Shavaripa not eat meat for a month. In this way the hunter and his wife abandoned their life-long habit of killing animals and became vegetarians. They learned how to meditate upon lovingkindness and compassion for all living creatures and, after being shown a vision of the self-inflicted torment their murderous way of life had prepared for them, developed sincere regret for their harmful deeds of the past.

After twelve years meditating upon sublime compassion in a state free of discursive thought, Shavaripa attained the supreme realization of mahamudra and received empowerment from Mahakala directly. Vajrayogini, Tara and many other deities also bestowed their blessings on him and Shavaripa became a great teacher of the dharma, transmitting his enlightening insights through song and dance, sound and symbol. It is said that Shavaripa will stay on this earth until Maitreya, the Buddha of Loving-kindness (Plate 32), appears and turns the wheel of dharma as the fifth of the one thousand Founding Buddhas of this world-age.

Dharmapala practices are very popular among the Tibetans but, as indicated, such powerful techniques are not without their dangers. It has been said, "If the practitioner ventures onto dangerous ground, unhealthy for his progress on the path, the dharmapala principle pulls him back violently."[54] Furthermore, only when we have acquired the confident strength of our personal meditational deity—such as Yamantaka or Chakrasamvara—are we fully qualified to call upon a protector like Mahakala for support. Otherwise, it is as if we were in possession of a vicious guard dog—if we do not treat it properly there is the danger that it will turn and attack us!

Up to this point dharma protectors such as Mahakala have been explained largely in terms of tantric practice. However, they can also play a significant role in the pre-tantric sutra path as well. According to Atisha, Je Tsong Khapa and other masters, the sutra path is divided into three graded scopes, each one corresponding to a different level of practitioner. The trainee of initial scope is mainly concerned with remaining detached from the enticing sensory desires of this lifetime. Since the main method for cultivating such detachment is meditation upon death and impermanence, such a trainee can rely on Dharmaraja (Plate 21), chief protector in the system of the "Slayer of the Lord of Death," Yamantaka.

For the person of middle scope, the main practices are the three higher trainings of morality, concentration and wisdom. Of these, the most fundamental is morality, and thus the practitioner of this level is protected by Vaishravana (Plate 15), the guardian who helps those attempting to keep pure moral discipline. Finally, for the trainee of highest scope, it is the development of the compassionate bodhichitta that is the most important. Mahakala, as an emanation of the supremely compassionate Avalokiteshvara, is therefore regarded as the protector of those engaged in cultivating such an altruistic motivation.

In terms of the advanced tantric practices themselves, the main role of Mahakala is to fulfill the four enlightened activities of pacifying interferences, increasing favorable circumstances, gaining control over situations and—if all else fails—destroying obstacles with wrathful force. Such powers, especially the last, are easily misused, and it has been suggested that the serious misapplication of these powerful techniques was partially responsible for the terrible devastation that Tibet has suffered at the hands of the Chinese invaders. Therefore, as His Holiness the Dalai Lama has said, those wishing a dharmapala practice should remember that the best protection of all is one's own development of a kind and loving heart. Just as Shakyamuni was protected from the onslaught of Mara by his meditation on love, we shall be safeguarded from outer and inner harm through our own generation of loving-kindness.

Still, for those who are properly qualified, a dharma protector such as Mahakala is of great importance. The following stanzas are among the many homages paid to this protector by famous practitioners. They were taken from a work by the First Dalai Lama, who, like Mahakala himself, was an emanation of Avalokiteshvara:

Homage to Mahakala, the Great Black One,
Wrathful emanation of the Bodhisattva of Compassion.
Homage to Mahakala, whose implements are
The skull-cup of blissful wisdom and the knife
Of penetrating methods severing negativity,
The Black Lord of ferocious appearance
Whose voice causes all on the earth to tremble.
O Mahakala, you appear in the form of a terrible demon
In order to overcome the endless hosts of demons.
Like the first day of the new moon,
You herald the destruction of the forces of darkness.
Protective lord, whose fangs are love, compassion,
    equanimity and joy,
Whose body blazes with fires of wisdom,
Your mantra is like the roar of a lion
Causing the jackals of evil to scatter.
Just as the angry yak catches its enemies on its horns
And then shakes the very life out of them,
Similarly do you destroy the inner forces
By which we obstruct our own path to liberation.[55]

6 A Living Tradition

The meditational deities illustrated in the preceding chapter serve as focal images for the supremely effective transformational methods of highest yoga tantra. Through skillful use of these methods it is possible to achieve full spiritual awakening very speedily, in some cases even within a few years. But the effectiveness of these practices does not lie primarily with the deities themselves. Instead, it depends upon the continuous transmission of enlightening insight from one mind to another through the medium of the guru-disciple relationship. Without such a relationship the would-be spiritual seeker remains isolated from the inspiring influence of those accomplished beings upon whom the power and indeed the very existence of these practices rely. As the Indian mahasiddha Naropa said:

> Before any guru existed
> Even the name of Buddha was not heard.
> All the buddhas of a thousand kalpas [eons]
> Only come about because of the guru.[1]

Thus in Vajrayana Buddhism reliance on the guru is of utmost importance and devotion to the guru is held to be the very root of the path. To appreciate the indispensable role of such wholehearted commitment and devotion it is necessary to realize that the term *guru* can be understood on several different levels. In the highest sense, *guru* refers to the indestructible union of the clear light mind of great bliss with the non-conceptual, unmistaken wisdom of emptiness: the ultimate nature of reality. In this sense, therefore, the guru is synonymous with the fully awakened mind of enlightenment itself, the unconditioned dharmakaya experience beyond thought or expression. In the ordinary sense, however, the guru is that which leads us from our present condition of confusion and limitation to the desired state of clarity and wisdom. Such a guru is our spiritual guide and mentor, inspiring us to follow the inner path to highest fulfillment.

Yet even the relative guru, our guide and inspiration, can be understood in two different but fundamentally interrelated ways. First of all there is the outer guru, the person who turns our mind towards the path, gives us instruction and advice, confers empowerment and guides our practice. It is such a skillful and compassionate friend to whom we are generally referring when we use the terms *guru* or its Tibetan equivalent, *lama*. But the final purpose of this outer guru is to introduce us to our own inner guru: the innate wisdom dwelling within our heart, uncontaminated by the delusions that currently obscure but cannot obliterate the fundamentally pure nature of our mind. It is this inner guru that is our final refuge, for our achievement of enlightenment depends primarily upon ourselves and our ability to awaken the wisdom-energy of our innermost being.

When we speak about the importance of establishing the proper guru-disciple relationship—especially in terms of highest yoga tantra practice—we are acknowledging the necessity of making contact with the particular outer guru, or gurus, who can capture the essence of our mind and heart. Not every spiritual master, no matter how highly realized, has this ability *in relation to us*. There must be a special bond established between guru and disciple to allow the necessary transmission of inspiration and insight to take place. Without such a bond or karmic connection, the guru will be unable to touch the deepest essence of the disciple's mind and the disciple will be unable to generate the heartfelt trust required for full surrendering of the ego and its neurotic preoccupations.

For such reasons, then, Tibetan lamas continually warn students not to choose a guru in the same indiscriminate way that a hungry dog runs after meat, pouncing on whatever happens to be available. Although there are numerous cases in which spiritual seekers have recognized their true gurus upon first sight—or even upon merely hearing their names—it is recommended that students examine a teacher well before taking on the commitments of a full guru-disciple relationship, particularly those commitments assumed upon receiving highest yoga tantra empowerment. If the relationship with the guru granting such empowerment is entered into too casually, it will prove extremely difficult if not impossible to maintain these commitments faithfully, to the extreme detriment of one's practice and general well-being both now and in the future.

What makes the Vajrayana buddhist tradition of Tibet so outstandingly valuable is that through it the delicate thread of the enlightening guru-disciple relationship has remained unbroken right up to the present day. Two thousand five hundred years after the passing of Shakyamuni Buddha there still exist living traditions of insight and instruction capable of leading qualified disciples to the same spiritual illumination that Shakyamuni himself attained under the Bodhi Tree. This is indeed remarkable when we consider that what is being transmitted through these various lineages is not mere knowledge about the spiritual path but the actual realizations leading to enlightened self-transformation. Through the agency of the guru, the qualified disciple is introduced to the deepest nature of his or her own mind, out of which eventually emerges a penetrative all-embracing wisdom that far outshines the ordinary conceptual understanding with which we are familiar. While other traditions of this ancient and timeless wisdom have become seriously weakened or even extinct, the Vajrayana has managed to remain alive and powerful.

Yet the survival of these precious lineages cannot be taken for granted. In India itself—where the Vajrayana reached its zenith when such monastic universities as Nalanda and Vikramashila were at the height of their influence, between the seventh and eleventh centuries—the living buddhist traditions were annihilated by successive waves of invaders who swept through the sub-continent from the twelfth century onwards. Fortunately, before this terrible destruction took place, the Vajrayana had been successfully transplanted to Tibet, the Land of Snow. The incomparable mahasiddha Guru Rinpoche, Padmasambhava (Plate 27), had been invited there in the eighth century and as a result of his powerful and far-reaching activities, Buddhism took firm root in the Tibetan culture.

However, even in the isolated Land of Snow the survival of the Vajrayana was endangered. Between 836 and 842 the anti-religious King Lang-darma led a brief but devastating persecution that virtually obliterated Buddhism from central Tibet. After his reign, the teachings staged a recovery, and the chief figure during this second flowering of the dharma was the Indian master Atisha (Figure 9) who, like Guru Rinpoche before him, was invited to Tibet to transmit the intact lineages of the Vajrayana.[2]

From these two Indian gurus and their Tibetan disciples emerged what came to be known respectively as the "old" (Tib. *nying-ma*) and "new" (Tib. *sar-ma*) translation traditions of the tantras. The Nyingma tradition that originated with Guru Rinpoche still survives, while Atisha's own Sarma tradition, the Kadam, no longer exists as a separate school. Instead, there eventually emerged three Sarma traditions—the Sakya, Kagyu and Geluk—which, along with the Nyingma, make up the four major schools of Tibetan Buddhism found today. To give a small idea of the flavor of these various Vajrayana traditions, this chapter contains brief selections from the biographies of the two outstanding Indian masters just mentioned, Guru Rinpoche and Atisha, as well as four of the major Tibetan lamas largely responsible for the character of the Sarma lineages. These latter include the Sakya Pandita (Plate 28) of the Sakya tradition, Marpa the Translator and his heart-son Jetsun Milarepa (Plates 29 and 30) of the Kagyu tradition and Je Tsong Khapa (Plate 31) of the Geluk tradition.

In the selections that accompany the illustrations of these spiritual masters, special attention has been paid to two themes of primary importance: the guru-disciple relationship as the indispensable foundation of the path to enlightenment, and the intimate role played in the lives of these masters by various meditational deities, especially those depicted in this work. Because the relationship with the guru, to be truly effective, must induce a profound transformation within the heart and mind of the disciple, and because the world of the meditational deities is so vastly different from the world we ordinarily inhabit, these brief biographies will necessarily be filled with much that appears extraordinary and even miraculous. Any attempt to dilute such passages to make them more palatable to the secular and decidedly skeptical tastes of the present day would be as misguided and inappropriate as depriving the painted images of their vivid and intense coloring. Whatever the Vajrayana is, it most certainly is *not* bland and pallid. To preserve at least a small flavor of the Diamond Vehicle's power and immediacy, passages of heightened expressiveness are reproduced here just as they appear in the standard biographies of these celebrated masters.

It is important to bear in mind that the four extant lineages, or schools, of Tibetan Buddhism—the Nyingma, Sakya, Kagyu and Geluk—are not self-contained, independent or opposing entities. They are all equally rooted in the teachings of Shakyamuni Buddha and, despite differences in approach and emphasis, each school preserves and transmits the insights and inspiration capable of guiding sincere practitioners to full enlightenment. Furthermore, if we examine the guru-disciple lineages of any one school we almost always find that they are inextricably intertwined with the lineages of one or more of the other schools.

Two brief examples will serve to illustrate this point. One of the deities practiced by many members of the Geluk tradition is Vajrayogini, specifically the form revealed by the Indian master Naropa and shown in Plate 24. Naropa himself was a forerunner of the Kagyu tradition, and through his Nepalese disciples this particular lineage of Vajrayogini passed first into the Sakya tradition and from there into the Geluk. In a similar fashion, the "Stages of the Path" (Tib. *lam-rim*) lineages of the Kadam master Atisha reached Je Tsong Khapa through two of his many illustrious gurus, one belonging to the Nyingma tradition and the other to the Kagyu. Such cross-fertilization of traditions still happens today and many of the highest lamas of one school have studied with and received empowerment from lamas of the other schools.

It is also important to realize that none of these schools was founded with the intention of competing with or supplanting any of the others. In fact, it may be misleading to think of the founding of these schools as a deliberate act at all; in a sense they merely evolved with time and changing events. Whenever a person of outstanding spiritual genius appears, it is natural that he or she will attract a core of followers who will train in the same practices or style favored by their mentor. Then, depending upon such diverse factors as the personal charisma of the guiding teacher, the temperament and abilities of the disciples, the establishment of a monastery or teaching institution in a particular place, the emergence of political or cultural boundaries and so forth, there may eventually evolve something having a distinct enough character for it to be called a separate spiritual tradition.

Yet no matter how strongly people may come to grasp onto such a tradition as something new and distinct, its true purpose far transcends the limitations of partisan feelings and sectarianism. Because individuals are so diverse, it is necessary that there be diverse traditions—whether buddhist or not—to appeal to and work with their individual aptitudes and inclinations.[3] Thus while with time there may evolve numerous schools, sub-schools and so forth, the sole legitimate reason for the existence of any one of them is just this: to keep the flame of enlightenment alive and ensure that it is passed from one generation to the next in a manner that brings temporary and ultimate benefit to as many beings as possible. As the great master Jamyang Khyentse Rinpoche (1820-1892) has written concerning the various Tibetan traditions of Vajrayana Buddhism:

> All of these many traditions, except for their having different names, do not in fact differ at all. In essence they all come together at one point: each and every one of them teaches methods for accomplishing the same ultimate goal, the full enlightenment of buddhahood.[4]

GURU RINPOCHE, PADMASAMBHAVA

Padmasambhava, the Lotus-born—popularly known as Guru Rinpoche, the Precious Master—is revered throughout the Himalayan ranges as a Second Buddha. Invited from India in the eighth century to subjugate the forces inhibiting the spread of Shakyamuni's teachings, he managed to transform hitherto hostile powers into guardians and protectors of the pure dharma and, in the process, left an indelible mark on the entire Himalayan region.

In quite a literal sense, Guru Rinpoche's mark is to be found throughout the Himalayan ranges in and around the many caves he used for meditation. At these sites one can still see handprints and footprints of the Precious Master impressed into solid rock, mute testimony to the extraordinary power this fully accomplished yogi and tantric magician exercised over the external and internal elements.

Guru Rinpoche embodies the ultimate attainment of the Vajrayana and the power, both temporal and spiritual, associated with this peerless attainment. These powerful attributes are reflected in Plate 27, which shows Guru Rinpoche wearing an expression of great force and concentration while holding various implements of power such as the vajra scepter, skull-cup and trident staff. He is dressed not only in the robes of a monk but also in the garments of a king to indicate that he is a member of both worldly and religious royalty. The artist has depicted the waters beneath Guru Rinpoche's throne as swirling and turbulent to enhance this impression of all-encompassing power.

Concerning his birth, Guru Rinpoche himself said:

Some people believe that I revealed myself upon the pollen bed of a lotus in the Dhanakosha Lake in the country of Orgyen; some people believe I was born as Prince of Orgyen; and others believe that I came in the flash of a thunderbolt to the Namchak hilltop; there are many distinct beliefs held by different individuals and peoples, for I have appeared in many forms.

However, twenty-four years after the parinirvana of the Buddha Shakyamuni, the Adibuddha of Boundless Light,

Amitabha, conceived the Thought of Enlightenment in the form of the Great Compassionate One [Avalokiteshvara], and from the heart of the Great Compassionate One, I, Padma, the Lotus Born Guru, was emanated as the syllable *HRI*. I came like falling rain throughout the world in innumerable billions of forms to those who were ready to receive me. The actions of the Enlightened Ones are incomprehensible! Who is to define or measure them![5]

As his biography relates, Guru Rinpoche was adopted by King Indrabhuti of Orgyen who made him his heir. This set the stage for Padmasambhava, as Prince of Orgyen, to perform many of the same deeds that Shakyamuni performed as Prince Siddhartha. He married the daughter of a neighboring king, lived luxuriously in the royal household and eventually, renouncing that life in favor of pursuing a greater destiny, departed from his father's kingdom to give himself over to austerities. He then went to Benares where he learned astrology from Arjuna, a member of the Shakya clan, and later studied medicine, languages, composition and various arts and crafts, mastering them all.

Finally he met Ananda, who had been the personal attendant of the Buddha, received ordination as a buddhist monk, and practiced both the sutra and tantra aspects of Buddha's teachings. From the guru Garab Dorje, an emanation of Vajrasattva, he received instructions on the Great Perfection, "the path of directly experienced intrinsic freedom." His experience of these Great Perfection (Tib. *dzogchen*) teachings has been described as follows:

Garab Dorje, good fountain of the Dharma, knew
   everything, and Padma assimilated it.
He concentrated on the Absorption in the Pure Void
And on the Plane of Essence which proceeds from it.
He practiced abstention from accepting or rejecting pain
   or Awakening.
He obtained, as fruit, salvation through oneself, free from
   renouncing or acquiring.[6]

Having become proficient in subduing hostile and destructive forces, Padmasambhava manifested in many different regions of India, China and Nepal where he established many beings in the pure practice of the buddhadharma.[7] Because his methods went far beyond what society conventionally deemed acceptable behavior for a religious practitioner, he often outraged the sensibilities of local rulers. On one famous occasion, after rumors were spread that Padmasambhava had acted improperly while giving instructions to Princess Mandarava and her attendants, her father—the king of Zahor— ordered her to be cast into a pit of thorns and her guru to be burnt at the stake. Then, the traditional accounts relate,

> All the deities and the buddhas came to Padma's aid. Some created a lake, some cast aside the wood, some unrolled the oil-soaked cloth, some fanned him. On the seventh day afterwards the King looked forth and, seeing that there was still smoke coming from the pyre, thought to himself, "This mendicant may have been, after all, some incarnation," and he sent ministers to investigate. To their astonishment they saw a rainbow-enhaloed lake where the pyre had been and surrounding the lake all the wood aflame, and at the center of the lake a lotus blossom upon which sat a beautiful child with an aura, apparently about eight years of age, its face covered with a dew-like perspiration. Eight maidens of the same appearance as Mandarava attended the child.[8]

Today this lake remains an important pilgrimage spot and is considered a particularly blessed site for meditative practice.

Of all Padmasambhava's enlightening deeds, those the Tibetan people cherish most relate to his introduction of Vajrayana Buddhism into the Land of Snow. King Trisong Detsen—himself considered an incarnation of Manjushri—invited him to Tibet to remove the obstacles hindering the construction and consecration of Samye, the first buddhist monastery in that land. Subjugating these evil forces and transforming them into protectors of the dharma, Padmasambhava not only established Samye (c. 779) as a center for the dissemination of Buddhism throughout Tibet, but laid the foundation for what later became known as the Nyingma tradition. His twenty-five closest disciples mastered and transmitted the various aspects of Guru

Rinpoche's teachings, and through a succession of such great lineage lamas as Longchen Rabjampa (1308-1363)[9] and Jigme Lingpa (1729-1798)[10] these teachings have been passed on and are still practiced today.

Within the Nyingma there are three lineages practiced in conjunction with one another: the Oral (Tib. *ka-ma*), Pure Vision (*dag-nang*) and Treasure Text (*ter-ma*) traditions. The first includes whatever was taught openly by Padmasambhava and the great bodhisattva Shantarakshita when they brought Buddha's teachings to Tibet for the first time. The second derives from visionary experiences of later masters who received instruction directly from Guru Rinpoche, Vajrasattva and so forth. And the third refers to those teachings hidden by Padmasambhava and revealed by later adepts. Because of the importance placed on this third lineage of instruction, the Nyingma tradition is sometimes referred to as the Treasure Text tradition.

TERMA   Termas are teachings, usually of the highest yoga tantra level, which Padmasambhava—often assisted by his consort Yeshe Tsogyal[11]—concealed for later discovery. Some were hidden in the earth while others were planted directly into the minds of his major disciples. When the time is ripe for the propagation of these hidden teachings, reincarnations of these same disciples appear and are inspired to discover and reveal them. Such discoverers of these hidden teachings are known as *tertons*, or treasure masters, and include not only such famous lamas of the past as Longchen Rabjampa, considered an emanation of Manjushri, Jigme Lingpa, and the Fifth Dalai Lama (1617-1682), but modern-day masters such as His Holiness Dudjom Rinpoche (1904-1987),[12] the late head of the Nyingma tradition, and the late Kyabje Dilgo Khyentse Rinpoche (1910-1991),[13] one of the most highly revered lamas of recent times.

At the end of one of his autobiographies—itself a treasure text written down by Yeshe Tsogyal and unearthed by the great terton Orgyen Chokyur Lingpa—Guru Rinpoche explains the circumstances of his departure from Tibet. He refers to a prophesy by Shakyamuni that savages from the Southwestern Island Continent would attack this world and states his intention to subdue these would-be invaders. However, the local prince, Murub Tsempo, son of King Trisong Detsen, became sad and tearful and begged me not to go, pleading that the people could not do without me. In great compassion I postponed my departure in order to assist the people of Tibet and bestow upon them essential teachings for the future. . . .

Then I, Padma, gave final instructions to my devotees and to those who would be reborn in the future: Future generations who cannot meet me must read this exposition of my spiritual practice and self-liberated existence in this world, and obtaining a clear view of its significance, live according to its implied command, becoming perfect in all things. . . .

Having exhorted the people to aspire to buddhahood in this manner, I, Padma, mounted the magical horse and was carried aloft by four dakinis. Again, I spoke to the people: I will come to remove the suffering of the people of the world on the tenth day of every moon but especially on the tenth day of the monkey month. Do not forget to pray!

Then, turning my face towards the southwest, I departed. The Prince Murub Tsempo and his subjects returned, each to his own home, each to his own practice.[14]

ATISHA

Just as Padmasambhava is beloved as the master primarily responsible for establishing Buddhism in Tibet, Atisha (982-1054, Figure 9) is revered as the one who revitalized it after the bitter persecution by King Lang-darma. Born the second son of a royal family in Bengal, Atisha showed such signs of intelligence and good character that he was chosen as heir to his father's throne. When he was eleven years old and, in accordance with the prevailing custom, about to be married, the deity Tara appeared to him vividly in a dream and warned him against committing himself to the worldly life. Atisha managed to avoid the intended marriage and, giving the excuse that he wished to go hunting, persuaded his parents to let him leave the palace grounds. His actual purpose, however, was to find a spiritual mentor.

He met a succession of teachers, including Vidyakokila the Elder and Avadhutipa, and eventually received initiation into the highest yoga tantra practice of Hevajra from the master Rahulagupta. When this great yogi saw that his young and eager disciple was still not free of his parents' worldly expectations for him, he devised a plan to win Atisha his release:

> [Rahulagupta] sent him back to the palace with eight of his disciples, four male and four female, dressed scantily in the bone ornaments of [advanced Vajrayana practitioners].
>
> For three months Atisha stayed in the environs of the palace with these strange new companions, behaving in a completely unconventional and outrageous manner. In the end his parents were forced to give up all hope for their precious son. Thinking him to have gone mad, they gave full permission for him to leave with his rather unsavory-looking friends and be gone once and for all.[15]

Atisha was now able to devote himself to intensive spiritual training. He studied the profound Middle Way view of reality under Avadhutipa, a lineage holder of the wisdom teachings, and received further empowerments into Vajrayana practice. At the age of twenty-nine he took the robes of a monk on the advice of Rahulagupta and received the ordination name Dipamkara Shrijnana, Lamp of

Figure 9: Atisha

Primordial Wisdom.

Although he continued to receive many profound teachings and deep realizations, Atisha remained dissatisfied. Then his vajra master Rahulagupta told him:

> It does not matter how many clear visions of tantric deities you receive, you must train to develop love, compassion and the totally dedicated heart of bodhichitta.[16]

Following this advice, Atisha devoted himself to the practice of Avalokiteshvara and set out to receive the instructions for developing the compassionate bodhichitta from Dharmamati, the lineage holder of these extensive teachings.

Dharmamati lived in the far-off land of Suvarnadvipa, the Golden Isles, and it took thirteen months of extremely difficult travel for Atisha to make his way there. When he finally arrived he did not go immediately to see this renowned teacher, but instead spent two weeks with a group of Dharmamati's disciples, using this time to check their master's qualifications before deciding to accept him as his guru. When the two of them finally met, Dharmamati presented Atisha with a buddha statue and predicted that one day he would be instrumental in taming the minds of those living in the northern Land of Snow.

Atisha stayed in Suvarnadvipa—identified by most scholars as modern-day Indonesia—for twelve years and received the complete transmission of the teachings and insights Dharmamati had gained from his own spiritual masters. Then, when he was forty-five years old, he returned to India and thereafter resided primarily at Vikramashila, one of the major North Indian monastic centers. It was there that emissaries of the Tibetan king Jangchub Wo found him and invited him to return with them to Tibet and reestablish the pure buddhadharma there. Upon consultation with Tara, Atisha agreed to go.

He was fifty-three years old when he set out from Vikramashila and it took two years to complete the arduous journey to Ngari, the capital city. There the king made a request whose sincerity and simplicity pleased Atisha very much:

> We do not want [teachings] that are so vast and profound we shall never be able to adopt them. What we need is

something that will tame our minds and enable us to deal with everyday impulsive behavior. . . . Please teach us the measures you yourself take.[17]

In response to this request Atisha began giving a set of discourses that later formed the basis of his most influential text, *Lamp of the Path to Enlightenment*. In this short work and his later autocommentary to it, Atisha organized the entire range of teachings he had received into a pathway for the progressive training of a disciple's mind. He was able to demonstrate that the vehicles of sutra and tantra, which many Tibetan practitioners had come to feel were so different as to be opposed to one another, in fact formed an integrated whole. He was further able to counter widespread misunderstandings concerning the Vajrayana by emphasizing that moral self-discipline is the foundation upon which all successful practice must be based. As Je Tsong Khapa wrote some four centuries later:

> Wherever the doctrine had disappeared he reestablished it; where it had diminished he revived it; and where it had become stained by wrong interpretations he purified it. Thus he brought dharma in Tibet into a state free from distortion.[18]

Of the many disciples Atisha gathered during his seventeen years in Tibet, it was the layman Dromtönpa who received and transmitted all of the master's major lineages. When Atisha passed away at the age of seventy-two—as predicted by Tara nearly twenty years earlier—Dromtönpa founded Radreng Monastery, where these precious lineages were preserved and perpetuated. Radreng thereby became the source of the Kadam tradition whose later masters, the Kadampa Geshes, followed the outwardly modest but inwardly advanced style of practice favored by Atisha himself.

The Kadampa Geshes placed special emphasis on the mind transformation teachings (Tib. *lo-jong*) that Atisha had received during his stay in the Golden Isles and had prized so highly. The following precepts have been selected from Atisha's lo-jong teachings because their direct, down-to-earth manner typifies the practical approach of the Kadam spiritual lineage:

Abandon sleepiness, dullness and laziness
And always exert enthusiastic effort.
With recollection, alertness and watchfulness
Always guard every door of the senses....
Conquer anger and arrogance
And possess a humble mind....
Whenever a pompous mind arises,
Flatten such arrogance;
Recall the teachings of your master.
When a cowardly mind arises,
Praise the sublimity of the mind.
Whenever objects of attraction or aversion arise,
Meditate upon the emptiness of both;
View them as illusions and emanations.
When hearing any offensive words,
View them as an echo....
Always stabilize [awareness of] your yidam and,
Whenever laziness or lassitude arise,
Enumerate these faults to yourself
And feel remorse from your heart....
When giving advice to others,
Have compassion and thoughts for their benefit.
Do not disparage spiritual doctrines[19]
And be intent on whichever you admire....
Examine your speech when amidst many people.
Examine your mind when living alone.[20]

SAKYA PANDITA

When Atisha was traveling northwards from Ngari in 1040, he paused for a while at a certain spot from which he could see two female yaks grazing. Shortly thereafter he made prostrations towards a mirror-like patch of gray earth upon which he had seen the syllables *HRIH, DHIH* and *HUM* appear. These are the seed-syllables of Avalokiteshvara, Manjushri and Vajrapani respectively. Atisha interpreted their appearance by predicting that emanations of these three deities would come to this place and work for the benefit of all living beings and that their work would be furthered by two forms of the protector Mahakala. It was in 1073 at this very site of gray earth (Tib. *sa-kya*) that Konchog Gyalpo of the influential Khon family founded the monastery in which the Sakya tradition, protected by two forms of Mahakala and adorned by an unbroken stream of enlightened beings, was to have its roots.

The distinctive teachings of the Sakya tradition are traced back to the ninth-century Indian mahasiddha Virupa. This great scholar and meditator, known previously as Shri Dharmapala, had become an abbot of the famous Nalanda Monastery in North India—some sources say he was the abbot of Vikramashila—and was a life-long practitioner of the *Chakrasamvara Tantra*.

However, after years of devoting himself to this meditational deity without any results, he decided to give up his practice and, in disgust, threw his rosary into the latrine! That night the female deity Nairatma (literally "selflessness"), who is the consort of Hevajra, appeared to Dharmapala in a clear vision in the form of a blue-colored woman who said:

> Precious son, cease this improper behavior. Fetch your rosary, wash it with perfume and continue your practice correctly. I am the deity with whom you have a karmic relationship and I shall guide you.[21]

She subsequently initiated Dharmapala into the mandala of Hevajra and over the next several days he made astonishing progress through practicing this tantric system.

The monastic community realized that something extraordinary was happening to their revered master, whose behavior had become eccentric and unpredictable. The authorities eventually felt compelled to ask him to leave and Virupa, the Ugly One—as he now called himself—gave up his robes, dressed himself in rags and flowers, and departed Nalanda. From this point on his life story is filled with numerous miraculous events such as his parting the waters of the Ganges, surviving execution attempts and even causing the sun to remain immobile in the sky. Having awakened the faith of a great number of people through his display of magical powers, Virupa was able to pass on to those who were ripe the lineage of pure Vajrayana practice.

From the view of succeeding generations, Virupa's greatest contribution was to transmit the teachings that came to be known as "The Path and Its Fruit" (Tib. *lam-dre*). These systemize the entire range of sutra and tantra instruction in terms of the meditational deity Hevajra. The viewpoint presented in these teachings is known as "the inseparability of samsara and nirvana." As a contemporary Sakya master puts it,

> Mind itself, the union of luminosity and emptiness, is the root of samsara and nirvana. When obscured it takes the form of samsara and when freed of obscurations it is nirvana. The key to buddhahood, the ultimate source of benefit for all beings, lies in this realization.[22]

The Lam-dre teachings eventually reached Tibet through the work of the translator Drogmi—a contemporary of Atisha and teacher of Marpa—who passed them on to Konchog Gyalpo (1034-1102), the founder of Sakya Monastery. They then passed to Konchog Gyalpo's brilliant son, Kunga Nyingpo (1092-1158), the predicted emanation of Avalokiteshvara, who wrote no less than eleven commentaries to their practice.

Kunga Nyingpo not only received instruction from Virupa in a clear vision but, when he was only twelve years old, also beheld Manjushri directly and received from him the verses known as "The Parting from the Four Attachments":

If you have attachment to this life,
　you are not a religious person.
If you have attachment to the world of existence,
　you do not have renunciation.

If you have attachment to your own purpose,
   you do not have the enlightenment thought.
If grasping arises, you do not have the view.[23]

These and other instructions—especially those of the new, or Sarma, translations of the tantras that were then being disseminated in Tibet—became the bases of the Sakya tradition's teachings and were given their characteristic form by Konchog Gyalpo's descendants, the Five Foremost Ones.[24] Of these, arguably the greatest was Kunga Gyaltsen (1181-1251), popularly known as the Sakya Pandita (Plate 28).

From an early age Kunga Gyaltsen gave many indications that he was an emanation of Manjushri, the embodiment of enlightened wisdom. He could speak Sanskrit before he was old enough to walk and mastered medicine and various other arts and sciences while still a boy. Once, while asleep in a stupa, he received a complete teaching on the *Treasury of Abhidharma* directly from its author, the great fifth-century master Vasubandhu! He studied widely and practiced such tantras as Chakrasamvara and Guhyasamaja, mastering them completely. He was instrumental in introducing the tradition of logical analysis into Tibet and some of his works were so acclaimed that they were disseminated in India in Sanskrit translation.

He also had extraordinary skill in debate and used this ability to eliminate misconceptions and correct faults in previous interpretations of the buddhist teachings. On several occasions he overcame non-buddhist masters. One of his vanquished opponents, who later became a buddhist monk, exclaimed:

It was not you that I could not defeat, but rather the orange being with the sword by your right shoulder.[25]

He was referring, of course, to Manjushri, who appeared next to Kunga Gyaltsen during the debate.

While still a young man Kunga Gyaltsen was told by his uncle,

In the latter part of your life, messengers will be sent to you from the far northern kingdom of Mongolia. . . . When they call you, do not hesitate. Go, for this will bring tremendous benefit to the dharma and to living beings.[26]

This prediction came true when the Mongol ruler of China, Prince Godan, requested that the Sakya Pandita, as the most famous sage of his day, come and serve as his spiritual guide. Thus when he was sixty-three years old he traveled to the Mongolian court in China where he lived out his remaining years, furthering the spread of the buddhadharma by devising a new Mongolian script into which the entire Tibetan buddhist canon was eventually translated.

At the end of a lifetime filled with teaching and benefiting others, the Sakya Pandita placed his hand on the head of his young nephew and dharma heir, Chogyal Pagpa—who was destined to be the spiritual tutor of Kublai Khan—and said, "Practice guru yoga, the one path followed by all the buddhas." He then assumed the full meditation posture, held a vajra and bell together at his heart, and entered the clear light of death. Though all signs of life had ceased, his body retained a radiant complexion for three days. During the cremation ceremony that followed, many auspicious signs appeared in the sky and were witnessed by everyone present. When his remains were later examined, images of such meditational deities as Hevajra, Manjushri, Chakrasamvara, Avalokiteshvara and Tara were clearly visible on his bones.

In terms of both his teachings and personal example, the Sakya Pandita demonstrated the need for a spiritual practice to combine both study and meditation. And the Sakya tradition continues to produce masters—such as its current head, His Holiness Sakya Trizin, Ngawang Kunga—famous for both their erudition and advanced realizations. Thus even after seven hundred years the members of this glorious spiritual tradition still take heed of the Sakya Pandita's admonition:

> "Meditate! there is no need to learn by instructions,"
> Says the shallow-minded fool.
> Contemplation without previous instruction
> Though diligently pursued, is the way of the beast.
>
> It is by the perfection of wisdom
> That omniscience differs from common knowledge.
> How would this infallible doctrine be true,
> If, without learning, one could become all-knowing?

Meditation without hearing [teachings beforehand],
Though it succeeds for a while, will soon fail.
You may melt gold and silver,
But, taken from the fire, they harden anew.[27]

Figure 10: The mahasiddha Tilopa

MARPA THE TRANSLATOR AND
JETSUN MILAREPA

Just as the greatly accomplished Virupa was the major Indian patri-
arch of the Sakya tradition, the mahasiddhas Tilopa (Figure 10) and
Naropa are the forefathers of the Kagyu. Tilopa (988-1069) received
the teachings of mahamudra directly from Buddha Vajradhara, and
from Vajrayogini he received the special dakini hearing lineage. Both
of these he transmitted to Naropa (1016-1100), who in turn passed
them on to his Tibetan disciple Marpa Chokyi Lodro (1012-1096),
popularly known as Marpa the Translator (Plate 29). Marpa's principal heart-son and dharma heir was the beloved Jetsun Milarepa
(1052-1135; Plate 30) and it was through these illustrious founding
fathers that the Kagyu, or Ear-Whispered, tradition came into existence. Thanks to an unbroken succession of great practitioners such
as Gampopa, Pagmo Drupa and the Gyalwa Karmapas, this tradition has remained alive and undegenerated right up to the present
day.

Milarepa's apprenticeship to Marpa is often held up as the epit-
ome of the guru-disciple relationship. These two differed from each
other in almost every respect except their intense dedication to the
dharma. Marpa was a solidly built, gruff householder with a large
family while Milarepa is often pictured as an emaciated ascetic, living alone in caves high up in the Himalayas, his skin having turned
the green color of the nettles that made up his meager diet. Yet, as
the translators of Marpa's biography have written:

> Each of them forged his own path based on who he was
> and what his resources were. Their life stories are exam-
> ples how one's life—anyone's life—could be devoted whole-
> heartedly to the practice and realization of the buddha-
> dharma.[28]

It would be impossible to do justice here to the eventful life stories of these two spiritual geniuses, but a few significant features can
be mentioned briefly. Marpa made his first journey to India because
he was frustrated in not being able to receive the dharma instructions he desired in Tibet. It was his intention to study the Vajrayana
at the monastic centers of northern India, but he had to pause in

Nepal for three years to acclimatize himself to the heat of the lower elevations. It was here that he met disciples of Naropa and immediately knew that this was the guru with whom he must train. In all, Marpa made three trips to India and spent twenty-one years there, sixteen of which were in the service of Naropa. He also studied with Maitripa and from this mahasiddha he received an additional mahamudra lineage.

As for mahamudra itself, this term encompasses a wide range of interrelated practices all leading to a direct, intuitive realization of the mind's ultimate nature. Through following these practices assiduously it is possible to come face to face with "suchness," the actual way things exist, devoid of preconceptions and elaboration, beyond the reach of words and intellect. We can glimpse the freedom attainable through mahamudra meditation from one of the songs Marpa sang to express his realizations, one stanza of which reads:

> The essence of realization is nowness,
> Occurring all at once, with nothing to add or subtract.
> Self-liberation, innate great bliss,
> Free from hope or fear is the fruition.[29]

During Marpa's last stay in India Naropa decided to test the Tibetan's ability to hold the lineage of his teachings. He therefore manifested the entire mandala of Hevajra, Marpa's main meditational deity, and said to him:

> Your personal yidam Hevajra with the nine emanation goddesses has arisen in the sky before you. Will you prostrate to me or to the yidam?[30]

Thinking that it was usual for him to see his guru while this was the first time he had ever directly beheld his meditational deity, Marpa prostrated to the bright and vivid mandala appearing before him. Naropa then dissolved the entire mandala back into his own heart and admonished Marpa that if it were not for the guru even the names of the enlightened beings would not exist. He then predicted that even though Marpa had eight sons, his dharma lineage would not be passed on by the descendants of his own family. But he also predicted:

Although in this life your family lineage will be interrupted, your dharma lineage will flow on like a wide river as long as the teachings of the Buddha remain. . . . All the future disciples of the lineage will be like the children of lions and garudas [birds of extraordinary power], and each generation will be better than the last.[31]

In particular Naropa prophesied that it would be Marpa's disciple Milarepa, whom Naropa had never met, who would be of special renown. When Marpa had first mentioned Milarepa to his guru, Naropa placed his joined hands on top of his head and said:

In the pitch-black land of the North
Is one like the sun rising over the snow.
To this being known as Thopaga [i.e. Milarepa]
I prostrate.[32]

Milarepa

When Milarepa first came to Marpa he certainly did not appear to be a fearless lion, or garuda, or radiant sun of the dharma. On the contrary, he was in a state of abject terror. Milarepa's father had been a prosperous land-owner. After he died, Milarepa's mother, sister and himself had their inheritance stolen by a wicked uncle and aunt and were thereby reduced to bitter poverty. To gain revenge on these people, Milarepa's mother urged him to learn the art of black magic, which he did. Using these powers he brought about the destruction of his mother's enemies, killing many people and animals in the process. Then, overcome by the horror of what he had done, and fearful of the fate that lay in store for him as a murderer, he desperately sought the refuge of a dharma master who could save him from the results of his misdeeds. It was in this state of mind that he entrusted himself to Marpa.

Marpa treated this would-be disciple very roughly. He mockingly called him "Sorcerer"—a name which stuck with him for a long time thereafter—and refused to give him any dharma instruction whatsoever. In fact, if Milarepa dared enter the room in which an empowerment or teachings were to take place, Marpa would descend from his throne in a rage, thrash Milarepa soundly and throw him out! Instead of teachings, Marpa gave Milarepa back-breaking tasks to perform. The most famous of these was the single-handed construction of a rock tower, which Milarepa was forced to tear down and rebuild three times.

Despite intense hardships Milarepa persevered in serving Marpa devotedly. After years of treating Milarepa so harshly, Marpa discerned that his methods had finally produced their desired effect. These tasks had acted as purification practices, cleansing Milarepa and preparing him to receive Marpa's most profound legacy.

Marpa then bestowed upon Milarepa the pith instructions of the teachings he himself had received from Naropa, particularly those related to the practices of Chakrasamvara, and sent him off to the mountains to do strict retreat. Through untiring effort and intense guru-devotion, Milarepa accomplished the supreme task of complete self-transformation, achieving the full enlightenment of buddhahood within a few short years. He then spent the remainder of his life wandering from place to place, revealing the dharma through spontaneous songs that touched the hearts of simple and learned alike. These songs are still sung by the Tibetan people, who, whatever their affiliation, regard Milarepa with abiding affection as one of their own.

To especially ripe disciples, Jetsun Milarepa—Mila, the Revered Cloth-Clad One—passed on the profound instructions handed down from Vajradhara, Tilopa, Naropa and Marpa. To Gampopa (1079-1153), a master of the Kadam tradition, he transmitted certain special teachings that Tilopa commanded be kept extremely hidden, to be passed from guru to only one disciple for thirteen successive generations. Yet one of the most powerful teachings that Milarepa ever gave Gampopa was completely non-verbal. Milarepa had sent Gampopa away to do retreat when suddenly he called his disciple back to him, explaining that he had one further set of instructions to pass on. He then lifted up his cloth garment and showed Gampopa his own scarred and calloused backside, testimony of the years of unstinting meditation he had engaged in to win the goal of full awakening. Deeply impressed by what he had seen, Gampopa departed, inspired to practice just as intensely.

Over the centuries the Kagyu tradition has continued to produce a succession of realized masters who have engaged in the same practices perfected by Marpa and Milarepa. Among them are the late head of the Kagyu tradition, His Holiness the Sixteenth Karmapa, Rangjung Rigpe Dorje (1923-1981), and His Eminence the late Kalu Rin-

.poche.(1904-1989), both recognized by members of all Tibetan traditions as yogis of exceptional attainment. In his last public discourse, Kalu Rinpoche described the attitude to be cultivated by the disciple toward his or her spiritual master as follows:

> . . .what we call the Buddha, or the Lama, is not material in the same way as iron, crystal, gold or silver are. You should never think of them with this sort of materialistic attitude. The essence of the Lama or Buddha is emptiness; their nature, clarity; their appearance, the play of unimpeded awareness. Apart from that, they have no real, material form, shape or color whatsoever—like the empty luminosity of space. When we know them to be like that, we can develop faith, merge our minds with theirs, and let our minds rest peacefully. This attitude and practice are most important.[33]

JE TSONG KHAPA

During China's so-called Cultural Revolution, when the Red Guards wreaked their greatest destruction in Tibet, among the many priceless treasures they desecrated and plundered was a tomb at Ganden Monastery near Lhasa. They were amazed to discover that the body it contained was uncorrupted, its hair and fingernails still growing after five centuries. These were the remains of Lama Je Tsong Khapa (1357-1419), one of the outstanding figures in Tibet's long and illustrious religious history.

The story of this remarkable yogi, teacher and prolific author begins at the time of Shakyamuni Buddha 2500 years ago. On one occasion a young boy offered Buddha a conch shell, symbol of the propagation of the dharma. Buddha then prophesied to his close disciple and attendant Ananda that in the future this boy would be reborn in the snowy north where he would found a great monastery, offer a crown to a sacred buddha statue and be instrumental in spreading the buddhist dharma. He also predicted that this future incarnation would be known as Sumati Kirti—Famous Pure Mind—the Tibetan for which is Losang Drakpa. More than a thousand years later the great Guru Rinpoche, Padmasambhava, predicted that a fully ordained monk by the name of Losang Drakpa would be born in the east of Tibet near China and that this bodhisattva emanation would attain the complete enjoyment body of a buddha.

All these things came about just as predicted. Je Tsong Khapa was born in Amdo in eastern Tibet amidst auspicious signs in the year 1357. Where his afterbirth was buried a tree sprang up bearing sacred syllables on its leaves and bark; this tree still stands and even skeptical present-day visitors to the site have reported seeing its self-arisen symbols for themselves. The district where he was born is called Tsong-kha, or Onion Land, providing Tsong Khapa with the name by which he is most commonly known.

A great teacher from Amdo named Choje Dondrub Rinchen had been away in Lhasa when he learned that upon his return home he would find a disciple who was an emanation of Manjushri. This proved to be Tsong Khapa, who while still very young began his formal dharma education under Dondrub Rinchen. At the age of three he received the lay buddhist vows from the illustrious Fourth Kar-

180

mapa, Rolpe Dorje,[34] and when he was seven his teacher ordained him as a novice monk and gave him the prophesied name, Losang Drakpa. By this early age Tsong Khapa had already received empowerment into such highest yoga tantra practices as Yamantaka and Hevajra and had completed a major meditational retreat on Chakrasamvara.

Eventually the time came for Tsong Khapa to journey to central Tibet to continue his spiritual training. Before he left, Dondrub Rinchen advised him which texts he should study initially and which meditational deities he should rely upon for the rest of his life. These latter included Yamantaka for the continuation of his practice, Vajrapani for freedom from interruptions, Manjushri for increase of wisdom, Amitayus for long life, and Vaishravana, Mahakala and Dharmaraja (of the Yamantaka mandala) for protection.

At the age of sixteen Tsong Khapa arrived at Drikung, a five-day journey from Lhasa, and there he received instruction in such subjects as the compassionate bodhichitta motivation and the profound mahamudra from the famous Drikung Kagyu master Chennge Chokyi Gyalpo. He also studied the major buddhist medical treatises at that time and soon became renowned for his abilities as a healer.

From this point onward Tsong Khapa's life story is filled with numerous accounts of the great teachers from all traditions with whom he studied and from whom he received tantric empowerment, the speed and thoroughness with which he mastered everything he was taught, and the miraculous visions that appeared as Tsong Khapa traveled from place to place to perfect his understanding and realizations. Particularly noteworthy was his relationship with the outstanding Sakya master Rendawa, from whom he received teachings on many profound topics, most especially the Middle Way (Skt. *madhyamika*) philosophy of the Indian mahasiddha Nagarjuna. Their relationship was such that each became the other's master, and throughout their lives they exchanged the various teachings they received from other gurus.

In honor of Rendawa, Tsong Khapa composed the following set of verses:

Manjushri, lord of stainless omniscience,
Avalokiteshvara, mighty treasure of immaculate love,

O Rendawa Zhonnu Lodro, crown jewel of Tibetan sages,
At your feet I make this request:
Grant protection to me, a fly seeking liberation.[35]

Rendawa felt that such praises were more applicable to Tsong
Khapa than to himself and rewrote them as follows:

Avalokiteshvara, great treasure of objectless compassion,[36]
Manjushri, master of flawless wisdom,
Vajrapani, destroyer of demons without exception:
Tsong Khapa, crown jewel of Snow Land sages,
Losang Drakpa, at your feet I make requests.[37]

It is still the practice of Tsong Khapa's followers to recite these verses
while visualizing Manjushri at Tsong Khapa's crown to symbolize
the enlightened qualities of his holy body, Avalokiteshvara at his
throat as a symbol of his speech and Vajrapani at his heart to indicate his limitless mind.[38]

The breadth of Tsong Khapa's erudition was exceptional. Not only
did he receive and give teachings based on the works of Shakyamuni
and the major Indian commentators—such as Nagarjuna, Asanga
and Dharmakirti—but he also transmitted the lineages of the great
Tibetan masters who came before him. These included the Hevajra
lineage of the Sakyas, mahamudra and the Six Yogas of Naropa from
the Kagyu tradition of Marpa and Milarepa, Kalachakra in the tradition of Buton Rinpoche, the various Chakrasamvara lineages held
by the Nyingma master Kyungpo Lhaypa, and many other teachings too numerous to mention. Tsong Khapa did not merely study
and transmit these lineages, but gained inner realization of them
through his practice of meditational retreat.

It was during one of his meditational retreats that Tsong Khapa—or
Je Rinpoche, the Revered Precious One, as he became known—
experienced clear, unfabricated visions of Manjushri. From that time
onwards he was in continual communication with the Buddha of
Wisdom and was able to clarify many difficult points of both sutra
and tantra by conferring directly with him. The intimate connection between the two of them is reflected in the usual depiction of
Tsong Khapa holding the sword and scriptural text emblematic of
Manjushri (see Plate 31). He is also depicted wearing the hat of a

pandit, symbolizing his mastery of the entire scope of buddhist teachings. The golden-yellow color of this hat—which is also the color of the earth element—indicates the importance Tsong Khapa placed on pure moral discipline as the ground, or foundation, of spiritual practice.

Following Manjushri's advice and his own desire to perfect his realization of the dharma, Tsong Khapa traveled south from Lhasa to Wolka Cholung with eight of his closest disciples to engage in strict retreat. During the first phase of this retreat the meditators concentrated on the various preliminary practices that purify and strengthen the body and mind in preparation for the more advanced tantric yogas that follow. So they would not have to rely on anyone else for food and could therefore remain completely isolated during their intensive practices, the meditators decided to restrict themselves to a diet of juniper berries.

These nine practitioners pursued their chosen task with great dedication and single-minded effort. Je Tsong Khapa himself performed three and a half million full-length prostrations and one million eight hundred thousand mandala offerings during this retreat. His practices were so intense that his prostrating form wore an impression in the ground and the forearm with which he rubbed the offering surface was often raw and bleeding.

At the end of this four-year retreat, during which Tsong Khapa and his companions received numerous direct visions of such enlightened beings as the Medicine Buddha, they traveled to the temple of Dzing-ji Ling where they found its central Maitreya statue in a sad state of disrepair. By selling their few possessions and making offerings to Vaishravana, the deity of wealth, they were successful in gathering a large number of people who assisted them in restoring this image. Through this act of devotion a strong link was forged with the Future Buddha to the benefit not only of those who assisted Tsong Khapa but of later generations as well.

Afterwards Tsong Khapa and his eight disciples went into the mountains to engage in further intensive practices. During this time they received visions not only of various deities but of such great mahasiddhas and pandits as Nagarjuna, Asanga, Tilopa and Naropa. On one famous occasion depicted in paintings to this day, Manjushri appeared and touched Tsong Khapa's chest with his sword. Immediately a stream of nectar flowed from the deity's heart into the meditator, filling him with indescribable bliss. This event was witnessed by his companions who, depending on the purity of their vision and their own spiritual progress, experienced varying degrees of similar bliss.[39]

It is said that there were four great deeds that Tsong Khapa performed, and restoration of the Maitreya statue is counted as the first. The others were giving particularly clear and complete explanations of Shakyamuni's teachings on ethical behavior (Skt. *vinaya*), thereby elucidating the path of pure moral discipline; presenting a crown of gold to the ancient buddha statue in the main temple in Lhasa, thereby fulfilling the prophesy made by Buddha Shakyamuni; and, towards the end of his life, founding and consecrating the monastery of Ganden near Lhasa, which became the fountainhead of the tradition that was to propagate Tsong Khapa's method of study and practice after his passing. Since its founding, this tradition and its followers have been known by several different names: "Gandenpa" recalls the tradition's first monastery; "New Kadam" acknowledges Tsong Khapa's devotion to and propagation of Atisha's lineage; and "Gelukpa"—the Virtuous—reflects the great emphasis this tradition has always placed on pure moral conduct.

Although even as a young man Tsong Khapa's learning was unexcelled and his fame as a teacher and meditation master widespread, he remained dissatisfied with his realization of the ultimate view of reality, the wisdom of emptiness. In particular, he felt there were subtle points relating to the profound madhyamika philosophy as propounded by the Indian masters Nagarjuna, Buddhapalita and Chandrakirti about which he still needed clarification. Therefore, at the age of forty he withdrew from active teaching and put himself into intensive retreat on these very points. Then, as related in a poem recounting his mystic experiences, written by one of his disciples and addressed to Je Rinpoche himself:

> One night you dreamed of Nagarjuna
> And his five spiritual sons
> Amongst themselves discussing
> The fabric of dependent origination.
> From their midst came Buddhapalita
> Who touched you with a scripture.[40]

Tsong Khapa awoke with a feeling of great bliss and immediately opened his copy of Buddhapalita's text. As recounted in his biography:

> While he was reading the words, "the self is not the same as the [mental and physical] aggregates, nor is it anything other than the aggregates" he effortlessly experienced the ultimate realization of absolute reality, along with perfect understanding of all the...subtleties concerning the authentic view.[41]

Overflowing with joy and faith in Shakyamuni Buddha, the original source of this enlightening realization, he wrote the poem entitled "In Praise of Dependent Arising," which contains the following stanzas:

> O wondrous teacher, O wondrous refuge,
> Supreme speaker, great protector.
> I pay homage to that great Teacher
> Who so clearly explained dependent-arising.
>
> O Benefactor, to heal all beings
> You proclaimed (dependent-arising),
> The peerless reason for ascertaining
> Emptiness, the heart of the teaching.[42]

These lines reflect Tsong Khapa's realization, insisted upon in his subsequent teachings and writings, that there is no contradiction between each and every phenomenon's complete lack of inherent self-existence—i.e. its ultimate truth of emptiness—and its valid conventional functioning according to the laws of cause and effect, or dependent arising.[43] The non-contradictoriness of the two truths, ultimate and conventional, is proclaimed by Tsong Khapa to be the most profound view of reality, the actual meaning intended by Shakyamuni, Nagarjuna and all enlightened beings.

Among the many people who came to see Tsong Khapa were some who wanted to test his understanding against their own and engage him in debate. One such would-be adversary was Gyaltsab Dharma Rinchen, a great scholar of the Sakya tradition. He arrived during one of Tsong Khapa's discourses and, filled with his own self-importance, sat down not with the disciples but on the guru's teaching throne itself. Tsong Khapa merely moved over to make room for him and continued his discourse. As Gyaltsab listened he became more and more impressed with the profundity of Tsong Khapa's wisdom and skill. First he took off his hat as a sign of respect, then he made prostrations and finally he humbly took his place among Tsong Khapa's disciples.

Although Gyaltsab's original action of taking Je Rinpoche's seat was arrogant, it proved to be an auspicious omen for the future; after Tsong Khapa's passing it was Gyaltsab Je who inherited the master's teaching mantle and became the first Throne Holder of Ganden (Tib. *Ganden Tri-pa*), the title by which the successive heads of the Geluk tradition are known.

Tsong Khapa is often depicted as flanked on his right by Gyaltsab Je and on his left by another of his foremost disciples, Khedrub Choje Gelek Palzangpo (Figure 11).[44] The latter was instrumental in propagating his master's most profound tantric lineages and succeeded Gyaltsab Je as head of the Geluk tradition. In one of the most commonly practiced guru-yoga visualizations among the Gelukpas,[45] Tsong Khapa and his two successors are seen as emanating from the heart of Maitreya Buddha; Tsong Khapa holds the implements of Manjushri while Gyaltsab Je wears the peaceful expression of the compassionate Avalokiteshvara and Khedrub Je the intense look of Vajrapani, Lord of the Tantras. Keeping this visualization in mind while developing strong faith in their personal guru as inseparable from Je Rinpoche, devoted practitioners then recite the verses of praise by Rendawa given earlier.

Another one of Tsong Khapa's highly realized disciples was Gendun Drub, founder of the famous Tashi Lhunpo Monastery that later became the seat of the Panchen Lamas, who were recognized as emanations of Amitabha Buddha. Gendun Drub himself was considered to be an incarnation of Atisha's chief disciple Dromtönpa and, like him, an emanation of Avalokiteshvara. He is the first in the line of fourteen incarnate masters known as the Dalai Lamas who, since the time of the great Fifth Dalai Lama in the seventeenth century, have been the temporal and spiritual leaders of the Tibetan people.

Although the Dalai Lama is the highest ranked lama in the Tibetan

Figure 11: Je Tsong Khapa with Gyaltsab Je (left) and Khedrub Je (right)

hierarchy, he is not the head of the Geluk tradition. This position is held by the successive Ganden Throne Holders, the ninety-eighth and present one being Ganden Tri Rinpoche Jampel Shenpen. The Dalai Lamas themselves have always been masters of a wide range of teachings and practices and the Great Fifth, to cite only one example, was a holder of many Nyingma lineages and a discoverer of treasure texts hidden by Guru Rinpoche, Padmasambhava.

Although Tsong Khapa passed away at the relatively early age of sixty-two, he left behind a powerful legacy. His eighteen large volumes of writings contain everything from devotional prayers to in-depth analyses of such advanced topics as the madhyamika view of reality and the illusory body practices of Guhyasamaja. But he is perhaps best remembered for his two encyclopedic works, *Great Exposition of the Stages of the Path* and *Great Exposition of Secret Mantra*. In these massive texts he ordered the complete paths of sutra and tantra into a coherent whole suitable for practice. In this endeavor he followed the example of Atisha[46]; indeed, while he was composing his *Stages of the Path* he received direct visions of this great master and of all the gurus of the lineage stretching back to Shakyamuni himself.

Even after Tsong Khapa showed signs that he was preparing to pass away from this life, he continued to give teachings and engage in his personal meditational practices. He persisted in this way until the morning of the twenty-fifth day of the tenth Tibetan month, a day of particularly great importance to practitioners of Chakrasamvara. At dawn he made a special series of tantric offerings after which he ceased breathing. His body then took on the vibrant appearance of youthful Manjushri and emitted light rays of variegated colors; this was a sign that, as predicted, Tsong Khapa achieved enlightenment after the clear light of death in the form of a complete enjoyment body. As is generally the case with highly realized teachers, his disciples took great care in their treatment of Tsong Khapa's body. Upon consultation with various oracles, they decided to enshrine it within a stupa, which remained intact until the events of the Cultural Revolution described at the beginning of this section.

Even after his demise, Je Tsong Khapa continued to be a living inspiration to many of his disciples. In particular, Khedrub Je received various visions of his departed master, who answered questions posed by this devoted disciple and encouraged him to overcome

Figure 12: Khedrub Je's vision of Je Tsong Khapa

difficulties he was having. In one of these visions (see Figure 12) Tsong Khapa appeared on a tiger, holding a sword and skull-cup, and told Khedrub Je that he was now residing in the Pure Land of Tushita, the abode of Maitreya Buddha. It is said that he will remain there until the time comes for him to appear as the eleventh of the one thousand Founding Buddhas predicted to appear during this present eon, at which time he will descend to turn the wheel of dharma just as Shakyamuni Buddha did and reveal the complete paths of sutra and tantra.

The esteem in which Manjushri Je Tsong Khapa, as he is often called, has been held by his contemporaries and succeeding generations is evident in many tributes to him written not only by members of his Geluk tradition, but by followers of other traditions as well. When the Eighth Karmapa, Mikyo Dorje (1507-1554), the great Kagyu scholar and meditator, was traveling through the Charida Pass in Tibet, as he himself wrote, "thoughts of the incomparable Tsong Khapa welled up" within him and he was moved to compose a poem of praise that includes the following stanzas:

> At a time when nearly all in this Northern Land
> Were living in utter contradiction to Dharma,
> Without illusion, O Tsong Khapa, you polished the
>   teachings.
> Hence I sing this praise to you of Ganden Mountain.

> When the teachings of the Sakya, Kagyu, Kadam
> And Nyingma sects in Tibet were declining,
> You, O Tsong Khapa, revived Buddha's doctrine,
> Hence I sing this praise to you of Ganden Mountain.

> In merely a few years you filled
> The land from China to India
> With peerless holders of the saffron robes.
> Hence I sing this praise to you of Ganden Mountain

> In person and in dreams you come to those
> Who but once recollect your image.
> Tsong Khapa, who watches with compassionate eyes
> I sing this praise to you of Ganden Mountain.

Manifesting sublime austerity and discipline,
The form and fragrance of your life were incomparable.
O Tsong Khapa, controlled one pleasing to the buddhas,
I sing this praise to you of Ganden Mountain.

By the strength of the sons of your lineage
And by my having faithfully offered this praise,
May the enlightened activity of Buddha Shakyamuni
Pervade the earth for ages to come.[47]

7 Maitreya, the Future Buddha

Just as love—the wish for others to be happy—is the motivation for entering the practice of the Vajrayana, so too is its open and boundless expression one of the most telling signs that this practice has been successful. The loving radiance of a spiritual master, even when cloaked in sternness or wrath, is the special quality that hooks the minds and hearts of others, and it is often said that the love of a guru for his or her disciples is far greater than the love they have for themselves. It is therefore fitting that this introduction to the world of the Vajrayana conclude with the Buddha of Loving-kindness, the Conqueror Maitreya (Plate 32).

The story of Maitreya begins incalculable ages in the past during the time of Buddha Ratna-chattra. One of his disciples was the monk Sthiramati, who had infinitely more concern for the welfare of others than he did for himself. He would often forsake taking food until he had established a vowed number of beings on the paths of pure moral discipline, concentration and wisdom. So strong was his dedication to others' happiness and so radiant his kindness and love (Skt. *maitri*), that even the gods of heaven praised him, giving him the title "Loving One," or Maitreya. Buddha Ratna-chattra predicted that in all his future rebirths as a bodhisattva he would be known by this name and that his fame would spread far and wide.

In addition to love, one of the main practices of Maitreya was the

Seven-Limbed Puja. This powerful method for countering the delusions, purifying negativity and accumulating meritorious energy is an integral part of buddhist practice, and its main features are outlined in the following prayer:

> With body, speech and mind I pay homage with devotion,
> And make offerings, both actual and mentally transformed.
> I declare all beginningless negative actions,
> And rejoice in the virtues all beings perform.
> O Gurus, please stay here until samsara ends,
> And turn the wheel of dharma for the benefit of all.
> Thus I dedicate the merit of myself and of all others
> That we may attain the enlightened beings' state.[1]

Through sincere performance of these seven limbs—prostration, offering, declaring non-virtue, rejoicing, entreating the guru-buddhas to remain, requesting teachings and the final dedication—Maitreya eventually achieved full enlightenment.

Although Maitreya realized buddhahood before Shakyamuni, he honored Shakyamuni as his guru and held him in highest esteem. In fact, one usual way of portraying Maitreya shows him adorned with a stupa on the crown of his head; the stupa symbolizes Shakyamuni and its position on Maitreya's crown demonstrates supreme respect. When Shakyamuni appeared in this world as the fourth Founding Buddha of the present age, Maitreya manifested as one of his disciples—along with Avalokiteshvara, Manjushri, and others—to demonstrate how the bodhisattva path should be followed.

Shakyamuni predicted that, through the inevitable degeneration of the times, his own teachings would last just five thousand years before disappearing from this world. People will grow more and more immoral and their lifespan will gradually decrease, as will their health, stature and fortune. While such delusions as miserliness, hatred and jealousy gain strength, the world will go through prolonged periods of famine, disease and continuous warfare until it eventually resembles a vast battlefield or graveyard. Thereupon Maitreya will appear, not in his fully evolved buddha form, but as a person of regal bearing, very handsome and taller than those around him. On seeing this unusual being, people will be filled with wonder and faith and will ask how he came to have such an attractive appearance. Maitreya will then reply, "Through the practice of patience, avoiding giving harm to others. If you too abide in love and tolerance, you shall also become similar to me."

Maitreya's appearance will mark a great turning point in the fortunes of this world. As more and more beings follow his example, their store of merit, and consequently their lifespan, will increase. Eventually people will live in health for such a long time that the sufferings of old age and death will scarcely be known. At that time, the observance of morality will grow lax as people become more and more engrossed in the pleasures of their existence. With this laxity will come another gradual shortening and degeneration of their lifespan until eventually beings once again will become suitably ripe to take sincere interest in the spiritual path. It is at this time that Maitreya Buddha will descend from the Tushita Buddha Field where he now resides to appear in this world as the fifth Founding Buddha of this world age.

Maitreya is depicted in Plate 32 in a posture symbolizing that he is ready to arise in response to the needs of the world and descend to turn the wheel of dharma, as Shakyamuni did before him. His hands are in the teaching mudra at his heart and hold the stems of two lotuses; these bear a wheel, indicating his role as the next wheel-turning Founding Buddha, and a vase, indicating that unlike Shakyamuni, who was born into royalty, Maitreya will be a member of the priestly, or brahmin caste. Above his head is an umbrella—one of the eight auspicious symbols—indicating Maitreya's ability to grant protection from evil influences. In this painting the artist has provided Maitreya with a brilliant aura to suggest that through the Buddha of Loving-kindness shines the light of hope for the future.

The first of the four great deeds of Je Tsong Khapa was the restoration of a Maitreya statue. In relation to this, one of Tsong Khapa's chief disciples, Gendun Drub, the First Dalai Lama, wrote:

> May the beings who contribute to the creation
> Of images of Maitreya, the Buddha of Love,
> Experience the dharma of the Great Way
> In the presence of Maitreya himself.[2]

In these verses the Dalai Lama gives expression to a wish common
among the followers of Mahayana Buddhism: that in the future they
might be reborn as disciples of Maitreya. An example of such a prayer
written by a modern-day Tibetan master is the following:

> In the past I have wandered down long lonely paths,
> But now, O Protector, by remembering you
> At the time when the light of my life comes to set
> May the hook of your mercy catch hold of my mind.
>
> When my mind travels on to my future rebirth
> May I sprout without hindrance from the heart of a lotus
> In the presence of Maitreya in Tushita Heaven,
> And may I be nourished on Mahayana's ambrosia.
>
> O Protector Maitreya, when you are the lama
> Of numberless beings at the site of Bodh Gaya
> May I too become one of your foremost disciples
> And be able to ripen all fortunate ones.
>
> In short, then, I dedicate all the white karma
> I gather in the past, the present and the future
> To be born in your presence, O mighty Protector.
> By developing insight on the Mahayana path
> And teaching to others, may I become a true refuge
> For every pathetic and depressed living being.[3]

Shakyamuni Buddha predicted that those who followed his teachings would be reborn in the first circle of Maitreya's entourage and
would be able to complete the spiritual path under his guidance. Thus
it is the custom when taking the vows to engage in the altruistic practices of a bodhisattva to recite the following verses:

> When like the sun rising over the mountains
> Maitreya Buddha appears at the Diamond Seat[4]
> And opens my lotus mind, may I fulfill
> All the needs of the swarms of fortunate disciples
> Who will cluster like thirsty bees longing to drink.

And when Maitreya Buddha with great pleasure extends
His right hand to my head and predicts where and when
I shall gain full enlightenment, may I achieve
This enlightenment quickly for everyone's sake.[5]

It is not always necessary to wait until Maitreya next appears in
this world to receive direct benefit from him. One of the most popular
stories illustrating how contact can be made with him even now concerns the Indian master Asanga,[6] who, along with Nagarjuna, is honored as one of the two Jewels of the World. Asanga had been experiencing difficulty in gaining an unmistaken understanding of the
Perfection of Wisdom sutras and decided that only from Maitreya
could he receive the instructions he desired. He therefore entered
into intensive retreat in hopes of gaining a direct vision of this buddha.
But after three years with no success he quit his retreat in disgust.
On his way back to town he saw an old man, who was in reality an
emanation of Maitreya, trying to remove a huge stone that blocked
the sun from his house by brushing it with a feather! Asanga took
this as a sign that, with enthusiastic perseverance, anything could
be accomplished, and reentered his retreat.

Three more years passed, then another three, all without results.
But each time Asanga gave up he would encounter someone performing an impossible task and would be inspired to return to his
practice. Finally, after twelve years with nothing to show for them,
Asanga gave up his practice for good. This time on his way into town
he saw a pitiful sight: on the ground lay a starving, mangy dog, its
wounds being eaten by maggots. Moved by compassion for the dog
and unwilling to kill the insects, he cut off a piece of his own flesh
and bent down to transfer the maggots to the meat with his tongue
so as not to harm them. He closed his eyes so he would not have to
look at what he was doing, and drew nearer. But although he leaned
over very far, he felt nothing. When he opened his eyes to see what
was wrong, the dog had disappeared and in its place stood Maitreya
in all his glory!

Asanga was so shocked he demanded, "Where were you all those
years I was meditating in that cave?" Maitreya replied that he had
been there next to him all that time and only delusions had prevented
Asanga from seeing him. Now that his compassionate act had re-

moved the veil of those delusions, there was nothing left to prevent their communicating with each other directly. Asanga was so over-joyed that, despite Maitreya's protestations, he lifted the buddha on his shoulders and ran through town crying, "Look everyone, here is Maitreya!" But except for one old woman, no one saw anything except an apparently insane man running up and down the streets. The woman herself, because her veil of delusions was somewhat thin-ner than those of the other townspeople, saw Asanga carrying a mangy dog on his shoulders.

Maitreya then took Asanga and transported him instantly to the pure land of Tushita. They spent one morning there, during which time Asanga received detailed instructions from Maitreya on the Per-fection of Wisdom sutras in the form of five texts that still make up an integral part of buddhist monastic education.[7] Having transmitted to Asanga these teachings, Maitreya returned him to this world, where Asanga discovered that fifty years had passed while he was away. Asanga then spent the remainder of his long life disseminating these teachings and his own commentaries to them, thereby bringing in-estimable benefit to others.

In one of the texts of Maitreya that Asanga revealed to the world—the *Uttaratantra*, or *Peerless Continuum*—there are detailed teachings about the buddha-nature, or buddha-potential, existing within the minds of all living beings. It is this potential that enables ordinary beings to be transformed, by means of the Vajrayana practices based on love and compassion, into fully awakened buddhas. Therefore it is fitting to bring this chapter on Maitreya, and this introduction to Vajrayana art and practice, to a close by reproducing one of the nine similes Maitreya gave for the existence within our limited minds of this unlimited potential for enlightenment:

> Under the floor of some poor man's house lies an
>   uncorroded treasure,
> But because he does not know of its existence
> He does not say that he is rich.
> Similarly, inside one's mind lies truth itself, firm and
>   unfading,
> Yet, because beings see it not, they experience a constant
>   stream of misery.

The pauper with a treasure buried under his shack
Does not say he has a treasure, for he knows it not:
Likewise, the treasure of truth lies within the house of the
    mind,
Yet we live impoverished through lack of it.
Therefore the seers take a pure birth into the world, so that
    this [treasure] may be made known.[8]

Figure 13: The eyes of Boudhanath Stupa

Artist's Afterword

My own introduction to the world of Tibetan tangka painting took place near the Boudhanath Stupa in the Kathmandu Valley of Nepal. In 1973 the surrounding village was much smaller than it is today and contained only a few buddhist temples. In contrast, Boudha is now the home of numerous temples and monasteries belonging to the various Tibetan traditions and the village has become a major stop on the pilgrimage route to Bodh Gaya, Sarnath, Kushinagar and Lumbini.[1] Despite these changes and the hectic "modernization" of Kathmandu, the Boudhanath Stupa itself remains a calm, commanding presence, its four pairs of eyes radiating compassionate wisdom to all four directions (Figure 13).

For nearly six years my home was within view of the stupa and it was always a great inspiration to wake up in the morning and look straight into those remarkable eyes. There was something in them that spoke wordlessly of clarity, insight and transcendence, of a beauty far beyond this world yet somehow tantalizingly near. Those eyes have left a huge imprint on my mind and even now the memory of them is deeply moving.

But I discovered while living in Boudha that inspiration alone was not enough; a key was needed to unlock the meaning, the mystery, of those haunting eyes. As we have tried to point out in the present work, this key to deeper understanding and appreciation was to be found in the living traditions of which Boudhanath Stupa itself is but one, albeit monumental, expression. Mention has been made of the various Tibetan lamas who were kind enough to provide spiritual guidance and meditational instruction; it was their undeniable and impressive wealth of compassion and wisdom that convinced me that what had been detected in the stupa's eyes was within reach of ordinary beings like myself. However, since my own path towards understanding has passed largely through the gateway of Vajrayana art itself, it would not be true to my sources of inspiration to neglect acknowledging the two Tibetan artists, Ludhup and Thargye, who guided me into this fascinating world.

Both of these teachers deserve a full measure of devotion and gratitude because they unhesitatingly gave me as much compassionate help as they could. This was not always easy because we were often forced to communicate through a translator and sometimes questions had to be repeated two or three times before we could be certain we understood one another. Despite these time-consuming difficulties, both teachers were extremely generous with their instructions and encouragement; without the foundation they provided, it would have been impossible for me to attempt the paintings presented here.

Ludhup was my first teacher. He was born in Amdo and escaped from Tibet when he was still a young monk. He had with him some scrolls, perhaps two hundred years old, that had been given to him in Tibet by his own teacher. These contained a number of different line-drawings together with the grid patterns (Tib. *tig-tsay*) upon which all such drawings are based. Because I had no previous training, these drawings became the basis of my entire artistic career; even today photocopies of these originals continue to provide me with immense inspiration.

It was Ludhup who taught me how to draw, introduced me to different painting styles and opened up a fascinating new world of buddhas, bodhisattvas, dakinis, protectors and so forth. The time spent with this good friend was joyous; it seemed impossible to get enough of the wonders he had to show me and every day was like an adventure. Unfortunately, less than a year after I began studying with him considerations of health forced him to leave the Kathmandu Valley and return to the mountains.

My second teacher was Thargye, a famous painter from Tsang in Tibet. He came from a long line of painters and both his father and grandfather had been considered great artists. While Ludhup initiated me into the world of Vajrayana art it was Thargye who provided a detailed map of that world. He remains one of the few artists capable of transmitting the entire range of skills needed to be a true master of this ancient artistic tradition.[2] His craftsmanship and expertise extends to such areas as mineralogy and botany, for the extraction of pigment from stones and plants, and even to astrology, for calculating the auspicious dates to commence and conclude his paintings.

Like many traditional artists, Thargye makes his own brushes, prepares his canvases himself and builds the frames on which they are stretched. Because he often has a company of apprentices to care for in addition to his family, he is also an enterprising merchant and businessman. Furthermore, his spiritual erudition enables him to explain the background and symbolism of what he creates in great detail and he knows many of the texts and rituals connected with these images. This compassionate master brought the entire artistic tradition of the Vajrayana alive for me, and over the years I trained with him I felt more and more linked to a powerful lineage that had its roots deep in the past.

One particular feature of Vajrayana art that goes back to the time of Shakyamuni Buddha himself is the use of grid patterns. The canvas or paper is marked with lines of specific dimension and spacing and the figure is then drawn on top of this grid to fit these specifications precisely. It is not a matter, for example, of guessing how tall or wide a buddha should be drawn; this is already determined by a long tradition that has remained unbroken throughout the centuries. This has not prevented each society into which Buddhism has entered from producing art which reflects its own cultural identity—simply compare a buddha image from Thailand with one from China—but it does raise the question, in Western minds at least, of the limits on artistic expression imposed by this tradition. This is a far-reaching question and I can only provide an answer from my own experience.

When my apprenticeship under Ludhup began, I was given grids of Buddha's face and body and instructed to copy my teacher's examples again and again (see Figures 1 to 3). This may sound stultifying, but it gave my hand and eye invaluable training and opened up previously unknown channels of creative energy. I also discovered how closely linked to my state of mind were the clarity and flow of the lines upon which the beauty of the image depended. If I was upset or unhappy, this would always be expressed somehow in the resulting drawing. Each buddha face was like a self-portrait, a mirror in which aspects of my being were clearly reflected. Even now in a class of new students it is easy to tell whose drawings are whose by this uncanny resemblance between creation and creator.

After a long process of training, which also included spiritual study and practice, something arose from inside me that was somehow removed from the ordinary ups and downs of my mind. Instead of being so strongly influenced by these shifts in thought and emotion, I tapped a source of balance and harmony that seemed to exist at a deeper level of being, untouched by superficial changes in mood or circumstances. Similar to the case of spiritual training, where the vows to avoid certain types of behavior appear at first to be restrictive but later are felt to be profoundly liberating, the apparent limitations of the grid format provided the context in which an extraordinary degree of freedom could be experienced.

For accomplished masters like Thargye there is no longer any need to rely on a grid at all; they make a few preliminary marks to indicate the desired size and spacing of the figures and then draw a perfectly proportioned buddha image freehand. In the case of such masters the discipline of a lifetime of training has liberated a spontaneous creative flow in the same way that spiritual training is said to bring to fulfillment one's innate buddha-nature.

Thus while artistic expression and creativity are definitely important in tangka painting, so-called self-expression—here referring to that which comes from the neurotic ego and its preoccupations—most certainly is not. Contrary to what we may think at first, this in no way diminishes the feeling of creative joy experienced while the work is in progress. In tangka painting, artistic freedom and joy are to be found in the *doing* of the art, in the concentration, love and devotion experienced during the act of creation itself. As these are spiritual qualities, the goal of artistic mastery cannot be reached through technical proficiency alone. Only by opening oneself up to spiritual inspiration can such progress be forthcoming.

In painting this series of tangkas I was primarily interested in presenting the individual figures in as clear and straightforward a manner as possible. I wanted the viewer to feel happy and comfortable about entering each picture so that he or she could appreciate the beauty of each deity without being overwhelmed or bewildered by a mass of extraneous detail. To this end I purposely avoided painting ornate auras around these deities, have kept the backgrounds as simple as possible and have eliminated all figures but the central one from nearly every canvas. The resulting paintings are therefore less elaborate than most traditional Tibetan tangkas but their essence and flavor are intended to be the same. Despite my years of training in the East, I remain a Westerner and necessarily look at these sacred figures from a Western perspective. If these paintings are in any way successful, they will communicate something from the world of Vajrayana art to those who, like myself, have grown up in a Western culture.

Although the paintings presented here are the work of someone who is still very much a beginner, it is hoped that through the inspiration of our spiritual and artistic masters some contribution has been made to the reader's understanding and well-being. Signs of degeneration are all around us—in Boudha itself, for example, factories of uninspired laborers supply the tourist trade with imitation sacred art having no authenticity whatsoever—but so too are indications that the spiritual quest, however disguised, is still very much alive in the human breast. Therefore, may all those searching for meaning behind the veil of transitory appearances be encouraged and inspired by the Vajrayana's unbroken transmission of blessings.

Andy Weber
July 6, 1989

List of Proper Names

Those wishing to consult other sources for further information on the material presented in *Images of Enlightenment* may find the following list of terms useful.

Most of these terms are Sanskrit proper names shown as they appear in this work, without diacritical marks; these names (eg. Vajrapani) have been provided with their Tibetan equivalents using the Wylie system of transliteration (eg. Phyag.na rDo.rje).

Tibetan names and terms appearing in this text in phonetic transcription (eg. Songtsen Gampo) are also provided with their Wylie counterparts (eg. Srong.btsan sGam.po).

Lastly, certain English terms and titles are provided with their Sanskrit and/or Tibetan equivalents.

Abhidharma (Tib. Chos.mngon.pa)
Akshobhya (Tib. Mi.bskyod.pa)
Amitabha (Tib. 'Od.dpag.med)
Amitayus (Tib. Tshe.dpag.med)
Amoghasiddha (Tib. Don.grub)
Ananda (Tib. Kun.dga'.bo)
Aryadeva (Tib. 'Phags.pa.lha)
Asanga (Tib. 'Phags.pa Thogs.med)

Atisha (Tib. Jo.bo.rje dPal.ldan A.ti.sha)

Avadhutipa (Rigs.pa'i Khu.byug Chung.ba, Sangs.rgyas dGongs.skyong)

Avalokiteshvara (Tib. sPyan.ras.gzigs)

Bhaishajyaguru Vaiduryaprabha (Tib. sMan.gyi.lha Bai.du.rya 'Od.gyi rGyal.po)

Bimbisara (Tib. gZugs.can sNying.po)

Bodh Gaya (Skt. Vajrasana; Tib. rDo.rje gDan)

Brahma (Tib. lHa Tshangs.pa)

Buddhapalita (Tib. Sangs.rgyas bsKyangs)

Buton Rinpoche (Bu.ston Rin.po che)

Chakrasamvara (Tib. 'Khor.lo sDom.pa)

Chakrasamvara Tantra (Skt. *Shri-mahasamvarodayatantra-rajanama*; Tib. *dPal bde.mchog 'byung.ba shes.bya.ba'i rgyud.kyi rgyal.po chen.po*)

Chandragomin (Tib. bTsun.pa Zla.ba)

Chandrakirti (Tib. Zla.ba Grags.pa)

Chennge Chokyi Gyalpo (sPyan.snga Chos.kyi rGyal.po)

Chogyal Pagpa ('Gro.mgon Chos.rgyal 'Phags.pa)

Choje Dondrup Rinchen (Tib. Chos.rje Don.grub Rin.chen)

Dalai Lama (Da.la'i Bla.ma, rGyal.ba Rin.po.che)

Dalai Lama I (rGyal.dbang dGe.'dun Grub)

Dalai Lama V (rGyal.mchog Ngag.dbang bLo.bzang rGya.mtsho)

Dalai Lama XIII (rGyal.dbang Thub.bstan rGya.mtsho)

Dalai Lama XIV (rGyal.dbang bsTan.'dzin rGya.mtsho)

Deer Park (Skt. Mrgadava; Tib. Ri.dvags.kyi Gnas)

Devadatta (Tib. lHas.byin)

Dharmakirti (Tib. Chos.kyi Grags.pa)

Dharmaraja (Tib. Chos.rgyal)

Dipamkara Shrijnana (Tib. dPal.ldan Ye.shes Mar.me mDzad)

Drikung (Tib. 'Bri.khungs)

Drogmi (Tib. 'Brog.mi)

Drogon Chagna Dragpa (Tib. 'Gro.mgon Phyag.na Grags.pa)

Dromtönpa ('Brom.ston rGyal.ba'i 'Byung.ngas)

Four Medical Tantras (Skt. *Amrita-ashtangahrdayopadeshatantra*; Tib. *bDud.rtsi snying.po yan.lag brgyad.pa gsang.ba man.ngag.gi rgyud, rGyud.bzhi*)

Gampopa (Dvags.po lHa.rje sGam.po.pa Zla.'od gZhon.nu)

Ganden (dGa.'ldan)

Ganden Tripa (dGa.ldan Khri.pa)

Geluk (dGe.lugs)

Gendun Drub *see* Dalai Lama I

Ghantapa (also Ghantapada; Tib. Slob.dpon rDo.rje Dril.bu.pa)

Great Exposition of Secret Mantra (sNgags.rim chen.mo)
Great Exposition of the Stages of the Path (Lam.rim chen.mo)
Great King of Prayers (Tib. *bZang.mchod smon.lam*)
Guhyasamaja (Tib. gSang.ba 'Dus.pa)
Guide to the Bodhisattva's Way of Life (Skt. *Bodhisattvacharyavatara*; Tib. *Byang.chub.sems.dpa'i.spyod.pa.la.'jug.pa, sPyod.'jug*)
Gyaltsab Dharma Rinchen (rGyal.tshab Dar.ma Rin.chen, rGyal.tshab rje)
Heart Sutra (Skt. *Bhagavatiprajnaparamitahrdaya*; Tib. *bCom.ldan.'das.ma shes.rab.kyi pha.rol.tu phyin.pa'i snying.po, Shes.rab snying.po*)
Heaven of the Thirty-three (Skt. Trayastrimsha; Tib. Sum.bcu.rtsa.gsum)
Heruka (Tib. He.ru.ka, bDe.mchog)
Hevajra (Tib. Kye'i rDo.rje, dGyes rDo.rje)
Indra (Tib. brGya.byin)
In Praise of Dependent Arising (Tib. *rTen.brel bstod.pa*)
Jamyang Khyentse Rinpoche ('Jam.dbyangs mKhyen.brtse Rin.po.che)
Jangchub Wö (lHa.btsun Byang.chub 'od)
Kadam (bKa'.gdams)
Kadampa Geshe (bKa.gdams dGe.bshes)
Kagyu (bKa'.brgyud)
Kalachakra (Tib. dPal Dus.kyi 'Khor.lo)
Kalarupa *see* Dharmaraja
Karmapa (rGyal.ba Kar.ma.pa)
Karmapa IV (rGyal.ba Rol.pa'i rDo.rje)
Karmapa VIII (rGyal.ba Mi.bskyod rDo.rje)
Karmapa XVI (rGyal.ba Rang.byung Rig.pa'i rDo.rje)
Karmapa XVII (rGyal.ba O.rgyan 'Gro.'dul 'Phrin.las rDo.rje)
Khedrub Gelek Palzangpo (mKhas.grub dGe.legs dPal.bzang.po, mKhas.grub rje)
Konchog Gyalpo (dKon.mchog rGyal.po)
Kunga Gyaltsen (Sa.chen Kun.dga' rGyal.mtshan)
Kunga Nyingpo (Sa.chen Kun.dga' sNying.po)
Lam-chung (Lam.chung.ba, Lam.'phran bsTan)
Lamp of the Path to Enlightenment (Skt. *Bodhipathapradipa*; Tib. *Byang.chub lam.gyi sgron.me*)
Lam-rim (lam.rim)
Land of Snow (Skt. Himavan; Tib. Gangs.can)
Lang-darma (Glang.dar.ma)
Longchen Rabjampa (Klong.chen Rab.'byams.pa Dri.med 'Od.zer)
Losang Drakpa (Blo.bzang Grags.pa)
Machig Labdron (Ma.cig Lab.sgron)
Magadha (Tib. Yul Ma.ga.dha)

Mahakala (Tib. mGon.po)
Maitreya (Tib. rGyal.ba Byams.pa)
Maitripa (Tib. Mai.tri.pa)
Manjushri (Tib. rJe.btsun 'Jam.dpal.dbyangs)
Mara (Tib. bDud)
Marpa (sGra.bsgyur Mar.pa Lo.tsa.ba)
Meru (Tib. Ri.rab, lHun.po)
Milarepa (rJe.btsun Mi.la.ras.pa bZhad.pa rDo.rje)
Nagarjuna (Tib. mGon.po Klu.sgrub)
Nairatma (Tib. bDag.med.ma)
Ngari (lNga.ris)
Nyingma (rNying.ma)
Offering to the Spiritual Master (Tib. *Bla.ma mchod.pa'i cho.ga*)
Padampa Sangye (Pha.dam.pa Sangs.rgyas)
Padmasambhava (Tib. Gu.ru Rin.po.che Slob.dpon Chen.po Padma
   'Byung.gnas)
Pagmo Drupa (Phag.mo gru.pa rDo.rje rgyal.po)
The Parting from the Four Attachments (Tib. *Zhen.pa bzhi.bral*)
The Path and Its Fruit (Skt. Margaphalanvitavavadaka; Tib. Lam
   'bras.bu.dang bcas.pa'i rtsa.ba rdo.rje'i tshig.rkang, Lam.'bras)
Perfection of Wisdom Sutra (Skt. *Prajnaparamitasutra*; Tib.
   Shes.rab.kyi pha.rol.tu phyin.pa'i mdo)
Praise to Dependent Arising see *In Praise of Dependent Arising*
Prajnaparamita (Tib. Shes.rab.kyi Pha.rol.tu Phyin.pa)
Radreng (Rva.sgreng)
Rahulagupta (Tib. Bla.ma Ra.hu.la, sGra.gcan 'Dzin.sbas)
Rajagriha (rGyal.po'i Khab)
Ralpachen (Ral.pa.can)
Ratnasambhava (Tib. Rin.'byung)
Rendawa (Red.mda'.ba gZhon.nu Blo.gros)
Sakya (Sa.skya)
Sakya Pandita (Tib. Sa.chen Kun.dga' rGyal.mtshan)
Samye (bSam.yas)
Shakyamuni (Tib. Sha.kya'i Thub.pa)
Shantarakshita (Tib. Zhi.ba.'tsho, Grags.pa'i.dpal)
Shantideva (Tib. gZhi.ba.lha)
Shariputra (Tib. Sha.ri'i.bu)
Sixteen Arhats (Skt. shodashasthvavira; Tib. gNas.brtan bCu.drug)
Six Yogas of Naropa (Tib. Na.ro chos drug)
Songtsen Gampo (Srong.btsan sGam.po)
Sukhavati (Tib. bDe.ba.can)

Suvarnadvipa (Tib. gSer.gling.pa Chos.kyi Blo.gros)

Tara (Tib. rJe.btsun sGrol.ma)

Taranatha (Tib. Kun.dga' sNying.po)

Tashi Lhunpo (bKra.shis lHun.po)

Thousand Founding Buddhas (Tib. sTong.pa'i Sangs.rgyas)

Treasury of Abhidharma (Skt. *Abhidharmakosha*; Tib. *Chos mngon.pa'i dzod*)

Trisong Detsen (Khrid.srong lDe.btsan)

Tsong Khapa (rJe Tsong.kha.pa, 'Jam.mgon La.ma Blo.bzang grags.pa)

Tushita (Tib. dGa'.ldan)

Ushnisha Vijaya (Tib. gTsug.tor rNam.rgyal.ma)

Uttaratantra (Tib. *rGyud Bla.ma*)

Vairochana (Tib. rNam.par sNang.mdzad)

Vaishravana (Tib. rNam.thos.sras)

Vajrabhairava (Tib. rDo.rje 'Jigs.byed)

Vajradhara (Tib. rDo.rje 'Chang)

Vajradharma (Tib. rDo.rje Chos)

Vajrapani (Tib. Phyag.na rDo.rje)

Vajrasattva (Tib. rDo.rje Sems.dpa')

Vajravarahi (Tib. rDo.rje Phag.mo)

Vajrayogini (Tib. rDo.rje rNal.'byor.ma)

Vasubandhu (Tib. dbYig.gnyen)

Vidyakokila the Elder (Tib. Rig.pa'i Khu.byug Che.ba)

Vidyakokila the Younger *see* Avadhutipa

Vultures' Peak (Skt. Grdhakutaparvata; Tib. Bya.rgod Phung.po'i Ri)

Yama (Tib. gShin.rje)

Yamantaka (Tib. gShin.rje gShed, 'Jigs.byed)

Yeshe Tsogyal (Ye.shes mTsho.rgyal)

Glossary

The terms listed below are provided with brief definitions according to their usage in this work. Wherever possible, Sanskrit and/or Tibetan equivalents have also been given.

abhidharma (Tib. *mngon.par chos*) the division of Shakyamuni Buddha's teachings dealing with the development of wisdom and the detailed analysis of phenomena

aggregates (Skt. *skandha*; Tib. *phung.po*) the five mental and physical constituents serving as the bases upon which a person is imputed—form (Skt. *rupa*; Tib. *gzugs*), feeling (Skt. *vedana*; Tib. *tshor.ba*), discrimination (Skt. *samjna*; Tib. *'du.shes*), compositional factors (Skt. *samskara*; Tib. *'du.byed*) and consciousness (Skt. *vijnana*; Tib. *rnam.shes*)

altruistic motivation see *bodhichitta*

arhat (*dgra.bcom.pa*) foe-destroyer; one who has achieved personal liberation from suffering, having overcome the forces of karma and delusion

bardo see *intermediate state*

bell (Skt. *ghanta*; Tib. *dril.bu*) implement employed by Vajrayana practitioners to symbolize penetrative wisdom into the nature of reality. It is held in the left hand and may be seen in representations of many meditational deities. Cf. *diamond scepter*

bodhi see *enlightenment*

bodhichitta (Tib. *byang.chub.kyi sems*) the compassionate motivation of wishing to attain full enlightenment for the sake of benefiting others; the mahayana motivation

bodhisattva (Tib. *byang.chub sems.dpa'*) a spiritual practitioner who has cultivated the bodhichitta motivation; a follower of the mahayana path

buddha (Tib. *sangs.rgyas*) one who has achieved full enlightenment, removing all the obscurations covering the essentially pure nature of the mind and developing all positive qualities limitlessly; first of the Three Jewels of Refuge

buddhadharma (Tib. *sang.rgyas.kyi chos*) the teachings of Shakyamuni Buddha

buddhahood (Skt. *buddhatvam, buddhapadam*; Tib. *sangs.rgyas nyid, sangs.rgyas.kyi go.'phang*) full enlightenment; the supreme spiritual attainment characterized by limitless compassion, limitless wisdom and limitless skillful means

buddha-nature (Skt. *tathagatagarbha*; Tib. *de.bzhin gshegs.pa'i snying.po*) the mind's potential to achieve full enlightenment

central channel (Skt. *shushumna, avadhuti*; Tib. *rtsa dbu.ma*) the axis of the vajra body along which are located the various chakras, penetrated during the completion stage practices of highest yoga tantra

chakra (Tib. *'khor.lo, rtsa.'khor*) wheel; channel-wheel; focal points along the central channel of the vajra body upon which one's concentration is directed during the completion stage of highest yoga tantra

channel (Skt. *nadi*; Tib. *rtsa*) see *vajra body*

chod rite (Tib. *gcod*) cutting-off rite; meditative practice originating with Padampa Sangye and Machig Labdron in which the practitioner confronts fearful situations causing ego-grasping and self-cherishing to arise, enabling them to be recognized and overcome

clear appearance (Tib. *gsal.snang*) visualization of oneself and one's surroundings in the purified form of a meditational deity and mandala; cf. *generation stage*

clear light (Skt. *prabhasvara*; Tib. *'od.gsal*) the very subtlest level of mind, arising naturally at the time of death and achievable through the completion stage practices of highest yoga tantra

compassion (Skt. *karuna*; Tib. *snying.rje*) the wish for others to be separated from suffering and its causes

completion stage (Skt. *sampannakrama*; Tib. *rdzogs.rim*) second of the two stages of highest yoga tantra practice, emphasizing the arousal of the subtlest level of mind through meditation on the vajra body; cf. *generation stage*

cyclic existence (Skt. *samsara*; Tib. *'khor ba*) the recurring round of death and rebirth, conditioned by ignorance and fraught with suffering

dakini (Tib. *mkha'.'gro.ma*) female sky-goer; one who helps arouse the blissful energy of wisdom in a qualified tantric practitioner

definite emergence (Skt. *nihsarana*; Tib. *nges.'byung*) the attitude of wishing to be rid of the sufferings of cyclic existence and their cause and to attain liberation; renunciation

deity yoga the practice, set forth in the tantras, of cultivating the clear appearance and divine pride of one's chosen meditational deity; cf. *emptiness yoga*

delusion (Skt. *klesha*; Tib. *nyon.mongs*) the mental and emotional afflictions responsible for suffering and dissatisfaction; chiefly ignorance, out of which desirous attachment, hatred, jealousy and all secondary delusions grow

dependent arising (Skt. *pratityasamutpada*; Tib. *rten.cing 'brel.ba*) the interdependent nature of phenomena as expressed in this statement by Shakyamuni Buddha: "due to the existence of this, that arises"; actual manner of existence as opposed to the ignorantly conceived inherent existence

desire realm (Skt. *kamadhatu*; Tib. *'dod.khams*) those states within cyclic existence in which beings are preoccupied with the objects of the five physical senses (i.e. sights, sounds, smells, tastes and tangible sensations); includes all hell beings, hungry spirits, animals, humans, demigods and the lower classes of gods

dharma (Tib. *chos*) spiritual teachings and realizations; that which holds one back from the unwanted experience of suffering; second of the Three Jewels of Refuge

dharmakaya see *truth body*

dharmapala (Tib. *chos.skyong*) fierce deity serving as protector of dharma practitioners

dharma protector see *dharmapala*

diamond scepter (Skt. *vajra*; Tib. *rdo.rje*) implement employed by Vajrayana practitioners to symbolize powerful and compassionate method. It is held in the right hand, and may be seen in the representations of many meditational deities. Cf. *bell*

Diamond Vehicle (Skt. *vajrayana*; Tib. *rdo.rje theg.pa*) see *Vajrayana*

divine pride (Tib. *lha'i nga.rgyal*) the cultivated identification of oneself as having actually become one's chosen meditational deity; cf. *generation stage*

drop (Skt. *bindu*; Tib. *thig.le*) see *vajra body*

dzog-chen (Skt. *mahasampanna, mahasandhi, atiyoga*; Tib. *rdzogs.chen*) great completion; great perfection; within the Nyingma tradition, dzog-chen is the supreme vehicle bringing the qualified practitioner into the sphere of that which spontaneously exists

ego-grasping (Skt. *atmagraha*; Tib. *bdag.'dzin*) the ignorant compulsion to regard one's I, or self, as inherently existent

eightfold path (Skt. *ashtangamarga*; Tib. *'phags.pa'i lam yan.lag brgyad.pa*) the path leading to the cessation of suffering; (1) right view, (2) right thought, (3) right speech, (4) right action, (5) right livelihood, (6) right effort, (7) right mindfulness and (8) right concentration; cf. *four noble truths*

emanation body (Skt. *nirmanakaya*; Tib. *sprul.sku*) the form in which the enlightened mind appears to benefit ordinary beings; cf. *form body*

empowerment (Skt. *abhisheka*; Tib. *dbang*) transmission received from a tantric master allowing a qualified disciple to engage in the practices of a particular meditational deity; initiation

emptiness (Skt. *shunyata*; Tib. *stong.pa nyid*) the absence of all false ideas about how things exist; specifically, the lack of the apparent independent, inherent existence of oneself and all other phenomena; the object of the wisdom cognizing the true nature of reality; selflessness

emptiness yoga the tantric practice of dissolving all ordinary appearances into emptiness as a necessary prerequisite for arising in the purified form of a meditational deity; cf. *deity yoga*

energy wind (Skt. *vayu, prana*; Tib. *rlung*) see *vajra body*

enjoyment body (Skt. *sambhogakaya*; Tib. *longs.spyod rdzogs.pa'i sku*) form in which the enlightened mind appears in order to benefit highly realized bodhisattvas; cf. *form body*

enlightenment (Skt. *bodhi*; Tib. *byang.chub*) full awakening; buddhahood; the ultimate goal of sutra and tantra practice

father-mother embrace (Tib. *yab.yum*) depiction of a highest yoga tantra deity together with consort, their embrace symbolizing the enlightened union of method and wisdom

father tantra (Tib. *pha.rgyud*) those highest yoga tantra practices, such as Guhyasamaja, in which generation of the illusory body is especially emphasized

five buddha families (Tib. *rigs.lnga*) the experience of full enlightenment as the transformation of the five aggregates and purification of the five delusions into the five wisdoms, represented by Vairochana (vajra family), Ratnasambhava (ratna), Amitabha (padma), Amoghasiddha (karma) and Akshobhya (buddha family).

form body (Skt. *rupakaya*; Tib. *gzugs.sku*) manifestation of a buddha's pure consciousness in a form beneficial to others. Of two types: enjoyment body and emanation body; cf. *truth body*

four classes of tantra the division of Vajrayana into (1) action tantra (Skt. *kriyatantra*; Tib. *bya.rgyud*), (2) performance tantra (Skt. *charyatantra*; Tib. *spyod.rgyud*), (3) yoga tantra (Skt. *yogatantra*; Tib. *rnal.'byor rgyud*) and (4) highest yoga tantra

four noble truths (Skt. *chatvaryaryasatyani*; Tib. *'phags.pa'i bden.bzhi*) the four truths of the noble ones; the subject matter of Shakyamuni Buddha's first discourse, namely (1) suffering, (2) the cause of suffering, (3) the cessation of suffering and (4) the path leading to the cessation of suffering

generation stage (Skt. *utpattikrama*; Tib. *bskyed.rim*) first of the two stages of highest yoga tantra practice, emphasizing cultivation of the clear appearance and divine pride of oneself as the meditational deity and initiating the transformation of death, the intermediate state and rebirth into the truth body, enjoyment body and emanation body of a buddha; cf. *completion stage*

geshe (Skt. *kalyanamitra*; Tib. *dge.bshes*) spiritual friend; title given the Tibetan masters of Atisha's Kadam tradition; title given those completing detailed study of the major buddhist treatises

Great Vehicle (Skt. *mahayana*; Tib. *theg.chen*) that aspect of Shakyamuni Buddha's teachings leading to the attainment of the full enlightenment of buddhahood, consisting of the common vehicle of sutra and the esoteric vehicle of tantra

grid pattern (Tib. *thig.mtse*) visual aid serving as a guide to the exact proportions of images in Vajrayana art

guru (Tib. *bla.ma*) spiritual master, mentor, guide; the root guru (Tib. *rtsa.ba'i bla.ma*) is that spiritual teacher to whom we chiefly entrust ourselves, the one who has been most helpful in taming our mind

guru-yoga (Tib. *bla.ma'i rnal.'byor*) the fundamental tantric practice whereby one's spiritual master is seen as essentially identical with the buddhas, one's personal meditational deity and the pure nature of one's own mind

highest yoga tantra (Skt. *anuttaratantra*; Tib. *rnal.'byor bla.med.kyi rgyud*) the most advanced of the four classes of tantra, capable of bringing fully qualified practitioners to full enlightenment within one lifetime; divided into the generation stage and completion stage

ignorance (Skt. *avidhya*; Tib. *ma.rig.pa*) misconception of the actual nature of things; the root cause of all suffering and dissatisfaction within cyclic existence; the obstacle overcome by the wisdom understanding emptiness

illusory body (Skt. *mayakaya, mayadeha*; Tib. *sgyu.lus*) a pure, subtle body achieved through the completion stage practices of highest yoga tantra

incarnate lama (Tib. *sprul.sku*) tulku; the reincarnation of a spiritual master

inherent existence (Skt. *svabhavasiddha*; Tib. *rang.bzhin.gyis grub.pa*) the mistaken conception that oneself and all other phenomena exist independently from their own side rather than being dependent upon causes, conditions, parts and the process of imputation; true existence; self-existence

initiation see *empowerment*

inner heat (Tib. *gtum.mo*) inner fire; energy residing at the navel chakra, utilized during the completion stage practices of highest yoga tantra as a means of bringing energy winds into the central channel and thereby arousing the subtlest level of mind: the blissful clear light

intermediate state (Skt. *antarabhava*; Tib. *bar.do*) the state between death in one life and rebirth in the next

karma (Tib. *las*) action; the workings of cause and effect whereby positive actions produce happiness and non-virtuous actions produce suffering

kaya (Tib. *sku*) "body" of a buddha; cf. *form body* and *truth body*

lama see *guru*

lam-rim stages of the path; a presentation of Shakyamuni Buddha's entire teachings in a form suitable for the step-by-step training of a disciple

liberation (Skt. *moksha, nirvana*; Tib. *thar.pa, mya.ngan.las 'das.pa*) freedom from delusion and karma achieved through the interrelated practices of higher discipline, concentration and wisdom

Lightning Vehicle see *Vajrayana*

lo-jong (Tib. *blo.sbyong*) mahayana thought transformation; practical methods for overcoming self-cherishing and cultivating the compassionate bodhichitta motivation

love (Skt. *maitri*; Tib. *byams.pa*) the wish for others to have happiness and its causes

madhyamika see *Middle Way*

mahamudra (Tib. *phyag.rgya chen.po*) great seal; profound meditational system dealing with the mind and the ultimate nature of reality

mahasiddha (Tib. *grub.thob chen.po*) a greatly accomplished tantric practitioner

Mahayana see *Great Vehicle*

Mahayana thought transformation see *lo-jong*

mandala (Tib. *dkyil.'khor, man.dal*) the celestial abode of a meditational deity, understood as an emanation of the wisdom of that deity. Also, a circular design symbolic of the universe, used during the practice of making offerings

mantra (Tib. *sngags*) protection of the mind; Sanskrit syllables recited in conjunction with the practice of a particular meditational deity

Mantrayana see *Vajrayana*

meditation (Skt. *bhavana*; Tib. *sgom*) the process of becoming thoroughly familiar with beneficial states of mind through both analytical investigation and single-pointed concentration

meditational deity (Skt. *ishtadevata*; Tib. *yi.dam*) personal deity; archetype deity; figure embodying particular aspects of enlightenment, such as universal compassion, and used as the focus of concentration and self-identification in Vajrayana practices

meditative concentration (Skt. *dhyana*; Tib. *bsam.gtan*) cultivation of particularly stable and penetrating states of mind; fifth of the six perfections

meritorious energy (Skt. *punya*; Tib. *bsod.nams*) the positive potential generated by virtuous actions of body, speech and mind

method (Skt. *upaya*; Tib. *thabs*) that aspect of the path to enlightenment dealing with compassion, bodhichitta and the first five of the six perfections, leading to the attainment of a buddha's form body; cf. *wisdom*

Middle Way (Skt. *madhyamika*; Tib. *dbu.ma*) the view presented in Shakyamuni Buddha's Perfection of Wisdom sutras and elucidated by Nagarjuna that all phenomena are dependent arisings, avoiding the mistaken extremes of inherent existence and non-existence (or eternalism and nihilism)

mind transformation teachings see *lo-jong*

mother tantra (Tib. *ma.rgyud*) those highest yoga tantra practices, such as Heruka Chakrasamvara, in which generation of the clear light mind is emphasized

mudra (Tib. *phyag.rgya*) gesture; the hand position of an enlightened being symbolizing an activity such as teaching, granting protection, etc.

naga (Tib. *klu*) a being dwelling in water or under ground, classified as an animal and often appearing in a serpent-like form

nirmanakaya see *emanation body*

nirvana see *liberation*

nyung-nay (Tib. *smyung.gnas*) powerful two-day purification practice centered upon the figure of 1000-armed Avalokiteshvara

obscuration (Skt. *avarana*; Tib. *sgrib.pa*) that which covers the essentially pure nature of the mind. Of the two layers of obscuration, kleshavarana (Tib.

nyon.sgrib) and jneyavarana (Tib. *shes.sgrib*), the former prevents liberation while the latter prevents the omniscience of full enlightenment

padma lotus

pandita (Tib. *pan.chen, mkhas.pa*) master of the various branches of knowledge

parinirvana (Tib. *yongs.su mya.ngan.las 'das.pa*) the passing away of an enlightened being

perfection (Skt. *paramita*; Tib. *pha.rol.tu phyin.pa*) one of the six major bodhisattva practices leading to full enlightenment: giving (Skt. *dana*; Tib. *sbyin.pa*), ethical self-discipline (Skt. *shila*; Tib. *tshul.khrims*), patience (Skt. *kshanti*; Tib. *bzod.pa*), effort (Skt. *virya*; Tib. *brtson.'grus*), meditative concentration and wisdom.

Perfection of Wisdom sutras (Skt. *prajnaparamitasutra*; Tib. *shes.rab.kyi pha.rol.tu phyin.pa'i mdo*) those teachings of Shakyamuni Buddha in which the wisdom of emptiness and the path of the bodhisattva are set forth

po-wa see *transference of consciousness*

prajnaparamita (Tib. *shes.rab.kyi pha.rol.tu phyin.pa*) perfection of wisdom

preliminaries (Tib. *sngon.'gro*) practices designed to remove hindrances and accumulate a store of meritorious energy, thus ensuring successful Vajrayana practice

puja (Tib. *mchod.pa*) offering ceremony

pure land (Skt. *buddhakshetra*; Tib. *sangs.rgyas.kyi zhing, dag.zhing*) state of existence outside samsara wherein all conditions are favorable for the attainment of full enlightenment

renunciation see *definite emergence*

rupakaya (Tib. *gzugs.sku*) see *form body*

sadhana (Tib. *sgrub.thabs*) literally, method of accomplishment; ordered practices relating to a chosen meditational deity

sambhogakaya see *enjoyment body*

samsara see *cyclic existence*

sangha (Tib. *dge.'dun*) the spiritual community; third of the Three Jewels of Refuge

Sarma traditions (*gsar.ma*) the New traditions of Tibetan Buddhism—the Kadam, Sakya, Kagyu and Geluk—as distinguished from the Old, or Nyingma, tradition

Secret Mantra Vehicle (Skt. *guhyamantrayana*; Tib. *theg.pa gsang.sngags*) see *Vajrayana*

seed-syllable in tantric visualizations, a Sanskrit syllable arising from emptiness and out of which a meditational deity in turn arises

self-cherishing (Tib. *rang gces.par 'dzin.pa*) self-centered attitude in which concern for one's own welfare outweighs concern for others; the chief obstacle to be overcome in cultivating the compassionate bodhichitta motivation

self-existence see *inherent existence*

seven-limbed puja (Tib. *yan.lag bdun*) practices designed to collect a store of meritorious energy and cleanse defilements of body, speech and mind: (1) prostration, (2) offering, (3) declaration of non-virtue, (4) rejoicing, (5) requesting the buddhas to turn the wheel of dharma, (6) beseeching the gurus not to enter parinirvana and (7) dedication to the attainment of enlightenment

shunyata see *emptiness*

six realms the various states of cyclic existence, consisting of the three upper realms of gods, demigods and humans and the three lower realms of animals, hungry spirits and hell-beings.

skillful means (Skt. *upayakaushalya*; Tib. *thabs.mkhas.pa*) methods for benefiting others according to their needs, capacities, etc.

stages of the path see *lam-rim*

stupa (Tib. *mchod.rten*) reliquary monument symbolizing the enlightened mind and generally containing the remains of a spiritual master

sutra (Tib. *mdo*) discourse of Shakyamuni Buddha; the division of Buddha's teachings dealing with the cultivation of meditative stabilization; the basic, pre-tantric aspect of the mahayana path emphasizing practice of the six perfections

tangka (*thang.ka*) Tibetan scroll painting, usually depicting meditational deities

tantra (Tib. *rgyud*) literally, thread or continuity; advanced, esoteric discourse of the Buddha presenting methods for achieving full enlightenment quickly through the practices of a particular meditational deity

Tantrayana see *Vajrayana*

tantrika (Tib. *rgyud.pa*) practitioner of the tantric teachings; commonly called a mantrika (Tib. *sngags.pa*)

tathagata (Tib. *de.bzhin.gshegs.pa*) one thus gone; one gone to thusness; an epithet of a buddha

terma (*gter.ma*) treasure text; teaching hidden by Guru Rinpoche, Padmasambhava, for later discovery

terton (*gter.ston*) one who discovers terma

Three Jewels of Refuge (Skt. *triratna, trisharana*; Tib. *dkon.mchog gsum*) Buddha, Dharma and Sangha

three principal aspects (Tib. *lam.gtso rnam.gsum*) essential elements of the sutra path that are to be cultivated for the successful practice of the more advanced tantric methods; namely, (1) definite emergence, (2) the compassionate motivation of bodhichitta and (3) the wisdom of emptiness

three trainings (Skt. *trishiksha*; Tib. *bslab.pa gsum*) the trainings in moral discipline, concentration and wisdom leading to an arhat's liberation from cyclic existence

transference of consciousness (Skt. *chyuti*; Tib. *'pho.ba*) the practice of directing one's consciousness at the time of death to rebirth in a pure land

true existence (Skt. *satyasiddha*; Tib. *bden.par.grub.pa*) see *inherent existence*

truth body (Skt. *dharmakaya*; Tib. *chos.sku*) the mind of a fully enlightened being, free of all obscurations, that remains meditatively absorbed in the direct perception of emptiness while simultaneously cognizing all phenomena; cf. *form body*

tulku see *incarnate lama*

tum-mo see *inner heat*

union (Skt. *yuganadda*; Tib. *zung.'jug*) advanced completion stage attainment in which the pure illusory body and the meaning clear light are achieved simultaneously, leading to the attainment of full enlightenment

Upanishads ancient Hindu scriptures

vajra see *diamond scepter*

vajra body (Tib. *rdo.rje sku*) the subtle system of channels, energy winds and red and white drops meditated upon during the completion stage of highest yoga tantra to arouse the blissful clear light experience: the subtlest level of mind

vajra position (Skt. *vajraparyaka*; Tib. *rdo.rje skyil.krung*) seated meditational posture in which one's legs are fully crossed

Vajrayana (Tib. *rdo.rje theg.pa*) Diamond Vehicle; the advanced, esoteric path presented in the buddhist tantras, leading qualified practitioners to the quick achievement of enlightenment for the sake of benefiting others; also known as the Secret Mantra Vehicle (Skt. *guhyamantrayana*), the Tantric Vehicle (Skt. *tantrayana*), the Mantra Vehicle (Skt. *mantrayana*) and the Lightning Vehicle

vinaya (Tib. *'dul.ba*) the division of Shakyamuni Buddha's teachings dealing with ethical self-discipline and the workings of cause and effect

visualization (Tib. *gsal.'debs*) the meditational technique of picturing in one's mind's eye a particular enlightened quality in the form of a meditational deity, etc.

vivid appearance see *clear appearance*

wang see *empowerment*

Wheel of Life (Skt. *bhavanachakra*; Tib. *srid.pa'i 'khor.lo*) visual representation of cyclic existence and the process by which ordinary beings, compelled by delusion and karma, take repeated rebirth

wisdom (Skt. *prajna*; Tib. *shes.rab*) that aspect of the path to enlightenment dealing with insight into the true nature of reality: emptiness; the last of the six perfections, leading to the attainment of a buddha's truth body; cf. *method*

yab-yum see *father-mother embrace*

yana (Tib. *theg.pa*) vehicle; means whereby a practitioner is led to the desired spiritual goal

yidam (*yi.dam*) see *meditational deity*

yoga (Tib. *rnal.'byor*) spiritual discipline

yogi (Tib. *rnal.'byor.pa*) male practitioner of yoga

yogini (Tib. *rnal.'byor.ma*) female practitioner of yoga

Notes

INTRODUCTION

1: Most of the colored illustrations appearing in this work are available in reproduction from Snow Lion Publications, P.O. Box 6483, Ithaca, N.Y. 14851 (1-800-950-0313). In the U.K., they can be ordered from Tharpa Publications, 15 Bendemeer Road, London SW15 1JX, England.

2: A recent example of a museum catalog which, although extensive and scholarly, does manage to relate Vajrayana art to the living spiritual tradition is Rhie and Thurman, *Wisdom and Compassion: The Sacred Art of Tibet*.

3: Traditional Tibetan classification schemes for the images of Vajrayana art can be found in Gega Lama, *Principles of Tibetan Art*.

4: See His Holiness the Dalai Lama, T. Gyatso, *Kalachakra Tantra: Rite of Initiation*, 24-29, for a more detailed definition of the term *yana* and for a discussion of the differences between sutra and tantra yanas.

5: See especially Waddell, *The Buddhism of Tibet*.

6: For the etymology of the term *mantra* and an explanation why the Vajrayana is called the Secret Mantra Vehicle, see His Holiness the Dalai Lama, Tenzin Gyatso, "Essence of Tantra" in Tsong-ka-pa, *Tantra in Tibet*, 47-48. (It should be noted that *mantra* also refers to the series of Sanskrit syllables recited when invoking tantric meditation deities; see Blofeld, *Mantras: Sacred Words of Power*. In the present work this latter usage appears in references to the mantra of Shakyamuni Buddha, the mantra of Avalokiteshvara, etc.).

7: For more detailed discussions of the history of Vajrayana and its movement from India to Tibet, see the texts cited in Chapter Six, note 2.

8: For explanations of the terms *self-existence* and *inherent existence* in relation to the central buddhist idea of emptiness, see the discussions of the Wheel of Life in Chapter One and the sections on Prajnaparamita and Manjushri in Chapter Two.

9: MacKenzie's *Reincarnation: The Boy Lama* gives an abbreviated biography of Lama Yeshe and a detailed account of the discovery of his incarnation, Tenzin Osel Rinpoche. A more extensive biography of Lama Yeshe is currently being prepared by Adele Hulse for Wisdom Publications.

CHAPTER ONE: THE FOUNDER AND HIS TEACHINGS

1: The various buddhist systems present different accounts of the way in which Shakyamuni achieved enlightenment; these are presented in Lessing and Wayman, *Introduction to the Buddhist Tantric Systems*, 17-39.

Of the many versions of Shakyamuni's life story currently available, the following three are of particular interest: Ashvaghosa's Sanskrit original, translated in Cowell, *Buddhist Mahayana Texts*; Arnold's popular nineteenth-century verse classic, *Light of Asia*; and Thich Nhat Hanh's recent *Old Path White Clouds*.

Commenting upon the compassionately motivated activities of buddhas in general and Shakyamuni Buddha in particular, His Holiness the Dalai Lama makes mention of what is known as the supreme emanation body, described as that which "brings about the welfare of disciples through twelve deeds in various world systems" (T. Gyatso, *Opening the Eye of New Awareness*, 101). These twelve, as they pertain to Shakyamuni Buddha, are listed in *Opening* as:

(1)   descent from Tushita Pure Land

(2)   entry into his mother's womb

(3)   birth in Lumbini

(4)   becoming skilled in the arts and playing the sports of youth

(5)   taking charge of the kingdom and keeping a harem

(6)   upon going to the four gates of the city, becoming discouraged with cyclic existence and leaving the householder's life

(7)   practicing austerities for six years

(8)   going to the Bodhi Tree

(9)   overcoming all the hosts of demons

(10) becoming fully enlightened on the fifteenth day of the fourth month

(11) turning the wheel of doctrine on the fourth day of the sixth month

(12) passing from sorrow in the city of Kushinagara.

2: Images of the severely emaciated Siddhartha are among the most striking examples of early Gandharan sculpture. See Zwalf, *Buddhism: Art and Faith*, 36 and Pal, *Light of Asia*, 95 for examples of such images.

3: In paintings depicting the attack of Mara's legions, the weapons hurled at Siddhartha are transformed into harmless flower petals as they approach the meditator's aura.

4: See Lati Rinbochay, *Meditative States*, for a detailed description of the advanced states of single-pointed concentration and their relation to the spiritual path.

5: For an extensive formulation of these four noble truths—more properly known as the Four Truths of the Noble Ones—see Walshe, *Thus Have I Heard*, 344-49.

6: To combat the many ignorantly produced conceptions interfering with a correct understanding of reality, Shakyamuni gave a wide range of teachings on conventional and ultimate truths. Based on these teachings there arose in India four schools of buddhist tenets of increasing subtlety and penetration: Vaibhashika, Sautrantika, Chittamatra and Madhyamika. For a discussion of these four, set in a context of a complete meditative practice, see Geshe Sopa, *Cutting through Appearances*. See also Hopkins, *Meditation on Emptiness*, 335-428.

7: Particularly popular are the Jataka Tales or birth stories that relate previous lives of Shakyamuni—often as an animal—and illustrate the practices of generosity, discipline, patience and so forth. For a collection of these stories see Dharma Publishing's Jataka Tales series as well as Aryasura, *The Marvelous Companion* and Speyer, *The Jatakamala*.

8: Byrom, *The Dhammapada*, 3.

9: This topic is discussed in detail in the chapter "How Delusions Arise" in Lama Yeshe, *Wisdom Energy*, 44-51.

10: These are discussed by H.H. the Dalai Lama, Tenzin Gyatso, in the chapter entitled "The Three Higher Trainings" appearing in Doboom Tulku, *Atisha and Buddhism in Tibet*, 51-70. The foundation of these trainings is the essential buddhist practice of mindfulness; see Walshe, 445-50; Nhat Hanh, *The Miracle of Mindfulness*; and Nyanaponika, *The Heart of Buddhist Meditation*.

11: Walshe, 270.

12: For a discussion of the four fearlessnesses of an Enlightened One, see

T. Gyatso, *Opening the Eye of New Awareness*, 105; Geshe Dhargyey, *Anthology*, 259-60; and Hopkins, *Meditation on Emptiness*, 210-11.

13: For a further discussion of lotus imagery, see the chapter entitled "The Flower Support" in Campbell's *The Mythic Image*, 221-35.

14: Buddhist scriptures enumerate 112 signs of a buddha's supreme emanation body; these are sometimes referred to as the thirty-two major and eighty minor marks. For a list and explanation of the thirty-two, see Dhargyey, 242-50. For their scriptural source, see Walshe, 441-60.

15: In another version of this story, the artists drew Buddha's image by tracing the shadow cast by his form on a piece of cloth. See Geshe Tharchin, *King Udrayana*, 13 and Kapsner, "Thanka Painting," 17.

16: The following instructions have been adapted from MacDonald, *How to Meditate*, 126-33.

17: For an expanded account of the origination of this diagram, see Tharchin, *King Udrayana*, 7-17.

18: In other representations of the Wheel of Life, the bird depicted is a rooster or another male fowl.

19: Shantideva, *Guide*, 45.

20: For a detailed discussion of the different ways the results of our actions can be experienced and of the factors influencing the heaviness of these actions, see Dhargyey, 334-43.

21: For a more detailed discussion of this point, see Lati Rinbochay, *Death, Intermediate State and Rebirth*, 55-56.

22: The twelve links of dependent arising can be explained in a variety of ways. As a result, the order of these twelve as they are depicted in the outer rim of the Wheel of Life can vary. For one such alternate version, see Geshe Rabten, *Treasury of Dharma*, 92. For further material on this complex subject matter, see Hopkins, *Meditation*, 161-73, 275-83, 707-11. A scriptural source for the twelve links is found in Walshe, 223-30 and an explanation in terms of meditation practice is in Yeshe, *Wisdom Energy*, 96-100. See also T. Gyatso, "Dependent Arising" and *The Meaning of Life*, 3-41.

23: T. Gyatso, *The Meaning of Life*, 12-13. For an alternate version of these lines, see Tharchin, *King Udrayana*, 13.

24: The following stanzas are taken from Dharma Publishing Staff, *Dhammapada*, 49-51.

25: Brief biographies of these sixteen arhats are found in the Central Institute of Buddhist Studies, *Manjushri*, 20-31 and in Yeshe De Research Project, *Light of Liberation: A History of Buddhism in India*, 150-55. This latter work gives two further references to material on the sixteen arhats (Loden

Sherab Dagyab, "The Sixteen gNas-brtan," in *Tibetan Relgious Art*, 60-118 and *Crystal Mirror VI*, 193-95 and 216-28) and contains the following statement of their function:

> Concerned for the Sangha's welfare, the Buddha requested that sixteen Great Arhats remain in the world and watch over the Dharma as long as beings were capable of benefiting from the teachings. Since then the Sixteen Great Arhats have appeared to encourage the devoted and support confidence in the Dharma.(150)

The present version of the arhat Lam-chung's story is adapted from Geshe Kelsang Gyatso, *Meaningful to Behold*, 72-74; for an alternate version see Tripitaka Master Hua, *A General Explanation*, 84-86.

26: These sites are described in Russell's "The Eight Places of Buddhist Pilgrimage" found in Mullin, *Teachings at Tushita*, 138-60. For the significance of pilgrimage in buddhist practice, see T. Gyatso, *My Tibet*, 139ff.

27: Lama Govinda, *Psycho-cosmic Symbolism of the Buddhist Stupa*, 4-5.

28: Taken from Gega Lama, *Principles of Tibetan Art*, Volume 2, 81.

29: Shakyamuni Buddha gave the following instructions when asked how to build a stupa: "In subsequent order at first (a-d) four terraces and after that (e) the receptacle for the pot are to be made. Then (f) the pot, (g) the vessel, (h) the pole, (i) the umbrella canopy—whether it be one or two or three or four up to thirteen umbrella canopies—and (j) the rain canopy are to be made." (Adapted from G. Roth, "Symbolism of the Buddhist Stupa," 184 in Dallapiccola, *The Stupa: Its Religious, Historical and Architectural Significance*.)

The first seven of these structural elements correspond to the thirty-seven harmonies with enlightenment: (a) the four establishments in mindfulness, (b) the four thorough abandonings, (c) the four legs of emanation, (d) the five faculties, (e) five powers, (f) the seven branches of enlightenment and (g) the eightfold path. These are discussed in detail in Dhargyey, *Anthology*, 267-74, 300-01 and T. Gyatso, *The Dalai Lama at Harvard*, 124-62.

As for the remaining elements, these symbolize (h-i) the ten heightened perceptions and special applications of mindfulness as well as (j) the great compassion of a fully enlightened being (see Dallapiccola, 188-90).

30: Received orally from various teachers. Other versions of this incident are found in T. Gyatso, *The Buddhism of Tibet*, 33 and Dhargyey, *Anthology*, 171-72 and Wallace, *Tibetan Buddhism*, 5-6.

31: The founding of this monumental structure is related in Dowman, *The Legend of the Great Stupa*.

CHAPTER TWO: THE BODHISATTVA PATH

1: As stated in Dhargyey, 199: "There are two major types of mental obscurations: (1) those due to disturbing attitudes [i.e. the delusions] and which prevent liberation and (2) those regarding all knowables and which prevent omniscience." For a discussion of these two obscurations, see Dhargyey, 222-23.

2: In addition to Avalokiteshvara, Manjushri and Vajrapani, these eight bodhisattva disciples were Maitreya (Plate 32), Samantabhadra, Kshitigarbha, Akashagarbha and Sarvanivarana-viskambini. These eight are evoked in the dedication chapter of Shantideva's *Guide*; see K. Gyatso, *Meaningful to Behold*, 361-62.

3: For a discussion of what is involved in the process of empowerment, see the chapter entitled "Abhisheka," 87-99, in Trungpa, *Journey without Goal*. See also the chapter "Inspiration and the Guru," 95-110, in Yeshe, *Introduction to Tantra*.

4: For an extensive list of terms used synonymously with "inherent existence," see Hopkins, *Meditation on Emptiness*, 36ff.

5: K. Gyatso, *Heart of Wisdom*, 29. It may be useful to compare the thoughts expressed in this quotation with the following two descriptions of ignorance, the root delusion that is the source of all mental and physcial suffering and dissatisfaction. The first description is by Shakyamuni Buddha himself and is found in his sutra entitled *The Rice Plants*:

> What, now, is ignorance? It is the notion that in these six elements [i.e. earth, water, fire, air, space and consciousness] there is a unity, substance, permanence, stability, enduringness, happiness, a self, a being, a soul, a living being, an individuality, a human being, a person, a man, a youth, an "I" or a "mine". These various kinds of misperception are called ignorance. When there is ignorance, lust, ill-will and bewilderment are set in motion within the objective field of consciousness. (Translated by Frye in Sciaky, "A General Presentation," 39.)

The second is found in Hopkins, *The Tantric Distinction*, 15-16:

> Ignorance is the conception of inherent or pointable concrete existence in things; it is also the conception that subject and object are inherently different entities. It is not a mere lack of knowledge about reality but an erroneous conception about the way things exist.... The ignorance that is the root of suffering is a conception discordant with reality, held with enormous conviction. We are convinced that persons and other phenomena exist

as solid, concrete or self-propelled units because that is how they appear to us. Yet this appearance is thoroughly deceptive, for people and things do not exist this way at all. Nonetheless, through our own ignorance we assent to their false appearance and base our lives on this misconstrued assent.

6: There is a debate among the different schools of buddhist tenets concerning whether or not the wisdom realizing emptiness as taught in the Perfection of Wisdom sutras is needed in order to attain liberation from cyclic existence. For detailed discussions of this issue, see Shantideva, *Guide*, 140-43 and T. Gyatso, *Transcendent Wisdom*, 43-54. See also Tsong-ka-pa, *Tantra in Tibet*, 38-46.

7: See the chapter "Nothingness Is Not Emptiness" by Kensur Lekden in Tsong-ka-pa, *Compassion in Tibetan Buddhism*, 70-74.

8: Zopa Rinpoche, *Chod*, 27.

9: K. Gyatso, *Heart of Wisdom*, 159.

10: *Ibid.*, 160.

11: *Ibid.*, 157.

12: *Ibid.*, 150.

13: Benard, "Ma-chig Lab-dron," 43.

14: The biography of Machig Labdron is presented in Allione, *Women of Wisdom*, 141-204 and Benard, 43-51. As for her predecessor, the great yogini Yeshe Tsogyal, see note 11 to Chapter Six.

15: For an account of Padampa Sangye's meeting with the great Tibetan yogi Milarepa, see Chang, *The Hundred Thousand Songs of Milarepa*, 606-13. And for a translation of teachings given by Padampa Sangye shortly before his passing, see Evans-Wentz, *Great Liberation*, 241-52.

16: This unpublished translation of the Tibetan prayer beginning "ma-sam jo-me" (Tib. *smar.bsam brjod.med*) is by Lama Thubten Yeshe.

17: Geshe Palden Dakpa, "An Explanation of the Name Avalokiteshvara," 90.

18: It is the common practice in Tibetan art for deities such as Avalokiteshvara to be adorned with crown ornaments containing five jewels. Before the fourteenth century, however, such ornaments commonly possessed three jewels, symbolizing the Three Jewels of Refuge—Buddha, Dharma and Sangha.

19: In some representations of the Wheel of Life, emanations of Avalokiteshvara are depicted leading sentient beings out of the six realms. See Lauf, *Tibetan Sacred Art*, 140-43.

20: For a discussion of this topic, see Blofeld, *Mantras*.

21: This explanation is based on one given orally by H.H. Sakya Trizin in Kensington, California, 1978. See also T. Gyatso, *Kindness, Clarity and Insight*, 116-17. Of related interest are the extensive explanations given by Lama Govinda in *Foundations of Tibetan Mysticism* and Dilgo Khyentze Rinpoche in Sakya Trizin, *Essence of Buddhism*, as well as Sogyal Rinpoche in *The Tibetan Book of Living and Dying*, 289-91. See also Bokar Rinpoche, *Chenrezig, Lord of Love*, 37-42.

22: K. Gyatso, *Heart of Wisdom*, xviii-xix.

23: Geshe Wangyal, *Door of Liberation*, 54-55.

24: *Ibid.*, 60.

25: *Ibid.*, 61.

26: This translation has been adapted from several sources, including the version published by Sogyal Rinpoche's Rigpa Fellowship.

27: This prayer is taken from an unpublished sadhana, translator unidentified. For further information concerning the various manifestations of the Bodhisattva of Compassion, see Piyasilo, *Avalokiteshvara*.

28: In Tibetan this color is described as red-yellow (*dmar.ser*).

29: Manjushri's birth and his relation to the Five-Peaked Mountain are described in Evans-Wentz, *Great Liberation*, 134-35, as follows:

> The Buddha once went to China to teach the dharma, but instead of listening to him the people cursed him. So he returned to Vultures' Peak, in India. Considering it to be useless to explain the higher truths to the Chinese, he decided to have introduced into China the conditional truths, along with astrology. Accordingly, the Buddha, while at Vultures' Peak, emitted from the crown of his head a golden yellow light-ray which fell upon a tree growing near a stupa, one of five stupas, each of which was on one of the peaks of the Five-Peaked Mountain. From the tree grew a goiter-like excrescence, whence there sprang a lotus blossom. And from this lotus blossom Manjushri was born, holding in his right hand the Sword of Wisdom and in his left hand a blue lotus blossom, supporting the *Book of Wisdom*.

30: Received orally from various teachers. For an alternate version of the story of Manjushri and the would-be arhats, where the questioner is identified as Shariputra instead of as Vajrapani, see Sakya Pandita, *Illuminations*, 126-27.

31: Translated by the author. For an alternate translation of this prayer, see Dhargyey, 95.

32: This story was related during a teaching given by Jack Kornfield in

Barre, Massachusetts. An expanded version is found in his *Living Buddhist Masters*, 35, where the meditation master is identified as Ven. Ajahn Chah. For a collection of his teachings, see Ven. Ajahn Chah, *Bodhinyana*.

33: Yeshe, *The Sadhana of Vajrapani*, 11.

34: Adapted from Mullin, *Path of the Bodhisattva Warrior*, 6. The image of the bodhisattva as a spiritual warrior is elaborated in Chogyam Trungpa, *Shambala: Sacred Path of the Warrior*.

CHAPTER THREE: THE FIVE BUDDHA FAMILIES

1: The buddhas of the five families—often referred to in western buddhist literature as the five dhyani, or meditation, buddhas—are presented here in their *nirmanakaya* aspects while in Plate 9 they appear in their *sambhogakaya* aspects. As explained in note 21 to Chapter Four and in the material for Table 6 in Chapter Five, enlightened beings manifest in various "form bodies" (Skt. *rupakaya*) to suit the various capacities of sentient beings. To those of lesser capacity, they appear as "emanation bodies" (Skt. *nirmanakaya*); iconographically these are depicted in the aspect of fully renounced monks, as in Figure 7. For disciples of greater capacity, they manifest as "complete enjoyment bodies" (Skt. *sambhogakaya*) and are shown wearing royal garments, adorned with jewels and occasionally, as in Plate 9, embracing consorts.

All form bodies arise from the unobstructed omniscient consciousnesses of enlightened beings. Such a fully enlightened consciousness is called the "truth body" (Skt. *dharmakaya*) of a buddha and is perceived only by other fully enlightened beings. Even though the truth body is formless, there are iconographic representations of buddhas in dharmakaya aspect. In the Nyingma tradition, such a dharmakaya buddha is Samantabhadra (not to be confused with the bodhisattva mentioned in note 2 to Chapter Two). As Chogyam Trungpa explains in *Visual Dharma*, 20, Samantabhadra "is depicted naked, symbolizing the formlessness and simplicity of the dharmakaya. He wears the topknot, is dark in color and holds his hands in the meditation mudra." The other major dharmakaya representation is Vajradhara, depicted in this work in Plate 16. Trungpa also explains that Vajradhara "appears wearing sambhogakaya garments and ornaments, the same as those of the peaceful yidams. Samantabhadra and Vajradhara are the primordial buddhas, who represent the totally unconditioned quality of enlightened mind. According to the New Translation School [Sarma], Shakyamuni took the form of Vajradhara to teach the tantras."

2: The following material on the relationship between color and spiritual transformation was received orally by the artist from his main painting teacher. It is presented in a form that owes much to the discussion found in Trungpa, *Visual Dharma*, 24-26. See also Trungpa, *Journey Without Goal*, 77-85. For a discussion of the five buddha families and the experience of color during the intermediate state, see Lama Lodo, *Bardo Teachings*. Finally, for an intriguing psychological and mythological interpretation of the five buddhas and the intermediate state experience, see Campbell, *Transformations of Myth through Time*, 171-88.

3: The five transcendent wisdoms associated with the five buddha families can be understood as the fully purified forms of the five basic wisdoms that absorb during the death evolution outlined in Chapter Five in the section on Yamantaka (Plate 20). These five basic wisdoms are briefly described in K. Gyatso, *Clear Light of Bliss*, 77-78, as follows:

> The basic mirror-like wisdom is so called because just as a mirror can simultaneously reflect many objects of various forms so too can one ordinary mind perceive many objects simultaneously. The mind that remembers experiences as having been pleasurable, painful and neutral is the basic wisdom of equality [equanimity]. The basic wisdom of individual analysis [discriminating wisdom] remembers individual names of one's friends and relatives and so forth. A mind that remembers normal external activities, purposes and so forth is the basic wisdom of accomplishing activities. And the fifth, the basic wisdom of dharmadhatu [all-encompassing wisdom], is the mind that is the seed of the wisdom truth body of a buddha.

4: In the scheme presented here, Akshobya occupies the center of the mandala and Vairochana is in the eastern direction. It should be noted that there are occasions when the positions of these two buddhas are reversed. And during empowerments into deities belonging to the lotus family, for example, it is Amitabha who occupies the central position.

5: For a discussion of these sutras, see Sangharakshita, *The Eternal Legacy*, 169-77 and *A Survey of Buddhism*, 354-80.

6: Sangharakshita, *A Survey of Buddhism*, 359. The legend of Dharmakara's vow before Lokeshvararaja is related in Campbell's *The Mythic Image*, pp. 221-24.

7: From a sadhana of the Five-deity Heruka Chakrasamvara, translator unidentified.

8: Translated by Glenn Mullin with Thepo Tulku; published in T. Chodron, *Pearl of Wisdom*, 48-56. See also T. Yeshe, *Transference of Consciousness at the Time of Death* and K. Gyatso, *Po-wa Sadhana*, both of which describe the transference practice in relation to Amitabha; and Sogyal Rinpoche, *The Tibetan Book of Living and Dying*, 214-43.

CHAPTER FOUR: ENLIGHTENED ACTIVITY

1: Adapted from T. Gyatso, *The Union of Bliss and Emptiness*, 153.

2: The legendary accounts state that two goddesses arose from Avalokiteshvara's pool of tears: Tara, representing his compassion, and Bhrikuti, representing his wisdom. Tibetans commonly identify the two goddesses as Green and White Tara, who themselves are linked with King Songtsen Gampo's two wives. See Willson, *In Praise of Tara*, 12 and 25, and also Wangyal, *The Door of Liberation*, 60.

3: Willson, 34. For Taranatha's version of the story of Princess Jnanachandra, see Templeman, *The Origin of the Tara Tantra*, 11ff.

4: Adapted from Willson, 180-81.

5: See Blofeld, *Bodhisattva of Compassion: The Mystical Tradition of Kuan Yin*.

6: See Galland, *Longing for Darkness: Tara and the Black Madonna*. See also Willson, 11-25, for a discussion of the various natures of Tara and her relationship to other female divinities.

7: See Galland, 59-67, for a description of a pilgrimage to this site and a photograph of the emerging image of Tara.

8: K. Gyatso, *Praise and Request to the Twenty-one Taras*, 9 and 13. For an alternate translation and commentary, see Willson, 136 and 149. See also the relevant pages in Beyer, *The Cult of Tara*.

9: Weber et al., *Tara's Colouring Book*, introduction.

10: Translated by the author. For an alternate version of this prayer, see Willson, 121.

11: Mullin, *Selected Works of the Dalai Lama I: Bridging the Sutras and Tantras*, 192.

12: It is interesting to note that for Green Tara, her outward appearance as a kriya tantra deity and as a highest yoga tantra deity can be identical. This is in contrast to the buddha of wisdom, for example, whose common kriya form, Manjushri (Plate 7) differs greatly from that of highest yoga tantra, Yamantaka (Plate 20). See note 3 to Chapter Five.

13: This prayer is taken from an unpublished sadhana, translator unidentified.

14: Adapted from K. Gyatso, *The Daily Practice of the Wish-fulfilling Circle*, 7.

15: For another version of this story, see Amdo Jamyang, *New Sun*, 7.

16: Adapted from Sciaky, "A General Presentation," 25-26.

17: This story was received orally from Geshe Ngawang Dhargyey.

18: From an unpublished manuscript, produced by the Rabten Choeling monastery in Switzerland, entitled *Ushnisha Vijaya Sadhana: The Method of Accomplishing the Totally Victorious Crown of the Head*, 4.

19: *Ibid.*, 4.

20: *Ibid.*, 10.

21: It should be noted that Amitabha is not always depicted in the nirmanakaya aspect of a monk, nor is Amitayus always shown in a bejewelled sambhogakaya aspect. Even Shakyamuni Buddha himself is sometimes portrayed in a glorified sambhogakaya aspect instead of as a fully renounced monk.

22: K. Gyatso, *The Yoga of Buddha Amitayus*, 12-14 and 22.

23: Depending upon the practice, the Lapis Healing Master is visualized together with six other buddhas, or seven if Shakyamuni himself is included. In K. Gyatso, *Medicine Guru Sadhana*, the six additional Medicine Buddhas are listed as: King of Clear Knowing, Melodious Ocean of Dharma Proclaimed, Supreme Glory Free from Sorrow, Stainless Excellent Gold, King of Melodious Sound, and Glorious Renown of Excellent Signs. See also Thubten Gyatso, *Medicine Buddha Sadhana*.

24: Birnbaum, *The Healing Buddha*, 80.

25: See Sangharakshita, *The Eternal Legacy*, 178.

26: Birnbaum, 164.

27: See Wallace, *Ambrosia Heart Tantra*.

28: *Ibid.*, 33.

29: *Ibid.*, 34.

30: See Donden, *Health through Balance*, and also Clifford, *Tibetan Buddhist Medicine and Psychiatry*.

31: Adapted from Thubten Gyatso, *Medicine Buddha Sadhana*, 9.

32: In the Pali sutra entitled *The Atanata Protective Verses*, the guardian of the North is referred to as King Vessavana, which in Sanskrit is Vaishravana. See Walshe, 471-78.

33: This story was received orally from various lamas.

CHAPTER FIVE: THE PATH OF BLISS AND EMPTINESS

1: This view is particularly evident in Waddell, *Tibetan Buddhism*, originally published in 1894. It also crops up in Getty, *The Gods of Northern Buddhism*, originally published in 1914.

2: See Moacanin, *Jung's Psychology and Tibetan Buddhism*.

3: The four classes of tantra, in ascending order of profundity, are: kriya (action), charya (performance), yoga and anuttara-yoga (highest yoga) tantra. For a discussion of their characteristic qualities, see Tsong-ka-pa, *Tantra in Tibet*, 52-53, 74-76, 129-38, 201-09. See also T. Gyatso, *Kalachakra Tantra*, 30-38 and Mullin, *The Practice of Kalachakra*.

4: Among the many works dealing with the preliminary practices are Tharchin, *Commentary on Guru Yoga and Offering of the Mandala*; Jamgon Kongtrul, *Torch of Certainty*; Rabten, *Preliminary Practices*; and Jig-me Ling-pa, *Innermost Essence*.

5: Translated by Sharpa Tulku and Alexander Berzin and appearing in T. Gyatso, *Kalachakra Initiation*, 71. For an alternate version, see T. Gyatso, *Kalachakra Tantra*, 426-27.

6: All Mahayana paths, whether of sutra or tantra, are a combination of method and wisdom, but only in highest yoga tantra are these two cultivated simultaneously as two aspects of the subtlest level of consciousness. For a detailed discussion of the significance of this in achieving the fully enlightened state of buddhahood, see T. Gyatso's "Vajrayana" and "Greatness of Mantra" in Tsong-ka-pa, *Tantra in Tibet*, 47-53, 60-66, and *Kalachakra Tantra*, 29. See also Hopkins, *The Tantric Distinction*.

7: T. Gyatso, *Kalachakra Initiation*, 73. See also T. Gyatso, *Kalachakra Tantra*, 431.

8: For a detailed discussion of these four, see Dhargyey, 77-80.

9: See Wayman, *Yoga of the Guhyasamajatantra*.

10: See Nalanda Translation Committee, *The Life of Marpa the Translator*, 15-17, 23, 52-54, etc.

11: Mullin, *Path of the Bodhisattva Warrior*, 286-87. On pages 287-93 of this work, the Thirteenth Dalai Lama outlines the practices of Guhyasamaja.

12: Tibetan Art Calender (Wisdom Publications) for December 1989, with explanation by Lokesh Chandra.

13: See Mullin, *Path*, 294, for the various Indian lineages of Guhyasamaja.

14: For more information on the generation stage and its union of emptiness and deity yoga, see Cozort, *Highest Yoga Tantra*; Tsong-ka-pa, *Tantra in Tibet*, 117-28; and Hopkins, *Tantric Distinction*, 155-64. See also Hopkins' discussion of this topic in T. Gyatso, *Kalachakra Tantra*, 23-38, 48-58.

As explained earlier, the term *mantra* means "mind-protection" (see Introduction, note 6) and the protection offered the mind by the generation stage practices of the Secret Mantra Vehicle is explained by the Dalai Lama, Tenzin Gyatso, as follows:

> There are two main factors in mantra training, pride in oneself as a deity and vivid appearance of that deity. Divine pride protects one from the pride of being ordinary, and divine vivid appearance protects one from ordinary appearances. (Tsong-ka-pa, *Tantra in Tibet*, 47.)

15: The ways in which a limited self-identity produces suffering and the tantric solution to this problem are discussed in Yeshe, *Introduction to Tantra*, 41-50.

16: For a detailed discussion of the completion stage, see Cozort, 65ff. and the entirety of K. Gyatso, *Clear Light of Bliss*. See also Mullin, *Path*, 290-92.

17: In discussing the various Vajrayana techniques "for manifesting the fundamental innate mind of clear light," the Fourteenth Dalai Lama writes:

> The *Guhyasamaja Tantra* . . . speaks mainly of putting concentrated focusing on the winds; the *Chakrasamvara Tantra* and the *Hevajra Tantra* speak mainly of the four joys; and the technique of manifesting the clear light by way of non-conceptual meditation is mainly found in the great completeness [dzog-chen] of the Nying-ma Order and the great seal [mahamudra] tradition of the Kagyu Order. All of these are modes of practice described in valid and reliable source-texts within Highest Yoga Tantra. (Adapted from T. Gyatso, *The Kalachakra Tantra*, 163.)

18: For another version of this story, see Getty, *The Gods of Northern Buddhism*, 152-53.

19: T. Gyatso, *Kindness, Clarity and Insight*, 98. Joseph Campbell, in *The Power of Myth*, 222, gives the following psychological interpretation of the appearance of peaceful and wrathful deities: "If you are clinging fiercely to your ego and its little temporal world of sorrows and joys, hanging on for dear life, it will be the wrathful aspect of the deity that appears. It will seem terrifying. But the moment your ego yields and gives up, that same meditation Buddha is experienced as a bestower of bliss."

20: The *lo-jong* literature is extensive and many texts and commentaries are currently available in English. Among these are: Rabten, *Advice from a Spiritual Friend*; K. Gyatso, *Universal Compassion*; and T. Gyatso, *Kindness, Clarity and Insight*, 100-15.

21: Dharmarakshita, *The Wheel of Sharp Weapons*, 17.

22: *Ibid.*, 17.

23: *Ibid.*, 27.

24: *Ibid.*, 38-39.

25: For a list and discussion of these categories, see Sangarakshita, *The Eternal Legacy*, 14-17 and Dhargyey, 293-94.

26: See Chapter One, note 29.

27: According to the most advanced school of buddhist philosophy, there is only one emptiness: the lack of inherent existence. However, different types of emptiness can be differentiated in terms of their bases, i.e. the phenomena that lack this inherent existence. See Hopkins, *Meditation on Emptiness*, 204-05.

As for the sixteen emptinesses, these are enumerated as follows: (1) the emptiness of internal entities, (2) of external entities, (3) of the internal and external, (4) the emptiness of emptiness, (5) of immensity, (6) of the ultimate, (7) of the conditioned, (8) of the unconditioned, (9) of that which is beyond extremes, (10) of that which has neither beginning nor end, (11) of that which is not to be discarded, (12) of a phenomenon's own nature, (13) of all phenomena, (14) of defining characteristics, (15) of the non-apprehensible and (16) the emptiness of non-things. These sixteen are explained in Lama Tsong Khapa's commentarial work entitled *Clear Illumination of the Intention* elucidating the thought of Chandrakirti's *Guide to the Middle Way*; see Geshe Rabten, *Echoes of Voidness*, 85-90.

28: The eight great accomplishments and the eight powers are given as follows. The great accomplishments are listed as the siddhis of the pill, of eye medicine, of going under the earth, of the sword, of the sky, of vanishing, of immortality and of destroying obstacles. The eight powers are those of body, speech, mind, magic, the ability to go anywhere, the power of the place, of being able to accomplish whatever one wishes, and the power of happiness.

29: Pabongka Rinpoche, *Liberation in the Palm of Your Hand*, 342. Another translation of this famous quotation is given in Sogyal Rinpoche, *The Tibetan Book of Living and Dying*, 40, as follows:

> In horror of death, I took to the mountains—
> Again and again I meditated on the uncertainty of the hour of death,
> Capturing the fortress of the deathless unending nature of mind.
> Now all fear of death is over and done.

30: The following material on the death process is from K.Gyatso, *Clear Light of Bliss*, 67-87. See also Lati Rinbochay, *Death, Intermediate State and Rebirth*, 32-48; Sogyal Rinpoche, *The Tibetan Book of Living and Dying*, 251-54; and Gedun Chopel, *Tibetan Arts of Love*, 95-120.

31: The use of the term "dissolves" here is merely figurative. The earth element does not actually dissolve into water at the time of death; instead, as the grosser element's ability to support consciousness weakens, the more subtle element appears to gain strength and become predominant. The

traditional texts say that the earth element dissolves into water, etc. as a way
of aiding one's meditative experiences.

As for the elements themselves, these are explained as follows:

> The first has the name "earth", but the main reference is to so-
> lidity and obstructiveness. The meaning of "water" is fluidity
> and moistening. "Fire" means heat and burning. "Wind" on
> the coarse level refers even to the air we breathe in and out, but
> on a subtler level it refers mainly to types of energies that promote
> development and change. (T. Gyatso, *Meaning of Life*, 28-29.)

32: From a privately distributed pamphlet containing two sadhanas of
Yamantaka, published in 1975 by Subterranean Vajrahammer Publications,
33.

33: Mullin, *Path*, 283.

34: The following material was taken from K. Gyatso, *Guide to Dakiniland*,
3ff.

35: Biographies of these eighty-four mahasiddhas are found in Robinson,
Buddha's Lions and in two works by Dowman: *Masters of Mahamudra* and
Masters of Enchantment. The latter work is beautifully illustrated by Robert
Beer; his painting of Ghantapa's ascent into space provides a vivid image
of the story presented below. See also K. Gyatso, *Guide to Dakiniland*, 10-
15, for accounts of the lives of Luipa, Ghantapa, Darikapa, Kusali and other
great practitioners of Chakrasamvara and Vajrayogini. It should be noted
that there are some differences between the version of Ghantapa's story
presented here (which follows that found in *Guide to Dakiniland*) and the
one appearing in *Masters of Enchantment*, 145-50.

For a discussion of the Luipa and Ghantapa lineages of Chakrasamvara,
see Mullin, *Path*, 296-98.

36: Dowman, *Masters of Mahamudra*, 34.

37: *Ibid.*, 34.

38: See Guenther, *The Royal Song of Saraha*.

39: Adapted from K. Gyatso, *Guide to Dakiniland*, 10.

40: Dowman, *Masters*, 272.

41: See Chang, *Six Yogas of Naropa* and Guenther, *The Life and Teachings
of Naropa*.

42: As Geshe Thegchok writes in his commentary to Je Tsong Khapa's
Praise to Dependent Arising, 45:

> In the *Sutra Requested by Dritarashtra*, Buddha taught non-
> inherent existence in relation to the *three* doors of liberation. The
> first door is that the *self-entity* of all phenomena is empty of in-

herent existence; the second is that *causes* are free from the sign of inherent existence; and the third is that *results* are not produced within the sphere of inherent existence. [Italics added.]

To the non-inherent existence of self-entity, cause and result can be added a fourth door of liberation, namely that *actions* are non-inherently existent.

43: The following material is based on an explanation received orally from Lati Rinpoche. For more information on the integrated practice of these three major deities, see T. Gyatso, *The Union of Bliss and Emptiness*, 12-15.

44: For a discussion of these four joys, see K. Gyatso, *Clear Light of Bliss*, 93-99.

45: A detailed description of this deity and her practice is found in K. Gyatso, *Guide to Dakiniland*. See also Yeshe, *Vajrayogini*.

46: The two other main forms of this deity—sometimes referred to as Vajradakini—were given in revelation to the Indian masters Indrabhuti and Maitripa.

47: K. Gyatso, *The Quick Path*, 119-20.

48: *Ibid.*, 10-11.

49: *Ibid.*, 11.

50: K. Gyatso, *Clear Light of Bliss*, 124.

51: *Ibid.*, 5. A similar point is made in Yeshe, *Introduction to Tantra*, 153.

52: The following material was received orally from various lamas and also extracted from Kalu Rinpoche, *Mahakala*.

53: See Dowman, *Masters of Mahamudra*, 60-62, from which the following material was extracted.

54: Trungpa, *Visual Dharma*, 22.

55: Gendun Drub, *Bridging the Sutras and Tantras*, 162-63.

CHAPTER SIX: A LIVING TRADITION

1: Nalanda, *The Life of Marpa*, 92.

2: For a concise history of the spread of Buddhism from India to Tibet and the evolution of the major traditions of Buddhism in Tibet—including selected teachings from these traditions—see Batchelor, *The Jewel in the Lotus*. See also Tarthang Tulku, "A History of the Buddhist Dharma," 127ff and "History," 75ff. For a history of the major Tibetan traditions and an examination of their artistic lineages, see Rhie and Thurman, *Wisdom and Compassion*, 26-32, 165-309.

3: For the views of His Holiness the Fourteenth Dalai Lama on this topic see T. Gyatso, *A Human Approach to World Peace*. On page 14 of that work he states: "...humanity needs all the world's religions to suit the ways of life, diverse spiritual needs, and inherited national traditions of individual human beings." Also see note 19 below.

4: Jamyang Khyentze Rinpoche, "The Opening of the Dharma," in T. Gyatso, *Four Essential Buddhist Texts*, 16.

5: Dowman, *The Legend of the Great Stupa*, 74. Elements of this account of Guru Rinpoche's miraculous birth appear in the following prayer by the Seventh Dalai Lama, Kelsang Gyatso (1708-1757) entitled "A Prayer to the Lotus Born":

> In the northwestern land of Urgyen [Orgyen],
> A magically produced valley of perfection,
> There springs forth a mighty lotus blossom
> And upon it appears a wondrous and magical transformation.
>
> There sits the Lotus Born Guru,
> A holder of diamond knowledge.
> Who wields in his hand a radiant vajra blazing
> With the fearless power of wisdom gazing boldly at truth.
>
> O Lotus Born One and your eight emanations
> Who inspire strength able to overcome every hindrance:
> Pacify the conditions that bring harm to living beings
> And unfold every circumstance conducive to goodness, light and
>   liberation.

(Mullin, *Selected Works of Dalai Lama VII*, 164.)

6: Yeshe Tsogyal, *Life*, 186.

7: For a description of the major manifestations of Guru Rinpoche, see Sogyal, *Dzogchen & Padmasambhava*, 29-35. Of particular interest are the eight manifestations of Guru Rinpoche often depicted on tangkas and in masked "lama dances" throughout the Himalayan region. These eight, with the characteristic activities of each, are described in material distributed by Lama Tharchin, a modern Nyingma master, as follows:

(a) Padmasambhava: appearing as the one born from a lotus, totally pure.
(b) Gyakar Panchen: displaying the qualities of a great Indian scholar.
(c) Loden Chokse: having an omniscient mind inseparable from Manjushri.
(d) Pema Gyalpo: manifesting as a king controlling all realms of existence.
(e) Nyima Oser: dispelling the darkness of ignorance.
(f) Shakya Senge: appearing as the monk who became the great liberator of all beings.

(g) Senge Dradok: destroying extreme wrong views and the demonic forces that arise when tantric vows are broken.

(h) Dorje Drolo: appearing as the fierce destroyer of enemies and the obstructions to enlightenment. It was in this form that Guru Rinpoche appeared when establishing the buddhadharma in Bhutan.

For further information on these eight manifestations, see Tarthang Tulku, "The Vajra Guru Mantra," 17-39; Olschak, *Mystic Art of Ancient Tibet*, 25-32; and Yeshe Tsogyal, *The Life and Liberation of Padmasambhava*, 191-218.

8: Evans-Wentz, *The Tibetan Book of the Great Liberation*, 146. The magically produced lake is identified as Rewalsar near the North Indian town of Mandi.

9: For examples of works by and about this great master, see Longchenpa, *You Are the Eyes of the World*, and Thondup Rinpoche, *Buddha Mind*.

10: See Jig-me Ling-pa, *The Dzogchen Innermost Essence Preliminary Practice*.

11: For biographies of this great yogini, see Tarthang Tulku, *Mother of Knowledge*, and Dowman, *Sky Dancer*.

12: For an extensive discussion of the history and teachings of the Nyingma tradition, see H.H. Dudjom Rinpoche, *The Nyingma School of Tibetan Buddhism*. The reincarnation of this great terton was born on October 9, 1990 and officially recognized by H.H. the Dalai Lama.

13. Among the published works of this master is his *Wish-fulfilling Jewel*.

14: Dowman, *Legend of the Great Stupa*, 104-07.

15: Dhargyey, 10-11.

16: Adapted from Dhargyey, 11.

17: *Ibid.*, 19.

18: Doboom Tulku, 11.

19: In Geshe Dhargyey's commentary to this verse of Atisha's *The Jewel Rosary of an Awakening Warrior* (found in Geshe Rabten and Geshe Dhargyey, *Advice from a Spiritual Friend*, 128) the following remarks are made concerning the importance of non-sectarianism:

> We should follow a spiritual system that suits our own abilities best and avoid criticizing other traditions. People with different dispositions naturally follow different traditions. It is not up to us, just because we follow one system, to discourage others from the path they have chosen and criticize them, discrediting their choice. In speaking disparagingly about other religious systems, we commit the serious non-virtue of abandoning dharma. Bud-

dha Shakyamuni said, "The consequences of religious sectarianism are far worse than killing saints or destroying as many religious monuments as there are grains of sand in the river Ganges."

20: *Ibid.*, 99-102.

21: Amipa, *A Waterdrop from the Glorious Sea*, 15.

22: C. Trichen, *The History of the Sakya Tradition*, x.

23: His Holiness Sakya Trizin, *Parting from the Four Attachments*, 40. This text contains several commentaries on these verses, one of which, by the fifteenth-century master Ngorchen Kunga Zangpo, also appears in Batchelor, *The Jewel in the Lotus*, 209-47.

24: The Five Foremost Ones are Konchog Gyalpo's son Kunga Nyingpo (1092-1158); Kunga Nyingpo's sons Sonam Tsemo (1142-1182) and Dagpa Gyaltsen (1147-1216); Kunga Nyingpo's grandson Kunga Gyaltsen (1181-1251) and his great-grandson Chogyal Pagpa (1235-1280).

25: Amipa, *A Waterdrop from the Glorious Sea*, 39.

26: *Ibid.*, 39-40.

27: Nagarjuna and the Sakya Pandita, *Elegant Sayings*, 112-13.

28: Nalanda Translation Committee, *The Life of Marpa the Translator*, xxiv.

29: *Ibid.*, xxxvii.

30: *Ibid.*, 92.

31: *Ibid.*, 99. For biographies of some of the most renowned lineage holders of Marpa's tradition, see Gyaltsen, *The Great Kagyu Masters*.

32: *Ibid.*, 89.

33: Sogyal Rinpoche, *Dzogchen & Padmasambhava*, 38. In his notes, Sogyal Rinpoche credits this quotation to The International Translation Committee, Drajur Dzamling Kunchab, *The Last Public Teaching of Lama Kalu Rinpoche*, Sonada, March 28, 1989.

The reincarnations of both H.H. the XVI Karmapa and H.E. Kalu Rinpoche have been recognized and enthroned. H.H. the XVII Karmapa, Ogyen Drodul Trinley Dorje, was enthroned at Tsurphu Monastery in Tibet on September 27, 1992. The reincarnation of H.E. Kalu Rinpoche, who passed away in May 1989, was enthroned on February 25, 1993, at Samdrup Darjay Choling Monastery in Sonada, India.

34: Rolpe Dorje (1340-1383), the Fourth Karmapa, gave the young Tsong Khapa the name Kunga Nyingpo and predicted, "This is a holy child who will be of great benefit to people. Therefore, he is like a second Buddha come to Tibet." (Karma Thinley, *History of the Sixteen Karmapas*, 66.)

35: Thurman, *Life and Teachings of Tsong Khapa*, 9.

36: The phrase "objectless compassion" does not mean compassion lacking an object. Rather it refers to the type of compassion that is conjoined with an understanding that its object, a suffering being, lacks or is empty of inherent existence. For a further discussion of this important phrase, see Tsong-ka-pa, *Compassion in Tibetan Buddhism*, 119-22 and Newland, *Compassion: A Tibetan Analysis*, 55, etc.

37: For an alternate version of this prayer, see Thurman, *Life*, 9. For a brief biography of Rendawa and an account of his relationship with Tsong Khapa, see Tharchin, *Nagarjuna's Letter*, 1-4.

38: For a depiction of this visualization, see the cover of Geshe Wangchen, *Awakening the Mind of Enlightenment*.

39: This scene is depicted on the cover of Thurman, *Tsong Khapa's Speech of Gold*.

40: Thurman, *Life*, 51.

41: *Ibid.*, 96.

42: Thegchok, *Praise to Dependent-Arising*, 34-36. See also Thurman, *Life*, 100.

43: For a detailed account of Tsong Khapa's view of the compatability of emptiness and conventional phenomena, see Napper, *Dependent-Arising and Emptiness*.

44: For a biography of Khedrub Je, see T. Gyatso, *Kalachakra Tantra*, 139-45.

45: Another widely practiced guru-yoga visualization is found in the *Guru Puja*, in which one's personal spiritual mentor is seen as inseparable from Je Tsong Khapa, with Shakyamuni Buddha in his heart and Vajradhara in Shakyamuni's heart. This visualization is described in detail in T. Gyatso, *The Union of Bliss and Emptiness*, 71-73.

46: Of all the texts that came to be written based on Atisha's *Lamp of the Path to Enlightenment*, Tsong Khapa's *Great Exposition of the Stages of the Path* is the most extensive. For a translation of Atisha's root work, see Atisha, *A Lamp for the Path and Commentary*. For a description of the eight major Geluk texts based on Atisha's original, see Dhargyey, xv-xvi, and T. Gyatso, *Path to Bliss*, 20-21. Texts in the Stages of the Path, or Lam-rim, genre are also prominent in traditions other than Atisha's Kadam and Tsong Khapa's Geluk; for examples see the Sakya Pandita's *Illuminations* and the great Kagyu master Gampopa's *Jewel Ornament*.

Of the many English translations now available of Lam-rim texts and commentaries, T. Gyatso's *Path to Bliss*, Pabongka Rinpoche's *Liberation* in the Palm of Your Hand, Geshe Ngawang Dhargyey's *An Anthology of Well-Spoken Advice* and K. Gyatso's *Joyful Path of Good Fortune* are of particular interest. For a particularly accessible rendering of these teachings presented by a qualified Westerner, see Wallace's *Tibetan Buddhism from the Ground Up*.

47: Thurman, *Life*, 243-45.

CHAPTER SEVEN: THE FUTURE BUDDHA

1: This brief version of the seven-limbed prayer, put into its present form by the author, is found inserted in a variety of tantric sadhanas. Much longer versions, in which each limb receives extensive treatment, are also in use. See T. Gyatso, *The Union of Bliss and Emptiness*, 92-116.

2: Gendun Drub, 160.

3: This prayer was written in the 1970s by Geshe Ngawang Dhargyey in response to a request by one of his disciples and was translated by Alexander Berzin.

4: "Diamond Seat" translates the Sanskrit name *Vajrasana*, the indestructible seat at the foot of the Bodhi Tree where Shakyamuni attained enlightenment. It is said that the other Founding Buddhas of this fortunate eon will also manifest their enlightenment at this very place. The species of tree growing there, however, will differ.

5: This is an alternate version of the stanzas following the one quoted earlier from Gendun Drub; see note 2 above.

6: For different versions of this popular story, see Wangyal, *The Door of Liberation*, 52-53; Dhargyey, 122-24; Willis, *On Knowing Reality*, 6-10; and Thurman, *Tsong Khapa's Speech of Gold*, 28-33.

7: These texts are listed with their Sanskrit titles in Thurman, *Tsong Khapa's Speech of Gold*, 29, as (1) *Ornament of Realizations*, (2) *Ornament of Universal Vehicle Scriptures*, (3) *Analysis of the Jewel Matrix*, (4) *Discrimination between Center and Extremes*, and (5) *Discrimination between Phenomenon and Noumenon*. Note that *Analysis of the Jewel Matrix* is referred to below as *Peerless Continuum* (*Uttaratantra*).

8: Acharya Konchog Gyatsen, "Nine Similes on Buddha-nature" in Mullin, *Teachings at Tushita*, 163.

ARTIST'S AFTERWORD

1: See J. Russell's "The Eight Places of Buddhist Pilgrimage" in G. Mullin, *Teachings at Tushita*.

2: The artist Thargye was one of the main informants for D. and J. Jackson, *Tibetan Thangka Painting*. This work gives a detailed description of the craftsmanship that goes into the production of a tangka and provides valuable insight into the range of skills required of a traditional Tibetan artist.

Bibliography

Ven. Ajahn Chah. *Bodhinyana: A Collection of Dhamma Talks*. Bung Wai Forest Monastery, 1982.

Allione, T. *Women of Wisdom*. London: Routledge & Kegan Paul, 1986.

Amipa, Sherab Gyaltsen. *A Waterdrop from the Glorious Sea: A Concise Account of the Advent of Buddhism in General and the Teachings of the Sakyapa Tradition in Particular*. Rikon: Tibetan Institute, 1976.

Arguelles, J. and M. *Mandala*. Berkeley: Shambhala, 1972.

Arnold, Sir Edwin. *The Light of Asia*. Wheaton: Theosophical Publishing House, 1969. First published in 1879.

Aryasura. *The Marvelous Companion: Life Stories of the Buddha*. Berkeley: Dharma, 1983.

Atisha. *A Lamp for the Path and Commentary*. Trans. Sherburne. London: George Allen and Unwin, 1983.

Avedon, J. *In Exile from the Land of Snows*. New York: Alfred A. Knopf, 1984.

Batchelor, S. *The Jewel in the Lotus: A Guide to the Buddhist Traditions of Tibet*. London: Wisdom, 1987.

_____. *The Tibet Guide*. London: Wisdom, 1987.

Beer, R. "Tibetan Thangka Painting." *The Middle Way* (August 1984), 103-08.

Benard, E. "Ma-chig Lab-dron." *Cho-yang, The Voice of Tibetan Religion and Culture*, No. 3. (n.d.), 43-51.

Beyer, S. *The Cult of Tara: Magic and Ritual in Tibet*. Berkeley: University of California Press, 1978.

Birnbaum, R. *The Healing Buddha*. London: Rider, 1980.

Blofeld, J. *Bodhisattva of Compassion: The Mystical Tradition of Kuan Yin*. Boulder: Shambhala, 1978.

—————— . *Mantras: Sacred Words of Power*. London: Unwin, 1977.

Bokar Rinpoche. *Chenrezig, Lord of Love: Principles and Methods of Deity Meditation*. San Francisco: ClearPoint Press, 1991.

Byrom, T., trans. *The Dhammapada: The Sayings of the Buddha*. London: Wildwood House, 1976.

Campbell, J. *The Mythic Image*. Princeton: Princeton University Press, 1974.

—————— . *The Power of Myth*. New York: Doubleday, 1988.

—————— . *Transformations of Myths through Time*. New York: Harper and Row, 1989.

Central Institute of Buddhist Studies. *Manjushri: An Exhibition of Rare Thankas*. Varanasi: CIBS, 1986.

Chang, G., trans. *The Hundred Thousand Songs of Milarepa*. Boulder: Shambhala, 1977.

—————— . *Six Yogas of Naropa and Teachings on Mahamudra*. Ithaca: Snow Lion, 1986. Originally published in 1963 as *Teachings of Tibetan Yoga*.

Chodron, T., comp. *Pearl of Wisdom: Buddhist Prayers and Practices*. 2 Volumes. Singapore: Amitabha Buddhist Centre, 1991.

Clifford, T. *Tibetan Buddhist Medicine and Psychiatry: The Diamond Healing*. York Beach: Samuel Weiser, 1984.

Conze, E., trans. *The Perfection of Wisdom in Eight Thousand Lines and Its Verse Summary*. Bolinas: Four Seasons Foundation, 1973.

Cowell, E., ed. *Buddhist Mahayana Texts*. New York: Dover, 1969. Originally published in 1894 as Volume XLIX of *The Sacred Books of the East*.

Cozort, D. *Highest Yoga Tantra: An Explanation to the Esoteric Buddhism of Tibet*. Ithaca: Snow Lion, 1986.

Dakpa, Geshe Palden. "An Explanation of the Name Avalokiteshvara," *Cho-yang, The Voice of Tibetan Religion and Culture*. No. 3 (n.d.), 88-91.

Dallapiccola, A.L. and Lallemant, S.Z., eds. *The Stupa: Its Religious, Historical and Architectural Significance*. Wiesbaden: Franz Steiner Verlag, 1980.

Dhargyey, Geshe Ngawang. *An Anthology of Well-Spoken Advice on the Graded Paths of the Mind*. Ed. A. Berzin. Dharamsala: Library of Tibetan Works & Archives, 1982.

Dharma Publishing Staff. *Dhammapada*. Berkeley: Dharma Publishing, 1985.

Dharmarakshita. *The Wheel of Sharp Weapons: A Mahayana Training of the Mind.* Dharamsala: Library of Tibetan Works and Archives, 1973.

Dilgo Khyentse. *The Wish-Fulfilling Jewel: The Practice of Guru Yoga According to the Longchen Nyingthig Tradition.* Boston: Shambhala, 1988.

Doboom Tulku and G. Mullin (trans.). *Atisha and Buddhism in Tibet.* New Delhi: Tibet House, 1983.

Donden, Dr. Yeshi. *Health Through Balance: An Introduction to Tibetan Medicine.* Ithaca: Snow Lion, 1986.

Dowman, K. *The Legend of the Great Stupa.* Emeryville: Dharma, 1973.

_____. *Masters of Enchantment: The Lives and Legends of the Mahasiddhas.* London: Arkana, 1988.

_____. *Masters of Mahamudra: Songs and Histories of the Eighty-four Buddhist Siddhas.* Albany: SUNY Press, 1985.

_____. *The Power-Places of Central Tibet: The Pilgrim's Guide.* London: Routledge and Kegan Paul, 1988.

_____. *Sky Dancer: The Secret Life and Songs of Lady Yeshe Tsogyel.* London: Routledge and Kegan Paul, 1984.

H.H. Dudjom Rinpoche, Jigdrel Yeshe Dorje. *The Nyingma School of Tibetan Buddhism.* Boston: Wisdom, 1992.

Evans-Wentz, W., ed. *The Tibetan Book of the Dead.* London: Oxford University Press, 1971.

_____. *The Tibetan Book of the Great Liberation.* London: Oxford University Press, 1954.

Fremantle, F. and Trungpa Rinpoche. *The Tibetan Book of the Dead.* Berkeley: Shambhala, 1975.

Galland, C. *Longing for Darkness: Tara and the Black Madonna, a Ten-year Journey.* New York: Viking, 1990.

Gampopa. *Jewel Ornament of Liberation.* Trans. H.V. Guenther. Berkeley: Shambhala, 1971.

Gedun Chopel. *Tibetan Arts of Love.* Introduced and translated by Jeffrey Hopkins. Ithaca: Snow Lion, 1992.

Gega Lama. *Principles of Tibetan Art.* 2 Volumes. Darjeeling: Jamyang Singe, 1983.

Getty, A. *The Gods of Northern Buddhism.* New York: Dover, 1988. Originally published in 1914.

Goddard, D., ed. *A Buddhist Bible.* Boston: Beacon Press, 1966. Originally published in 1938.

Govinda, Lama Anagarika. "Entering the Realm of the Sacred: Buddhist Art and Architecture; the Mandala of the Dhyani-Buddhas." *Gesar* (Spring 1980), 10-13.

_____. *Foundations of Tibetan Mysticism.* London: Rider, 1983.

_____ . *Psycho-cosmic Symbolism of the Buddhist Stupa*. Berkeley: Dharma, 1976.

Guenther, H., trans. *The Life and Teaching of Naropa*. London: Oxford University Press, 1963.

_____ . *The Royal Song of Saraha*. Berkeley: Shambhala, 1973.

Karma Thinley. *The History of the Sixteen Karmapas of Tibet*. Boulder: Prajna Press, 1980.

Khenpo Konchog Gyaltsen, trans. *The Great Kagyu Masters: The Golden Lineage Treasury*. Ithaca: Snow Lion, 1990.

Gyatso, Geshe Kelsang. *Clear Light of Bliss: Mahamudra in Vajrayana Buddhism*. London: Tharpa, 1990.

_____ . *The Daily Practice of the Wish-fulfilling Circle*. Ulverston: Manjushri Institute, 1988.

_____ . *Guide to Dakiniland*. London: Tharpa, 1990.

_____ . *Heart of Wisdom: A Commentary to the Heart Sutra*. London: Tharpa, 1986.

_____ . *Joyful Path of Good Fortune: The Stages of the Path to Enlightenment*. London: Tharpa, 1990.

_____ . *Meaningful to Behold: A Commentary to Shantideva's* Guide to the Bodhisattva's Way of Life. London: Tharpa, 1986.

_____ . *Medicine Guru Sadhana: The Method for Making Requests to the Assembly of Seven Medicine Gurus*. Buxton: Tara Centre, 1987.

_____ . *Po-wa Sadhana*. Ulverston: Manjushri Institute, 1981.

_____ . *Praise and Request to the Twenty-one Taras*. Ulverston: Manjushri Institute, 1985.

_____ . *The Quick Path to Great Bliss* and *The Feast of Great Bliss* by Je Phabongkha. Ulverston: Manjushri Institute, 1987.

_____ . *Universal Compassion: A Commentary to Bodhisattva Chekawa's* Training the Mind in Seven Points. London: Tharpa, 1988.

_____ . *The Yoga of Buddha Amitayus*. Ulverston: Manjushri Institute, 1986.

Gyatso, Tenzin (His Holiness the Fourteenth Dalai Lama). *The Bodh Gaya Interviews*. Ithaca: Snow Lion, 1988.

_____ . *The Buddhism of Tibet*. Ithaca: Snow Lion, 1987.

_____ . *The Dalai Lama at Harvard*. Ithaca: Snow Lion, 1988.

_____ . "Dependent Arising." *Cho-yang, The Voice of Tibetan Religion and Culture*. No. 3 (n.d.), 26-42.

_____ . *Four Essential Buddhist Texts*. Dharamsala: Library of Tibetan Works and Archives, 1982.

_____ . *Freedom In Exile*. New York: Harper Collins, 1990.

_____ . *A Human Approach to World Peace*. London: Wisdom, 1984.

_____ . *Kalachakra Initiation*. Madison: Deer Park, 1981.

_____ . *Kalachakra Tantra: Rite of Initiation*. London: Wisdom, 1989.

_____ . *Kindness, Clarity and Insight*. Ithaca: Snow Lion, 1984.

_____ . *The Meaning of Life from a Buddhist Perspective*. Boston: Wisdom, 1992.

_____ . *My Tibet* (Photographs by G. Rowell). Berkeley: University of California Press, 1990.

_____ . *Opening the Eye of New Awareness*. Trans. D. Lopez. London: Wisdom, 1985.

_____ . *Path to Bliss: A Practical Guide to Stages of Meditation*. Ithaca: Snow Lion, 1991.

_____ . *Transcendent Wisdom: A Commentary on the Ninth Chapter of Shantideva's Guide to the Bodhisattva's Way of Life*. Trans. A. Wallace. Ithaca: Snow Lion, 1988.

_____ . *The Union of Bliss and Emptiness: A Commentary on the Lama Choepa Guru Yoga Practice*. Ithaca: Snow Lion, 1988.

Gyatso, Thubten. *Medicine Buddha Sadhana*. Ulverston: Wisdom, 1982.

Hopkins, J. *Meditation on Emptiness*. London: Wisdom, 1983.

_____ . *The Tantric Distinction: An Introduction to Tibetan Buddhism*. London. Wisdom, 1984.

Tripitaka Master Hua. *A General Explanation of* The Buddha Speaks of Amitabha Sutra. San Francisco: Buddhist Text Translation Society, 1974.

Jackson, D. and J. Jackson. *Tibetan Thangka Painting: Methods and Materials*. London: Serindia Publications, 1984.

Amdo Jamyang. *New Sun Self-learning Book on the Art of Tibetan Painting*. Mussoorie: published by artist, 1982.

Jig-me Ling-pa. *The Dzogchen Innermost Essence Preliminary Practice*. Dharamsala: Library of Tibetan Works and Archives, 1982.

Jung, C.G. *Mandala Symbolism*. Princeton: Princeton University Press, 1972.

H. E. Kalu Rinpoche. *The Gem Ornament of Manifold Oral Instructions Which Benefits Each and Every One Appropriately*. Ithaca: Snow Lion, 1986.

_____ . *Mahakala: The Awakened Energy of Compassion*. San Francisco: Kagyu Droden Kunchab, 1977.

Kapsner, M. "Thangka Painting." *Cho-yang, The Voice of Tibetan Religion and Culture*. No. 3 (n.d.), 17-24.

Kongtrul, Jamgon. *The Torch of Certainty*. Boulder: Prajna Press, 1983.

Kornfield, J. *Living Buddhist Masters*. Santa Cruz: Unity Press, 1977.

Kunga Rinpoche and B. Cutillo (trans.). *Miraculous Journey: New Stories and Songs by Milarepa*. Novato: Lotsawa, 1986.

Lati Rinbochay and J. Hopkins (trans.). *Death, Intermediate State and Rebirth in Tibetan Buddhism*. London: Rider, 1979.

_____ . *Meditative States in Tibetan Buddhism: The Concentrations and Formless Absorptions*. London: Wisdom, 1983.

Lauf, D. *Tibetan Sacred Art: The Heritage of Tantra*. Berkeley: Shambhala, 1976.

Lessing, F. and A. Wayman, trans. *Introduction to the Buddhist Tantric Systems*. New York: Samuel Weiser, 1960.

Lhalungpa, L., trans. *The Life of Milarepa*. Boston: Shambhala, 1984.

Lodo, Lama. *Bardo Teachings: The Way of Death and Rebirth*. Ithaca: Snow Lion, 1987.

Longchenpa. *You Are the Eyes of the World*. Novato: Lotsawa, 1987.

MacDonald, K. *How to Meditate: A Practical Guide*. London: Wisdom, 1984.

MacKenzie, V. *Reincarnation: The Boy Lama*. London: Bloomsbury, 1988.

Mascaro, J. *The Dhammapada: The Path of Perfection*. Harmondsworth: Penguin, 1973.

Moacanin, R. *Jung's Psychology and Tibetan Buddhism: Western and Eastern Paths to the Heart*. London: Wisdom, 1986.

Mullin, G., ed. *Death and Dying: The Tibetan Tradition*. London: Arkana, 1987.

_____ . *Meditations on the Lower Tantras*. Dharamsala: Library of Tibetan Works and Archives, 1983.

_____ . *Path of the Bodhisattva Warrior: The Life and Teachings of the Thirteenth Dalai Lama*. Ithaca: Snow Lion, 1988.

_____ . *The Practice of Kalachakra*. Ithaca: Snow Lion, 1991.

_____ . *Selected Works of the Dalai Lama I: Bridging the Sutras and Tantras*. Ithaca: Snow Lion, 1985.

_____ . *Teachings at Tushita: Buddhist Discourses, Articles and Translations*. New Delhi: Mahayana Publications, 1981.

Nagarjuna and the Sakya Pandita. *Elegant Sayings*. Berkeley: Dharma, 1977.

Nagarjuna and the Seventh Dalai Lama. *The Precious Garland and the Song of the Four Mindfulnesses*. London: George Allen and Unwin, 1975.

Nalanda Translation Committee. *The Life of Marpa the Translator*. Boulder: Prajna Press, 1982.

Napper, E. *Dependent-Arising and Emptiness: A Tibetan Buddhist Interpretation of Madhyamika Philosophy Emphasizing the Compatability of Emptiness and Conventional Phenomena*. Boston: Wisdom, 1989.

Neumann, E. *The Great Mother: An Analysis of the Archetype.* Princeton: Princeton University Press, 1963.

Newland, G. *Compassion: A Tibetan Analysis.* London: Wisdom, 1984.

Nhat Hanh, T. *The Miracle of Mindfulness: A Manual on Meditation.* Boston: Beacon Press, 1976.

_____. *Old Path White Clouds: Walking in the Footsteps of the Buddha.* Berkeley: Parallax Press, 1991.

Nyanaponika Thera. *The Heart of Buddhist Meditation.* York Beach: Samuel Weiser, 1988. Originally published in 1962.

Olschak, B. *Mystic Art of Ancient Tibet.* London: George Allen and Unwin, 1973.

Pabongka Rinpoche. *Liberation in Our Hands.* Trans. Geshe Lobsang Tharchin. Howell: Mahayana Sutra and Tantra Press, 1990.

_____. *Liberation in the Palm of Your Hand: A Concise Discourse on the Path to Enlightenment.* Trans. Michael Richards. Boston: Wisdom, 1991.

Pal, Pratapaditya. *Light of Asia: Buddha Sakyamuni in Asian Art.* Los Angeles County Museum of Art, 1984.

Piyasilo. *Avalokiteshvara: Origin, Manifestations & Meaning.* Petaling Jaya, Malaysia: Dharmafarer Enterprises, 1991.

Rabten, Geshe. *Echoes of Voidness.* London: Wisdom, 1983.

_____. *The Preliminary Practices.* Dharamsala: Library of Tibetan Works and Archives, 1974.

_____. *Song of the Profound View.* London: Wisdom, 1989.

_____. *Treasury of Dharma: A Tibetan Buddhist Meditation Course.* London: Tharpa, 1988.

_____ and Geshe Ngawang Dhargyey. *Advice from a Spiritual Friend: Buddhist Thought Transformation.* London: Wisdom, 1984.

Rhie, Marylin and Thurman, Robert. *Wisdom and Compassion: The Sacred Art of Tibet.* New York: Harry N. Abrams, 1991.

Robinson, J., trans. *Buddha's Lions: The Lives of the Eighty-four Siddhas.* Emeryville: Dharma, 1979.

Sakya Pandita. *Illuminations: A Guide to Essential Buddhist Practices.* Novato: Lotsawa, 1988.

His Holiness Sakya Trizin and Ngawang Samten Chophel (trans.). *A Collection of Instructions on Parting from the Four Attachments: The Basic Mind Training Teaching of the Sakya Tradition.* Singapore: Sakya Tenphel Ling, 1982.

Sakya Trizin, et al. *Essence of Buddhism.* New Delhi: Tibet House, 1986.

Khetsun Sangpo Rinbochay. *Tantric Practice in Nying-ma.* Trans. and ed. Jeffrey Hopkins. Ithaca: Snow Lion, 1986.

Sciaky, K. "A General Presentation of the Doctrine of Karma and of the Differences Posited by the Theravada and Mahayana Schools." *Dreloma*, XIII (Jan. 1985), 8-32.

Shantideva. *A Guide to the Bodhisattva's Way of Life.* Trans. S. Batchelor. Dharamsala: Library of Tibetan Works and Archives, 1979.

Silananda, Ven. U. *The Four Foundations of Mindfulness.* London: Wisdom, 1990.

Sogyal Rinpoche. *Dzogchen & Padmasambhava.* Berkeley: Rigpa, 1989.

_____ . *The Tibetan Book of Living and Dying.* San Francisco: Harper, 1992.

Sopa, Geshe Lhundup and J. Hopkins. *Cutting Through Appearances: Practice and Theory of Tibetan Buddhism.* Ithaca: Snow Lion, 1989. Revised publication of *Practice and Theory of Tibetan Buddhism* (London: Rider, 1976).

Speyer, J. S., trans. *The Jatakamala, or Garland of Birth Stories of Aryasura.* Delhi: Motilal Benarsidass, 1971.

Tarthang Tulku. "History." *Crystal Mirror*, IV, 3-99.

_____ . "A History of the Buddhist Dharma." *Crystal Mirror*, V, 3-307.

_____ . *Mother of Knowledge: The Enlightenment of Ye-shes mTsho-rgyal.* Berkeley: Dharma, 1983.

_____ . *Sacred Art of Tibet.* Berkeley: Dharma, 1972.

_____ . "The Vajra Guru Mantra." *Crystal Mirror*, II, 17-39.

Templeman, D., trans. *The Origin of the Tara Tantra by Jo-nan Taranatha.* Dharamsala: Library of Tibetan Works and Archives, 1981.

Tharchin, Geshe Lobsang. *A Commentary on Guru Yoga and Offering of the Mandala.* Ithaca: Snow Lion, 1987.

_____ . *King Udrayana and the Wheel of Life: The History and Meaning of the Buddhist Teaching of Dependent Origination.* Freewood Acres: Mahayana Sutra and Tantra Press, 1984.

_____ . *Nagarjuna's Letter.* Dharamsala: Library of Tibetan Works and Archives, 1979.

Thegchok, Geshe Jampa. *Lama Tsongkhapa's Praise to Dependent-Arising.* Melbourne: Nalanda Monastery, 1990.

Thondup Rinpoche. *Buddha Mind: An Anthology of Longchen Rabjam's Writings on Dzogpa Chenpo.* Ithaca: Snow Lion, 1989.

_____ . *Hidden Teachings of Tibet: An Explanation of the Terma Tradition.* Boston: Wisdom, 1986.

Thurman, R., ed. *The Life and Teachings of Tsong Khapa.* Dharamsala: Library of Tibetan Works and Archives, 1982.

_____ . *Tsong Khapa's Speech of Gold in the "Essence of True Eloquence"*. Princeton: Princeton University Press, 1984. Republished in paperback as *The Central Philosophy of Tibet*.

Trichen, Chogay. *The History of the Sakya Tradition*. Bristol: Ganesha Press, 1983.

Trungpa, Chogyam. *Journey Without Goal: The Tantric Wisdom of the Buddha*. Boulder: Prajna, 1981.

_____ . *Shambala: Sacred Path of the Warrior*. Boulder: Shambhala, 1984.

_____ . *Visual Dharma: The Buddhist Art of Tibet*. Berkeley: Shambhala, 1975.

Tsering, P. "The Age of Maitreya, the Coming Buddha." *Tibetan Review* (Sept. 1981), 15-19.

Tsogyal, Yeshe. *The Life and Liberation of Padmasambhava*. Emeryville: Dharma, 1978.

Tsong-ka-pa. *Compassion in Tibetan Buddhism*. Ed. and trans. Jeffrey Hopkins. Ithaca: Snow Lion, 1980.

_____ . *Tantra in Tibet: The Great Exposition of Secret Mantra*. London: George Allen and Unwin, 1977.

Tsongkapa. *The Principal Teachings of Buddhism*. Trans. Geshe Lobsang Tharchin. Freewood Acres: Mahayana Sutra and Tantra Press, 1988.

Waddell, L. *Tibetan Buddhism: With Its Mystic Cults, Symbolism and Mythology, and Its Relation to Indian Buddhism*. New York: Dover, 1972. First published in 1894 as *The Buddhism of Tibet, or Lamaism*.

Wallace, A., trans. *The Ambrosia Heart Tantra: The Secret Oral Teaching on the Eight Branches of the Science of Healing*. Dharamsala: Library of Tibetan Works and Archives, 1977.

_____ . *A Passage from Solitude: Training the Mind in a Life Embracing the World*. Ithaca: Snow Lion, 1992.

_____ . *Tibetan Buddhism from the Ground Up: A Practical Approach to Modern Life*. Boston: Wisdom, 1993.

Walshe, M., trans. *Thus Have I Heard*. London: Wisdom, 1987.

Wangchen, Geshe Namgyal. *Awakening the Mind of Enlightenment: Meditations on the Buddhist Path*. London: Wisdom, 1987.

Wangyal, Geshe. *The Door of Liberation*. New York: Maurice Girodias, 1973. Reprinted, New York: Lotsawa, 1978.

Wayman, A. *Yoga of the Guhyasamajatantra: The Archane Lore of Forty Verses*. Delhi: Motilal, 1977.

Weber, A., N. Wellings and J. Landaw. *Tara's Colouring Book*. London: Wisdom, 1979.

Willis, J. *On Knowing Reality: The Tattvartha Chapter of Asanga's* Bodhisattvabhumi. New York: Columbia University Press, 1979.

Willson, M. *In Praise of Tara: Songs to the Saviouress.* London: Wisdom, 1986.

Yeshe, Lama Thubten. *Introduction to Tantra: A Vision of Totality.* London: Wisdom, 1987.

_____ . *The Sadhana of Vajrapani: Lord of the Secret.* Boulder Creek: Vajrapani Institute, 1977.

_____ . *Vajra Yogini.* London: Wisdom, 1984.

_____ . *Transference of Consciousness at the Time of Death.* Boston: Wisdom, 1985.

_____ and Zopa Rinpoche. *Wisdom Energy: Basic Buddhist Teachings.* London: Wisdom, 1982.

Yeshe De Research Project (comp.). "Light of Liberation: A History of Buddhism in India." *Crystal Mirror,* VIII (1992).

Zopa Rinpoche, Lama Thubten. *Chod: Cutting Off the Truly Existent I.* London: Wisdom, 1983.

Zwalf, W., ed. *Buddhism: Art and Faith.* London: British Museum Publications, 1985.

Index